THE
BOSTON
MARATHON
HANDBOOK

HELP US KEEP THIS GUIDE UP TO DATE

Every effort has been made by the author and editors to make this guide as accurate and useful as possible. However, many things can change after a guide is published—regulations change, facilities come under new management, and so forth.

We would love to hear from you concerning your experiences with this guide and how you feel it could be improved and kept up to date. While we may not be able to respond to all comments and suggestions, we'll take them to heart, and we'll also make certain to share them with the author. Please send your comments and suggestions to falconeditorial @rowman.com.

Thanks for your input!

THE
BOSTON
MARATHON
HANDBOOK

An Insider's Guide to Training for and
Succeeding in the Ultimate Road Race

MARC W. POLLINA

FALCON

ESSEX, CONNECTICUT

An imprint of Globe Pequot, the trade division of
The Rowman & Littlefield Publishing Group, Inc.
4501 Forbes Blvd., Ste. 200
Lanham, MD 20706
www.rowman.com

Falcon and FalconGuides are registered trademarks and Make Adventure Your Story is a trademark of
The Rowman & Littlefield Publishing Group, Inc.

Distributed by NATIONAL BOOK NETWORK

British Library Cataloguing in Publication Information available

Library of Congress Cataloging-in-Publication Data

Names: Pollina, Marc W., author.
Title: The Boston Marathon handbook : an insider's guide to training for and succeeding in the
    ultimate road race / Marc W. Pollina.
Description: Essex, Connecticut : FalconGuides, 2024. | Includes index.
Identifiers: LCCN 2023035390 (print) | LCCN 2023035391 (ebook) | ISBN 9781493079025 (paperback)
    | ISBN 9781493079032 (epub)
Subjects: LCSH: Boston Marathon. | Marathon running—Training.
Classification: LCC GV1065.22.B67 P65 2024 (print) | LCC GV1065.22.B67 (ebook) | DDC
    796.42/52071—dc23/eng/20230919
LC record available at https://lccn.loc.gov/2023035390
LC ebook record available at https://lccn.loc.gov/2023035391

♾️™ The paper used in this publication meets the minimum requirements of American National
Standard for Information Sciences—Permanence of Paper for Printed Library Materials, ANSI/NISO
Z39.48-1992.

Boston Marathon and the B.A.A. unicorn logo are trademarks of the Boston Athletic Association. *The
Boston Marathon Handbook* is not an official publication of the Boston Athletic Association.

For all courageous souls who chase unicorns

(except you, Rosie Ruiz)

In Memory of Patricia Wainwright Pollina

Stop fretting about the Boston Marathon forecast. Decide right now that the only storm on Monday will be you.

Tommy Rivers "Rivs" Puzey
16th Place, 2:18:20, Boston Marathon (2017)
24,799th Place, 6:31:54, Boston Marathon (2022)
Cancer Survivor (2020–present)

CONTENTS

CHAPTER 7

CHAPTER 8

CHAPTER 9

CHAPTER 10

FOREWORD

Marc Pollina and I met in the spring of 2023, but in a sense we've known each other for 20 years. With our collective mutual friendships in the Boston running scene, particularly our respective affiliations with the Boston Marathon Charity Program and our mutual love of the Boston Marathon, we truly are kindred spirits.

When Marc described *The Boston Marathon Handbook* and asked me to write its foreword, I was quite surprised and especially honored. I was also thrilled about the opportunity to offer homage to our beloved Boston Marathon from a perspective I'll refer to as "reverently whimsical," a point of view Marc so effectively captures in this tongue-in-cheek collection.

The Boston Marathon Handbook is an indispensable guide for Boston Marathoners past, present, and future. Whether you're a wily veteran, retired from marathoning, preparing for your next Boston, or a newbie planning to take on Grossman's Hill, Heartbreak Hill, the Haunted Mile, the long stretch to the Citgo sign, right-on-Hereford-left-on-Boylston, and the other famous milestones along the way, Marc's book is a must.

Every Boston Marathoner's supportive network of family, friends, and fans will find an endless array of helpful and humorous anecdotes to enhance their experience of the Boston Marathon. The non-marathoners in that network can soak up inside information for their own pleasure or to dominate trivia night at the local pub. This book is for you, too.

Marc has run 18 Bostons, most of them for which he qualified and with consistent finishes within close range of each other. I've run only 14 Bostons with finishes ranging from first to last (yes, really, though unofficially), DNF'd (did not finish), and pretty much everything in between, so I can attest to having at least a little perspective on the course. Like Marc and most other multi–Boston Marathon veterans, I've roasted in the baking hot sun, shivered in the spitting snow, been blown home to fast times, and held up nearly straight from a biting east wind off the Boston Harbor.

In 1976, my bib number disintegrated mid-race from the cascade of garden hoses cooling us off, so when I took the lead near the 18-mile mark, the photographers on their open-air truck couldn't identify me. Despite their incessant inquiries as to my name, I would not confess. Our little game provided a short-lived pleasant distraction, as I was soon found out.

When defending my title the next year, I once again ran the race without a number. Having arrived late to Hopkinton, my bib was nowhere to be found. Race officials promised to hand my #1 bib to me along the course. That never happened. When finish line officials weren't convinced I was "official," nearby runners vouched that I had run the entire race. It all worked out in the end. "Someday we'll look back on this and it will all seem funny" is a well-known refrain, and here we are, to be educated and entertained by the engaging Boston Marathon stories and lessons Marc shares.

As a long-standing, dues-paying, card-carrying member and former employee of the B.A.A., I've acquired quite a collection of marathon hats. Yet, even more of that collection comes from the Dana-Farber Marathon Challenge team I've coached since 1990. It was by way of Marc having run Boston for the Project Hope Marathon Team, as a qualified runner no less, that brought us together in our shared sphere of mutual running friends.

Boston charity runners fundraise and run with a boldness and sense of purpose that expands and amplifies their marathoning experience. They aren't just fighting the cold, the heat, the wind, the rain, the fatigue, or injuries, they're fighting to improve and/or save the lives of family members and friends, many of whom they have not met and may never meet.

We marathoners know a little levity is necessary to offset the gravity of the challenge. And if laughter really is some of the best medicine, Marc Pollina's *The Boston Marathon Handbook* is our indispensable panacea.

Jack Fultz
1976 Boston Marathon Men's Champion
Member, B.A.A.

ACKNOWLEDGMENTS

Publishing a book is like racing a marathon. There will be pain, inevitably. Patience is a virtue, generally. And the more support you have, the more successful you'll be. Always.

Many generous contributors banded together to give birth to this book, support its journey to publication, and nurture it to ensure it fulfills its potential. In true Boston Marathon fashion, my gratitude extends from start to finish.

Mile 1
Special thanks to the B.A.A. for creating, hosting, organizing, and executing the race we love. Our lives would be far less fulfilling without you.

Mile 2
Lisa Birnbach, you have no idea how enamored I was with *The Official Preppy Handbook*. I am grateful for your heartening book and hopeful we can meet in matching Tretorns for a coffee on the UWS.

Mile 3
Many thanks are owed to my agent, Matt Wagner at Fresh Books Literary Agency. Matt believed in this book when it was a nervous first-timer fresh off the bus in Hopkinton. You are my spirit animal. Thank you for shepherding this book the entire distance and beyond.

Mile 4
A huge shout-out to my editor, Dave LeGere, who embraced the vision Matt and I shared and provided the perfect blend of guidance, resources, and freedom to bring it to life and send it out into the world with self-assurance and hope.

Mile 5
I am fortunate for family, namely the fiercely talented pair of Isabella and Sienna Berg. When you're not creating something magical of your own, you're always in my corner, eating my confident (but sometimes questionable) cooking and smiling (occasionally) at my jokes. Thank you for lifting my spirits and keeping me young at heart.

Mile 6

I am indebted to legions of runners who trained and raced with me in all manner of Boston's wicked weather. These hearty and inspiring souls include Rich "Shifter" Horgan, Bernie Alcock, Gina Fiandaca, Courtney and Ryan Fine, Joe Findaro, Breno Melo, Jay Warner, Dan Montero, Gordon Pilotte, and Dr. Alan Cherkasky. Thank you for sharing in the fun and amplifying my joy of running to "11."

Mile 7

Long before I rediscovered running at age 34 in Massachusetts, I fell in love with running at age 12 in Pennsylvania. My first and only running coaches, Central Columbia's Joe Kelly and the late Irv Zablocky, turned my nightmare of running long distances into an unforeseen dream. Not sure how that happened, but thank you.

Mile 8

The Boston Marathon introduced me to two of the kindest, most generous humans, the late Russell Leblang and Jake Kennedy. Both were taken from this world far too early. Rest in peace, Russell and Jake. We miss you.

Mile 9

I would like to thank the following Boston-area companies and key executives for their continued support and encouragement: DMSE Sports and Dave McGillivray, Tracksmith and Lou Serafini, Heartbreak Hill Running Company and Dan Fitzgerald, and Marathon Sports and Shane O'Hara.

Mile 10

Friends lift you up and tether you to the ground. Brandon and Mary Ruth Thompson and Jason and Jennifer Tribush, you are the best of them. Thank you for gifting me with your encouragement, friendship, beachtails, tennis, golf, and bourbon. My heart is as swollen as my liver.

Mile 11

Tom Derderian, Michael Connelly, Paul Clerici, John Brant, et al. authored must-read Boston Marathon–themed books that complement this book. I share your love of this great race and am honored this book joins your timeless classics on bookshelves.

Mile 12

Can a pub change your life? That's a rhetorical question. Anyone in Boston who ran the Eliot Lounge or Crossroads runs each Thursday from January through mid-April knows it can. Rest in peace, Eliot Lounge and Crossroads Pub. Your spirits live on.

Mile 13

I am grateful for Felicity Tucker, Jason Rossi, Josh Rosenberg, Melissa Evarts, and the entire team at Rowman & Littlefield/Globe Pequot/Falcon Guides. From the cover design to the page layout and beyond, you built upon the ideas in my head and delivered a beautiful book worthy of being held in the salt-stained hands of generations of glycogen-depleted marathoners. Well done.

Mile 14

Jack Fultz, you are a legend to me. Not because you're the 1976 Boston Marathon champion (which is epic), but because you embody all that is good about this amazing race that we love. The Boston Marathon is our red thread, and I'm thankful to it for connecting us and to you for capturing so eloquently why others might be interested in exploring what we found.

Mile 15

To all of the financial services firms that attempted to ensnare my soul, you failed. Thank heavens.

Mile 16

Kara Goucher, Alison Mariella Desir, Christine Yu, and Lauren Fleshman et al. penned books that inspired the running community to question what the future of running should look like. Thank you for your continued efforts to improve and preserve the integrity of our sport.

Mile 17

Props to Marc "O" Caminetsky, Heather Caminetsky, Richard "TFFD" Snyder, Brett Gordon, Norman Lang, Tim "McLovin" McLean, Scott "Scum E." Kaplan, Jennifer "JJ" Davis, Ron Golub, Mimi "Mulva" Golub, Glen "GG" Hartford, Bob "VB" Gifford, and all members of the Project Hope Marathon Team for teaching me that training for a marathon can be an absolute blast.

Mile 18

I'm grateful for Rachel Anderson, Kathleen Auclair, Mary Darling, Jill Dellorco, Cris Gutierrez III, Sumner Jones, Kate Kennedy, Ronald Kmiec, Amanda and Ian Nurse, Becca Pizzi, Nick Renfro, Jamie Sarkisian, Heather Schulz, Andrea Smiley, Amy and Paul Sole, Huy Son, Toby Tanser, John Young, and Hayley Yudelman. Your generous contributions went above and beyond. Thank you.

Mile 19

Hampden-Sydney College is an educational utopia that fell from the heavens into the middle of a field in southern Virginia. Thank you, Hampden-Sydney. You're a writer's nirvana and I'm beholden to you.

Mile 20

This one is for you, Chase Pollina. A photo of you at age seven handing me a Gatorade at Mile 20 in 2004 is my all-time favorite. Please know I'd be happy to return the courtesy when you're ready to chase a unicorn of your own.

Mile 21

So many Boston Marathon luminaries opened their hearts and provided memorable quotes for us all to enjoy: Dick Beardsley, Peter Bromka, Amby Burfoot, Fernando Cabada, Bobbi Gibb, George Hirsch, Bob Hodge, Deena Kastor, Meb Keflezighi, Nico Montañez, Alexi Pappas, Uta Pippig, Dathan Ritzenhein, Lonah Salpeter, Joan Benoit Samuelson, Kathrine Switzer, and Mike Wardian. Thank you for believing in the book and for following through so generously after you promised to contribute. I am filled with gratitude.

Mile 22

To my inimitable sister, Connie Pollina, we've come a long way since "Seven-Up Land." Your love and encouragement are invaluable to me always, including throughout the writing of this book. As brothers go, I'm the luckiest.

Mile 23

It's hard to believe "the best way to help yourself is to help others" until you "Run for the Nun" and discover it's true. Thank you to Project Hope's founder, Sister Margaret Leonard, whose huge heart and compassion inhabited me in 2011 and are with me today.

Mile 24

I pulled all-nighters in empty classrooms to finish short stories that would impress Dr. James M. Schiffer, the catalyst for my love of writing. Thank you for encouraging me. I hear your voice in my head whenever my fingers hover atop a keyboard.

Mile 25

Huge respect to the communities of Hopkinton, Ashland, Framingham, Natick, Wellesley, Newton, Brookline, and Boston. Thank you for transforming a paved road into the paradise of our road racing dreams.

Mile 26

To my parents, Richard G. Pollina and the late Patricia W. Pollina, I'm speechless. Thank you for your patience, unlimited love, and top-shelf genes. Dad, I can't wait to raise a glass of the finest with you. Mom, I look forward to an overdue hug when I'm done down here.

Mile 26.2

This book wouldn't have made it to Hopkinton or Copley Square without the superhuman love and support of my wife, Susan M. Simmons. You captivate and inspire me. Your smiling eyes reduce the world to the two of us. With all my wild heart, thank you. We did it. Let's celebrate for a hot second and do it again.

INTRODUCTION

At 7:32 a.m. on Marathon Monday, April 16, 2018, I shivered in the flooded, remarkably empty streets of Hopkinton Town Center. Below-freezing windchills, violent rain, and gale-force squalls had shredded the garbage bags duct-taped to my legs, torn apart my umbrella, numbed my hands, and bricked my phone.

With 15 consecutive Boston Marathons under my belt, I was no stranger to Hopkinton, but the ghost town surrounding me bore little resemblance to the festive streets of years gone by. The start of the race I love was hours away, and I was miserable.

"Are you okay?" asked a complete stranger from her front porch. I stood there saturated and speechless. I was anything but okay. The woman (from a distance, a doppelgänger for my mom) swung her door open wide and motioned for me to come inside. She gave me fresh clothes to wear while she dried everything clinging to me moments before.

My mother had passed away in 2016, but there she was, reincarnate, treating me to hot coffee and toasted bagels. Her perfect doses of encouragement and friendly conversation warmed me from the inside as her fire thawed me from the outside. She put a smile on my face before the race that set the tone for the remainder of my day.

I learned her name was Kathleen, but it wasn't until I reconnected with Kathleen five years later after wandering the streets of Hopkinton with just her picture and first name that I discovered she was related to George Brown, the legendary 33-time starter and 11-time manager of the Boston Marathon. What seemed like a once-in-a-lifetime act of kindness was, for the Boston Marathon and its uncanny way of connecting disparate people, quite ordinary. But, as you'll learn, even when it's ordinary, Boston is extraordinary.

Kathleen, thank you. Your huge heart, genuine concern, and selfless generosity are still with me today. Without the Boston Marathon, we never would have crossed paths. I am a far better human because they did.

To each of you readers, I hope this handbook helps you collect Boston Marathon memories of your own. Your memories will pile atop one another like baseball teammates celebrating victory on the pitcher's mound after the final out of the World Series. It will be difficult to pick one from the heap to call your favorite.

It's a bit cliché to say "the Boston Marathon transforms you." It does. The surprise isn't that transformation happens; it's how it happens. My experience tells me it will occur in a way you won't expect. It's only then that a favorite will emerge.

Until then, please make full use of *The Boston Marathon Handbook* throughout your journey. Knowing this guide is dog-eared and revisited as you prepare for, race, and recover from Boston (and repeat, as you desire) pleases me more than having a golden olive branch wreath placed atop my head in Copley Square.

So, devour this book and go forth. Your own defining Boston Marathon moment awaits you. It will transcend a negative split, perfect tailwind, and whatever the clock says above your head at the finish line. You won't see it coming. But if you open your heart to Boston and its beloved race, you'll be sure to feel it overwhelm you when it occurs. And, like a last-minute change in the Marathon Monday weather forecast, you can rest assured it will.

Marc and Kathleen, "Perfect Chaos" (2018)   *Marc and Kathleen, Reunion (2023)*

CHAPTER 1

Why Is the Boston Marathon Special?

Who better than Boston Marathon legends, qualifiers, dignitaries, innovators, and finishers to share what it feels like to have a unicorn medal placed around your neck?

Here and throughout the book, Boston luminaries provide one-sentence answers to the following question:

Why is the Boston Marathon special to me?

Sometimes it's best to hear it from the mouths of others before you form an answer of your own.

> *"The Boston Marathon is special not only because you have to earn your place on the starting line, but also in the energy of the race that wills you to achieve your highest potential."*

Rachel Anderson
8 Marathons
1 Boston Marathon

> *"The Boston Marathon was my first marathon (1965, 25th place) and may be my last some day; if so, that would make fitting bookends."*

Amby Burfoot
Winner, Boston Marathon (1968)
Former Editor in Chief, *Runner's World* Magazine
9-Time Winner, 60-Consecutive-Time Finisher,
Manchester Road Race (Manchester, CT)

"The Boston Marathon is an iconic global event, a king and queen maker for the champions, a test of will and speed for amateur athletes, and a display of raw humanity for every person who gets the opportunity to run; whether raising funds or racing for time, athletes from every corner of the globe and every walk of life—a collective of 30,000—and their overlapping personal stories are what make me love the race year after year."

Dan Fitzgerald

2 Marathons

1 Boston Marathon (2014)

Cofounder and Head Coach, Heartbreak Hill Running Company

"Having traveled the globe to run marathons, nothing compares to Boston . . . the history, the pageantry, the crowds, and the enthusiasm all rolled into one race; there's nothing like lacing up and running with the best of the best at the same time, on the same course, in the same conditions as if you're in the Super Bowl or Game 7 of the World Series, playing with and competing against the world's greatest."

Brett Gordon

34 Marathons

23 Consecutive Boston Marathons

Six Star Medalist

"The Boston Marathon is special to me because it is an incredible race that brings community together, celebrates history, and is all the greatness that running can be."

Kara Goucher

3rd Place, Boston Marathon (2009)

3rd Place, New York City Marathon (2008)

9th Place, 10,000m (2008) and 11th Place, Marathon (2012), Olympic Games

Marc Pollina

George Hirsch

Above: Kara Goucher with fellow authors Christine Yu, Alison Mariella Désir, and Lauren Fleshman at the 2023 Boston Marathon expo

Left: George Hirsch and Joan Benoit Samuelson run stride for stride in the 1979 Boston Marathon.

"The Boston Marathon is the first race I ever ran back in 1969 when the entry fee was $2 and all you needed was a letter from a doctor saying that you were fit enough to cover the distance."

George A. Hirsch
40 Marathons
5 Boston Marathons
Chair, New York Road
Runners Board of Directors

"As a young athlete the Boston Marathon loomed large and the pull of its force and my own trajectory collided as they must, for a lifelong love affair with the race and the top competitors from around the globe who created its history."

Bob Hodge
3rd Place, Boston Marathon (1979)
7-Time Winner and 2-Time Record Setter, Mount Washington Road Race
3rd Place, US Cross-Country Championships (1979)

"Winning the Boston Marathon in 2014 is a very special achievement for me, representing not only a career highlight but also a meaningful tribute to the victims of the 2013 bombing on Boylston Street, which had strengthened the resolve of the running community worldwide and become a symbol of our resilience."

Meb Keflezighi
Winner, Boston Marathon (2014)
Winner, New York City Marathon (2009)
Silver Medalist, Olympic Marathon (2004)

"After dropping out my first year (1972) then coming back and finishing my second year (1973), I made a commitment that day to run this race every year for the rest of my life, and this year (2023) was my 51st consecutive Boston Marathon finish . . . can't get any more special than that."

Dave McGillivray
More Than 165 Marathons
51 Consecutive Boston Marathons
Race Director, Boston Marathon

"The Boston Marathon holds a special place in my heart because of the rich Mammoth Track Club history—from Meb winning in 2014 to Deena placing 5th overall to maybe not as well known, my former teammate Daniel Tapia placing 9th overall; the club is very successful at Boston, and I love continuing that heritage of success."

Nico Montañez
2 Boston Marathons
13th Place, Boston Marathon (2023)
Ranked 5th Fastest American Marathoner (2021)

"The city comes alive and our sport thrives with the Boston Marathon; to this day, after 24 marathons since 2010 when it made me a runner, Boston is, and always will be, my favorite race!"

Amanda Nurse
24 Marathons
10 Boston Marathons
Founder, Wellness in Motion (WIM) Coaching

"The Boston Marathon stands in my heart for freedom I so enjoy with every single step on the peaceful roads from Hopkinton to downtown Boston while the freedoms of each person create a symphony of sharing joy and love of our sport."

Uta Pippig
Winner, 3 Consecutive Boston Marathons (1994–1996)
3-Time Winner, Berlin Marathon (1990, 1992, 1995)
Winner, New York City Marathon (1993)
2-Time Olympian, Germany, 10,000m (1992) and Marathon (1996)

"The Boston Marathon is special because there is no experience for dedicated marathoners like the Hopkinton to Boylston journey; it builds from a quiet sleepy New England village to a roaring crowd with an epic finish . . . and there is no feeling like the last 600m of the Boston Marathon after the journey it took to get there."

Dathan Ritzenhein
3-Time Olympian (10,000m, 2004; Marathon, 2008; 10,000m, 2012)
7th Place, 1st American, Boston Marathon (2015)
Head Coach, On Athletics Club (OAC)

"With its rich history and tradition, the Boston Marathon is special to me in so many wonderful ways: It launched my marathon career when I won unexpectedly in 1979 (despite never having seen the course), it forged numerous friendships over the many years I participated as a runner, commentator, and in various other capacities, it strengthened my connection to my parents (who grew up in suburban Boston) and our daughter (who reminds me she never missed a Boston Marathon, even in utero, until COVID hit), and it created a very meaningful family memory when our children and I ran together at the 2014 Boston Marathon (helping the city heal after the 2013 bombing)."

Joan Benoit Samuelson
2-Time Winner, Boston Marathon (1979 and 1983)
Gold Medalist, Olympic Marathon (1984)
Winner, Chicago Marathon (1985)

5

"I love the Boston Marathon's rich history, and because it focuses on fitness and well-being and brings the community together on a day that everyone aspires to be a runner, never more so than in 2014 as the community rallied in unison after the bombing."

Jamie Sarkisian
25 Boston Marathons
The "Beer Can Guy"

"This race, where the entire city and its people come together, is bigger than any one runner; it's the highest stage for an amateur marathoner and the pinnacle of our sport."

Lou Serafini
10 Marathons
10th Place, USATF Marathon Road Championships (2022)
Director of Community, Tracksmith

Lou Serafini holds court behind the Eliot Lounge bar at the Trackhouse, Tracksmith's headquarters at 285 Newbury Street.

"The Boston Marathon is special to me because it shows me I'm stronger and more resilient than I ever thought possible—qualifying for Boston at all (which I never thought I would do), much less running it multiple times."

Andrea Smiley
6 Marathons
2 Boston Marathons

"The Boston Marathon changed my life; it was the spark that ignited the women's running revolution that has now transformed the world."

Kathrine (K.V.) Switzer
First Woman to Run the Boston Marathon as an
Officially Registered Competitor (1967)
Winner, 1974 New York City Marathon
Board Chair, 261 Fearless

Bestowed upon heroes, the Marathon Milestone Medallion was granted to Kathrine in 2022 on the 50th anniversary of her legendary finish in 1972.
Kathrine Switzer

John Young digs deep on his way to finishing the 2018 Boston Marathon (aka "Perfect Chaos"). John Young

"Starting along with other athletes in the very first wave, prior to 8:30 a.m., I was able to have the best view of the race as a runner where I got to be in the lead group greeting the spectators all the way to Boston; better yet, I was on the course running as the wheelchair athletes, hand-cyclists, and then the elite women and men passed me—what a rush!"

John Young
6 Boston Marathons
Mobility Impaired Division

CHAPTER 2

There's Only One Boston

"Have you run Boston?"

That's the one question every distance runner is asked. Think of it as a rite of passage, as inevitable as puberty or death. On the surface, it's an innocuous question. Either you have or you haven't. But the question is a veiled litmus test, and your answer communicates far more than your "yes" or "no."

Is running the Boston Marathon necessary to be considered a runner? Of course not. If you lace up your shoes and run around the block, you're a runner. But the question is a sly means (whether intentional or not) for the inquirer to discern the degree of your zeal. Even the way you answer the question is as important as the answer itself.

"Oh, heavens, no" communicates you have no desire of subjecting yourself to such a masochistic endeavor. "How far is that?" is an admission you're new to this whole running thing and have yet to learn some standard distances and lingo. "I wish" articulates you'd like to, but have little faith you'll ever be fast enough to earn a bib.

On the affirmative side, "Yep, 2018, what a beast" means, yes, you ran it, but suffer from residual PTSD. "Every year since 2003" is your way of admitting you're a streaker. And "no, but I BQ'd minus 10 at London, so I can't wait for September" means you're not only savvy enough to know the vernacular, but you're chomping at the bit for registration to open so you can run Boston for the first time next year.

It's nothing short of amazing how one question can convey so much. Hey, Boston is special. You hear that a lot. But we're not here because the Boston Marathon is simply special.

There's no other marathon in the world like the Boston Marathon. That's closer to the mark. Known as the "The Granddaddy of All Marathons," the Boston Marathon is unique. There's only one Boston.

Emil Zatopek, voted by *Runner's World* magazine as the "Greatest Runner of All Time," once said, "If you want to run, run a mile. If you want to experience a different life, run a marathon." Zatopek was right. Run 26.2 miles anywhere and you will come face-to-face with your weaknesses. You will dig deeper than you thought imaginable to find your strengths. And you will traverse a spectrum of emotions you weren't aware even existed. The marathon alters you in a way other races don't. The person at the finish is often markedly different than the person at the start. Which brings us back to Boston.

If running any marathon has the power to change your life, what is it about the Boston Marathon that sets it apart and transforms you to a degree unmatched by the thousands of other races of the same length?

There is no universal answer. Asking a runner to describe Boston is like asking a mother to explain what makes her child special. Where does one even begin?

It can be hard to articulate. And the answer is unique to each runner. It's heartfelt. It's personal. *The Boston Marathon Handbook* will help you find your answer.

Herein lies a treasure trove of Boston knowledge, anecdotes, suggestions, advice, and more. You'll navigate your way from Eastie to the Back Bay to the South End to the North End to Southie and back, blending seamlessly with the locals from neighborhood to neighborhood like a Boston Sand & Gravel worker nicknamed Sully who throws back "regulahs" at Dunks by day and Jameson picklebacks at Murphy's Law by night. Even better, you'll be prepared to race from Hopkinton to Copley Square with nary a faux pas, even when your glycogen stores are tapped, the Citgo sign is wicked blurry, and that last gel you forced down in Coolidge Corner is reversing its direction.

If you feel the Boston Marathon is as out of reach and as elusive as the unicorn on its finisher's medal, you can find solace and inspiration within the forthcoming pages. Home to many of the world's most esteemed colleges and universities (including Harvard and MIT in neighboring Cambridge), Boston is known to be a city that rewards intelligence. And, in true Boston fashion, to have success in the wildly challenging Boston Marathon, you have to be a scholar of the race, invest in your success, and learn the nuances of the course. There are no shortcuts.

The seeds of success at Boston are scattered haphazardly across the globe: offline (passed down from generation to generation) and online (stumbled across from site to site). As if actually training for the Boston Marathon weren't tricky enough, scouring the earth for knowledge on the race adds layers of complexity and tedium beyond long runs and tempos.

Wouldn't it be better if these real-world and digital scavenger hunts weren't necessary? Wouldn't it be awesome if everything you needed was in one place, a place you could enjoy and revisit like an old friend? Even better, what if you could pass all of this ageless Boston Marathon information along in one fell swoop to fellow runners, loved ones, or anyone you deem worthy?

"If you're not smiling, you're doing it wrong" is Joe Findaro's MO at Boston. Joe Findaro

That would be more than a book. That would be an heirloom, as timeless and special as the race itself. That's why we're here.

Have you run Boston?

If you've heard or anticipate ever having to answer that inescapable question, you're reading the right book. Welcome to *The Boston Marathon Handbook*.

We begin our journey by taking a closer look at what makes the Boston Marathon extraordinary. From Heartbreak Hill to the Scream Tunnel to Patriots' Day and beyond, there's a lot to love. Let's explore the Boston Marathon's unique identifiers so you can contemplate them and establish a love affair of your own.

B.A.A.

Formed in 1887, the nonprofit Boston Athletic Association states its mission is "promoting a healthy lifestyle through sports, especially running." That's a pretty modest mission considering the organization is responsible for and hosts the oldest, most prestigious marathon in the world. That's as humble as Tom Brady saying he leads a healthy lifestyle through throwing things, especially footballs.

Without the B.A.A., there wouldn't be a Boston Marathon. The inaugural race was held on April 19, 1897, with a field of 15 runners, 10 of whom crossed the finish line. With recent fields often larger than 30,000 runners representing more than 120 countries, the Boston Marathon has come a long way since its unassuming beginnings when John McDermott won with, by today's standards, a pedestrian 2:55:10 over an abbreviated 24.5-mile course.

Today, true to its mission, the B.A.A. manages training clinics, youth programs, online communities, and a host of popular road and cross-country races ranging from one mile to 26.2 miles. In addition to its races, the B.A.A. has a three-tiered Running Club: the High Performance Team (professional athletes), Racing Team (top-performing regional runners), and Club Level (Age-Group dominators).

The Boston Marathon's beloved unicorn logo/mascot, affectionately coined "Spike" by B.A.A. members, traces its roots to the B.A.A., too. Jack Fleming, the B.A.A.'s president and chief executive officer, describes the unicorn as "a myth-ological figure that is meant to be pursued, but, in that pursuit you never catch [it]," adding "so it inspires you to continue to try—to race harder in the case of running—and though it may be elusive, it really is the pursuit of the unicorn that makes you better and better and better." That pretty much nails the essence of the Boston Marathon and those who covet it. We're all chasing a unicorn.

Who knew a mascot chosen in the 1800s would be so spot-on appropriate for how chimerical it is to BQ and gain entry, as well as how magical it is to turn right on Hereford and left on Boylston on your way to the finish line? Well done, B.A.A. Well done.

JOHNNY ADELBERT KELLEY (AKA "THE ELDER")

There are Boston Marathon personalities aplenty, and there are legends in abun-dance, too, and then there's Johnny Kelley. We may never see a résumé quite like Kelley's ever again.

A three-time US Olympian (1936, 1940, and 1948), Kelley competed in 61 Boston Marathons, finishing 58, winning two (1935 and 1945), earning second place seven times, and placing in the top 10 an astounding 18 times. Sound impressive? That's an understatement. Kelley was named "Runner of the Century" by *Runner's World* magazine in 2000. That's rarified air.

If you fail to master the Boston Marathon course on your first try, take solace in knowing Kelley failed to finish in his first two attempts (1928 and 1932). Hard to believe, but a testament to how tricky the course can be to runners, no matter their paces or levels of talent.

A native of West Medford, Massachusetts, Kelley was nicknamed "The Elder" to avoid confusion with the unrelated Johnny J. Kelley (aka "The Younger"), the winner of the 1957 Boston Marathon and member of the 1956 and 1960 US Olympic teams.

No offense to The Younger or Boston winners before and after, but no one can match the cumulative affection The Elder received throughout his six decades of participation. Beyond his success on the roads, The Elder endeared himself to Boston with his salt-of-the-earth Irish charm, infectious smile, and zest for running and life.

Local marathoners training for Boston on the marathon course pay homage to The Elder at the statue commemorating him just past Mile 19 at the corner of Commonwealth Avenue and Walnut Street in Newton. The statue is at the base of the third of four Newton hills, approximately one

"Young at Heart" is dressed for success on every occasion.

mile before Heartbreak Hill, the hill Kelley was responsible for making famous.

Young at Heart depicts a 27-year-old Kelley, winning in 1935, clasping hands with an older Kelley finishing his 58th Boston Marathon at age 84. It's a ritual among locals to keep Kelley festive, dressing him in holiday-appropriate gear, draping medals around his neck, and making wishes while reaching up to tap the inside of the hat the older Kelley holds in his outstretched left hand. Be sure to visit his statue and make a wish of your own before race day. Or, if things are rough during the race, take a quick detour on your way. There's Johnny, in bronze and in spirit, when you need him the most. Ready to lift you up and over Heartbreak.

WILLIAM HENRY RODGERS (AKA "BOSTON BILLY")

The running boom is often attributed to Frank Shorter's gold medal victory in the 1972 Olympic Marathon in Munich, Germany. There's no doubt Shorter's win was a catalyst that inspired Americans to run. Running was no longer just a source of punishment in other sports. And there's no debating Steve Prefontaine's charisma and passion transformed the sport even further; distance running became cool. But when another legend shocked the running world (and himself), winning the first of four Boston Marathons in 1975 in a then-American record 2:09:55, he captured the hearts of Bostonians in a way that endeared him to the city like few have before or after. His name is William Henry Rodgers, or "Boston Billy" as he was christened following his Boston success.

Bill Rodgers catapulted the city and the race into renewed prominence on the world running stage. The Boston Marathon's allure was on the rise just as a new era of prize money and corporate sponsorship arrived. In addition to winning four Boston Marathon titles (1975, 1978, 1979, 1980), Rodgers won four consecutive New York City Marathons (1976–1979), appearing on the cover of *Sports Illustrated* in 1978 and 1979.

Despite his worldwide fame, Rodgers is a humble, gritty local who wore a headband, painter's gloves from a hardware store, and a cotton T-shirt with a handwritten "GBTC" (Greater Boston Track Club) on his chest on his way to victory in 1975.

He owned and operated the family-owned Bill Rodgers Running Center in Faneuil Hall Marketplace in downtown Boston for decades. Don't be surprised if you see "Boston Billy" on your shakeout run along the Esplanade or Emerald Necklace. He's in high demand during race week, but he's still no stranger to his favorite routes around town.

THE DUEL IN THE SUN

The adjective *epic* is thrown around often when describing the Boston Marathon. Sometimes it's deserved, and sometimes it's a hyperbolic way to describe something worthy of a less-grandiose descriptor. Well, 1982's race was epic. We're talking pre-prize-money bloodsport: the road racing equivalent of Ali vs. Frazier in the "Thrilla in Manila." The drama didn't occur in the confines of a ring; it unfolded mile by mile on the fabled streets of Boston, captivating concentric layers of its suburbs until it reached its climax downtown.

The race is known as much for the downfall of its combatants as it is for the heart they displayed in their fight to the finish on that momentous day, April 19, 1982. Alberto Salazar was a brash running prodigy and already a big deal on the racing scene, earning multiple NCAA All-America honors, making the 1980 Olympic team at 10,000 meters, and running the then fastest debut in US marathon history (2:09:41) as the winner of the 1980 New York City Marathon.

By contrast, Dick Beardsley, the underdog, never lettered in track or cross-country in high school or college. He was a dairy farmer and fishing guide in Minnesota, albeit an increasingly fast one. Beardsley debuted with a 2:47:14 at the 1977 Paavo Nurmi Marathon in Hurley, Wisconsin, and proceeded to run 13 straight personal records (PRs), culminating with a 2:09:37 at the 1981 Grandma's Marathon in Duluth, Minnesota.

So, at Mile 17, at the base of the Newton hills, when Salazar and Beardsley found themselves in the lead, side by side and separated from the field, it was easy to assume Salazar would wear down the farmer and more or less coast to certain victory. Beardsley had a different plan.

Up the hills and down the hills, Beardsley didn't just match Salazar stride for stride; he led Salazar, doing the lion's share of the work, pulling Salazar along in his slipstream. Because it was a noon start and the sun was positioned slightly behind the runners later in the race, Beardsley didn't have to turn around to see Salazar. He kept an eye on his whereabouts by studying the shadow Salazar cast on the pavement in front of him.

Alberto Salazar and Dick Beardsley putting on a show in the final stages of the 1982 Boston Marathon. Dick Beardsley

One could argue Beardsley's decision to push the pace and lead the race cost him in the end, but it's likely Salazar's decision to draft was tactical and he would have stayed on Beardsley's shoulder regardless of the pace. As it played out, Beardsley's aggressiveness was instrumental in delivering a finish that forced both competitors to dig deeper than they could have ever imagined possible without one another.

Most epic finishes occur late in a race, with competitors straining for the tape. The Duel in the Sun was special because the drama of the finish ratcheted up its suspense over nine miles, arguably the most renowned nine miles in road racing. And it wasn't a pack of runners rambling into town; it was 1:1 Beardsley vs. Salazar, mano a mano. The David vs. Goliath dynamic between the two heightened the theater.

Because it was such a beautiful day (sunny with mid-60-degree temps) in an era before metal barricades were used en masse to separate runners and spectators outside the city, crowds were not only shoulder to shoulder and dozens deep, but spectators were on top of the runners, creating a narrow chute allowing runners and their motorcycle escort to pass as the clock ticked and miles passed. This crucible of time and space created an electric atmosphere difficult to recapture in modern times due to heightened safety precautions and increased use of barricades.

Tension built as the warriors passed Kenmore Square, Salazar in his familiar position, one step in arrears as if tethered to Beardsley by a lifeline. The crowds roared as Salazar finally made his move after stalking his prey for more than 25 miles. Just before the right turn on Hereford Street, Salazar passed Beardsley and opened up a three- or four-meter lead before they navigated the last turn to the finish on Ring Road. (**Note:** The finish line as we know it moved to Boylston Street in 1986.) Beardsley retaliated, surging to within a stride in the homestretch before Salazar finally switched gears one last time to eke out a 1.6-second victory (2:08:51 to 2:08:53).

Unbeknownst to them, spectators that day witnessed perhaps the greatest drama in road racing history. And because Salazar was a mere 23 years old and Beardsley just 26 (both incredibly young to achieve such marathon success), the running world assumed the magic that unfolded was the beginning of a rivalry for the ages. Instead, the 1982 race serves as a reminder to everyone to enjoy and make the most of the moment you're in. Running and racing are gifts, as beautiful for their transience as they can be for their endurance.

When I started running as a junior in high school, I knew about the Boston Marathon but never thought once I'd ever be good enough to run it, let alone almost win it; the history of the race, the towns we run through, all of the people that come to cheer all the runners create memories that never fade . . . I can't remember what I had for breakfast this morning but I can remember Boston April 19, 1982, like I just got done running it!

Dick Beardsley
Runner-Up, Boston Marathon (1982)
Co-Winner, London Marathon (1981)
Founder, Dick Beardsley Foundation

In more ways than one, Salazar and Beardsley "won" that day. Their names are often recited together like McEnroe and Borg, Johnson and Bird, or Palmer and Nicklaus. But, much like the Boston Marathon's ancient Greek roots, the Duel in the Sun has its tragic elements, too. It's not an exaggeration to say the duo never was the same after the race, failing to reach the heights of success this epic battle portended. Many feel the 1982 race and the depths to which they drained their reservoirs that day were largely responsible for their decline.

Personal and professional challenges haunted the pair off the roads, too. Beardsley became entangled in the auger on his dairy farm in 1989. He mangled his left leg before managing to stop the machine just before losing conscious-ness. Subsequent car accidents (one in 1992 while driving and one in 1993 while running) did further damage, resulting in an addiction to highly addictive nar-cotic painkillers. At his worst, Beardsley was popping 80–90 pills a day.

Salazar experienced a heart attack in 2007 when his heart "stopped" for 14 minutes. When he survived and continued coaching the Nike Oregon Proj-ect (NOP), Nike's elite team of Olympic-caliber athletes (including Galen Rupp, Mo Farah, Kara Goucher, Jordan Hasay, Mary Cain, and Dathan Ritzenhein), all seemed to be well. But in 2015, Salazar was the subject of an investigation into doping allegations. Salazar denied wrongdoing, but several of his NOP athletes testified, resulting in the American Arbitration Association issuing a guilty verdict and sentencing Salazar to a four-year ban for doping violations.

In 2020, Salazar incurred further sanctions; the US Center for SafeSport ruled him "temporarily ineligible" from coaching after allegations of sexual and emo-tional misconduct were investigated. Upon further review in 2021, Salazar was ruled "permanently ineligible," banning him indefinitely.

The jury is still out on how or if Salazar can atone for his transgressions. Per-haps he should follow the lead of Beardsley who, a stride ahead of him once again, has been drug-free since 1997 and travels the world as a motivational speaker. It's clear from their unforgettable performance on April 19, 1982, the two have incredible resolve. And Beardsley has proven redemption is attainable. The ques-tion is whether Salazar can dig deep before the finish and summon the strength for one last surge of his own.

DIVERSITY, EQUITY, AND INCLUSION

In its 1890 Yearbook Constitution, the B.A.A. stated its objective: "to encourage all manly sports and promote physical culture." In retrospect, *manly* seems like an unfortunate word choice at best (*courageous* would have worked just fine) and insensitive, nay, offensive, at worst.

The Boston Marathon is my second family, and it never ceases to amaze me that people come here from all over the world, all races, all genders, all ethnic groups, religions and political persuasions, and we all love each other, we're all hugging each other and talking with each other and loving to be together, so if we can do this in the Boston Marathon, we can do this in the world and form a network of friendships around the globe that will lead to peace, prosperity, and human rights for everyone in the world.

Roberta "Bobbi" Gibb

First Woman in History to Complete the Boston Marathon (1966)

3-Time Pre-Sanctioned Women's Winner, Boston Marathon (1966, 1967, 1968)

Inductee, Road Runners Club Long Distance Running Hall of Fame

The good news is *manly* has been rightfully removed from the B.A.A.'s modern mission statement and we can all breathe a sigh of relief when reading the current version: "Committed to a world where all people can access and benefit from running and an active lifestyle." The all-encompassing "all people" now applies to athletes in many divisions (e.g., Vision Impaired, Lower Limb Impaired, Upper Limb Impaired, Wheelchair, Nonbinary, and Masters). And we have the strength and courage of a few pioneering women to thank for propelling the Boston Marathon into its new era of diversity, equity, and inclusion.

- **Women**—In February of 1966, the Amateur Athletics Union (AAU) sent a letter to 23-year-old Roberta Louise "Bobbi" Gibb stating women are "not physiologically able to run a marathon." Bobbi knew this wasn't true. She had run up to 40 miles in white leather Red Cross nurses' shoes in a given day on training runs in the Rocky Mountains. In October of 1926, a British woman, Violet Piercy, ran the London Marathon course in 3:40:22, the first women's marathon time recognized by the International Association of Athletics Federations (IAAF). Bobbi wouldn't be the first women's marathoner, but she was determined to be the first to break the Boston Marathon's gender barrier and be the first woman in history across the finish line in Copley Square.

  On April 19, 1966, Gibb hid like a crafty bandit in a forsythia bush in Hopkinton. She joined the field of 540 official (all-male) entrants as they streamed by the start. To her surprise, Gibb was cheered by the crowds as she made her way toward Boston. Word spread among spectators that a woman was running, and the press soon became aware and began to report on her progress. Gibb finished ahead of two-thirds of her competitors in an unofficial 3:21:40. The then-governor of Massachusetts, John Volpe, shook Gibb's hand after she crossed the line.

  A May 2, 1966, *Sports Illustrated* article written by Gwilym S. Brown entitled "A Game Girl in a Man's Game" memorialized the moment with well-meaning but, in hindsight, awkward compliments (describing Gibb as "a tidy-looking and pretty 23-year-old blonde") and heartfelt congratulations (explaining how Gibb ran "fast enough to finish ahead of no fewer than 290 of the event's 415 starters").

In 1967 on a day that featured snow squalls the first five miles, another groundbreaking woman, Kathrine Virginia Switzer, joined Gibb at Boston. Unlike Gibb, Switzer had a bib on her chest, #261 to be precise, procured by signing her entry form as "K. V. Switzer." Despite spectators' warm reception to Gibb's run the previous year, race rules still forbade female participation. When news spread mid-race that Switzer was running with an official race number, race manager Jock Semple, in attempts to remove Switzer's bib, repeatedly assaulted Switzer on the course. Famously, Switzer's then-boyfriend, Tom Miller, a linebacker-sized football player and elite hammer thrower who was running with her, tackled Semple, allowing Switzer to finish the race in approximately 4:20:00 (nearly an hour behind Gibb).

Unfortunately, because of Switzer's official entry into and completion of the 1967 Boston Marathon, the AAU made the decision to prohibit women from all competitions with male runners. Even worse, the AAU stipulated violators would lose the right to compete in races of any length.

Gibb returned to Boston, winning in 1968 for the third time in a row before passing the baton to Sara Mae Berman, who won successive pre-sanctioned titles in 1969, 1970, and 1971. By the time Nina Kuscsik claimed victory in 1972 at the first officially sanctioned Women's division event, momentum created by her predecessors, namely Gibb, Switzer, and Berman, opened the floodgates for generations of women to come.

Joan Benoit Samuelson, Lisa Rainsberger, Desiree Linden, Uta Pippig, Fatuma Roba, Catherine Ndereba, and many more Boston winners and contenders owe a debt of gratitude to the women who made it possible for them to shine on the world's most celebrated running stage.

- **Wheelchair Athletes**—The advent and evolution of wheelchair racing at the Boston Marathon are as madcap as the beginnings and advancement of the Women's division. The first wheelchair marathoner in history, Eugene Roberts, a Vietnam veteran and double amputee, picked a wicked weather day, April 20, 1970, to pioneer an event that has produced some of the highest drama and closest finishes in recent Boston Marathon memory.

Much like Bobbi Gibb four years prior, Roberts was an unofficial entrant who chose to bandit the race, albeit with a hospital-issued wheelchair. The weather was severe, even by Boston standards—rain mixed with sleet, high winds, and temperatures below 40 degrees Fahrenheit. That sounds challenging enough for runners, but it's even harder to imagine navigating a rudimentary wheelchair 26.2 miles over treacherous hills and icy roads with numb hands. (**Note:** Though the Boston Marathon is an international sport involving participants from many countries that use the Celsius scale, for simplicity all temperatures will be given from here on in degrees Fahrenheit.)

Roberts started his trek from Hopkinton to Boston roughly an hour before the noon start. Despite the inclement conditions, he persevered and crossed the finish line in just over seven hours. Unlike the Women's division, whose field doubled in size from one to two the subsequent year, no wheelchair athletes dared to toe the line again until 1975.

Bob Hall, a 24-year-old Belmont, Massachusetts, native who was disabled at an early age by polio, wrote a letter to Boston Marathon race director Will Cloney and asked whether he could enter the 1975 race in a wheelchair. Cloney wrote back to inform Hall that he was unable to grant him an official number, but he'd recognize Hall as an official finisher if he could cross the line in under 3:30:00.

Unlike Roberts, who fought severe weather, Hall had Mother Nature squarely on his side. The 1975 edition had nearly perfect race conditions—temps in the low to mid-50s and strong northwest tailwinds with gusts of 25 mph. We should all be so lucky.

The race was so fast that 43 percent of runners in the field had sub-three-hour finishes and 90 percent of the field broke 3:30:00. Hall picked a perfect year for his debut, and when he crossed the line in 2:58, he became the first official finisher in the Wheelchair division of the Boston Marathon. And in 1977, just five years after Nina Kuscsik became the first official Women's division finisher, Sharon Rahn raced to victory to be crowned the first official women's finisher in the Wheelchair division.

Little did trailblazers like Roberts, Hall, and Rahn know that future wheelchair competitors would yield some of the greatest finishes in Boston Marathon history. Who can forget 2016 when Marcel Hug (1st), Ernst van Dyk (2nd), and Kurt Fearnley (3rd) all recorded the same time (1:24:06) on their mad dash to the finish? Or Louise Sauvage's sneak attack and surprising win against legend (and already celebrating) Jean Driscoll in 1998 (both finished in 1:41:19)?

The Boston Marathon is the first major marathon to include a wheelchair competition. In 1984, the B.A.A. sanctioned the Wheelchair division, and in 1986, in tandem with then-sponsor John Hancock Financial Services, prize money was awarded. The multi-decade success of the Wheelchair division proved to be a gateway for Boston's most recent additions: Para Athletics divisions for athletes with vision, lower-limb, and upper-limb impairments, Adaptive Programs for athletes with a variety of other impairments (e.g., autism, cerebral palsy, multiple sclerosis, muscular dystrophy, ALS, and Parkinson's disease), and rules and policies to accommodate transgender athletes.

- **Handcycles**—Launched in 2017, the Handcycle Program of the Boston Marathon provides an alternative means of participation for athletes who, due to the nature of their impairments, are not able to use a racing wheelchair or run with prostheses. Prior to the formation of the Handcycle Program, handcyclists often participated at Boston, but did not compete for prize money and were not recognized as official winners if they were first across the finish line.

    Tom Davis (58:36) and Michelle Love (2:39:05) were crowned the first champions of the Handcycle division in 2017. The field size is typically capped at around 40 participants, and athletes must either qualify or gain invitational entry. Drafting is not permitted on the course, and speeds no faster than 12 mph are allowed during the race's opening (downhill) half-mile on the narrow streets of Hopkinton. Top male and female finishers receive an award and a stipend of recognition.

    The inclusion of handcycles in marathons in general, and Boston in particular, has polarized the running community. Advocates believe athletes who can't run or operate a push-rim (racing) wheelchair deserve opportunities to race marathons. Critics are convinced that handcycling is cycling and should be part of cycling events, not running events, logic supported by the Paralympics, which considers handcycling a cycling sport and wheelchair racing a track and field sport.

    There is a divide between handcyclists and push-rim wheelchair racers, too. Handcycles have gears and cranks that resemble a bicycle. Push-rim wheelchairs have one gear and are synonymous with adaptive running. They are two distinct pieces of adaptive equipment requiring two separate divisions when raced within the same event. Despite the ongoing controversy regarding whether or not handcycling deserves to be included at marathons, the B.A.A. has grown increasingly accommodating; handcycle athletes now have their own awards, prize money, and share a start time with duo teams (typically after the start of the Wheelchair division and before the start of the Elite Men).

- **Duo Teams**—Legendary father and son Dick and Rick Hoyt (aka "Team Hoyt") were the first tandem to race the Boston Marathon, in 1981, pioneering a new "Duo Team" division. According to the B.A.A. definition, "a Duo Team Is comprised of a runner pushing a non-ambulatory person with a permanent physical impairment in a customized racing wheelchair."

  As with all official participants, the duo runner and the duo rider must be at least 18 years of age on race day. Both members of a Duo Team must qualify (or obtain invitational entry), register, and compete together as a team if accepted. Team Hoyt pioneered a new way to race, paving the way

The Yes You Can! *Team Hoyt statue a block from the starting line in Hopkinton, Massachusetts*

for future generations of duo teams, including the first all-female team (Marie Boudreau-Ninkov and Onni Peck) in 2017 and the first mother-daughter team (Barbara Singleton and Beth Craig) in 2021.

The names of both Duo Team members will appear in the official race results. With only a dozen or so Duo Teams participating each year, prize money has yet to be awarded to the fastest teams. But it's possible sponsors would be inclined to allocate funds to top finishers if participation and competition continue to rise.

- **Para Athletics**—The B.A.A. introduced its Para Athletics divisions in 2021, defining them as "competitive divisions that implement the principles of the International Paralympic Committee (IPC) Classification Code." The Boston Marathon's Para Athletics divisions include the following:
  - Vision Impairment T11/T12 and T13
  - Lower Limb Impairment T61–T64
  - Upper Limb Impairment T45, T46

Each Para Athletics division has specific eligibility requirements, classification profiles, qualifying standards, high-performance standards, rules of competition, field size limitations, scoring, awards, and prize money.

The Boston Marathon is the first major marathon to offer prize money and awards for Para Athletes. Or, as the B.A.A. states more eloquently, "The Boston Marathon aims to be a platform that showcases the athleticism, achievements, and competition of aspiring and elite Para Athletes beyond the already established wheelchair division."

Allowing athletes who have a visual, upper, or lower limb impairment to compete for prize money on Boston's illustrious stage creates an opportunity to showcase participants and grow and expand Para Athletics around the world.

Adrianne Haslet, who lost her leg in the 2013 Boston Marathon bombing, is doing her share to honor fellow victims and raise awareness of the race's Para Athletics divisions. A ballroom dancer turned runner, Haslet, with the help of a prosthetic blade and her coach and support runner (marathon legend Shalane Flanagan), finished the 2022 Boston Marathon in 5:18:41, a podium finish (3rd place) in her division and a triumphant and seminal moment for the sport.

- **Nonbinary**—What began as a race organized by men for men in 1897 and transformed to unofficially (1966) and officially (1972) accommodate women has become increasingly more inclusive as it has matured. In another step forward toward further gender inclusion, the B.A.A. declared, beginning in 2023, athletes applying for entry into the Boston Marathon have the option to register as male, female, or nonbinary (i.e., not identifying exclusively as male or female).

Critics would argue that changes recently implemented are long-overdue and further improvements are necessary, but gender equality and inclusion in sports are human rights that the B.A.A. is committed to honor and advance. The Boston Marathon provides a powerful global platform for the B.A.A. to embrace change and lean into its responsibility to help lead the world in a more gender-balanced and inclusive direction.

Allowing athletes to identify as nonbinary when registering for the Boston Marathon is a big step forward, but the B.A.A. has indicated it must roll out further amendments to solve the gender equality and inclusion challenges more completely.

- **Guide and Support Runners**—Guide or Support Runners provide on-course support to athletes with visual, physical, or intellectual impairments in the Boston Marathon. Guide Runners provide verbal cues and navigation support to athletes with vision impairments on the marathon course. Support Runners provide verbal instructions, directions, and/or cues that support orientation and/or decision-making for athletes with physical or intellectual impairments.

The B.A.A. does not match, assign, or provide Guide or Support Runners to athletes. Each eligible athlete is responsible for finding a Guide or Support Runner who best meets his, her, or their personal needs. Runners who are interested in being Guide or Support Runners should reach out to athletes directly to offer their services. Selection and registration procedures and rules of participation are highlighted on the B.A.A. website. Several high-profile runners have been Guide and Support Runners, including Olympian Alexi Pappas, ultra pioneer Scott Jurek, and prolific marathoner and ultramarathoner Mike Wardian.

Para Division and Adaptive Program athletes and their respective Guide and Support Runners often share accommodations in Hopkinton before the race. It's a Boston Marathon tradition for many families in Hopkinton to open their houses to charity teams, organizations dedicated to transforming the lives of people with disabilities, and their volunteer guides and supporters. As comfortable as Athletes' Village is, being pampered in a warm,

Olympian Alexi Pappas guides Lisa Thompson to a 3:42:00 finish in 2023.
Kevin Gunawan

quaint New England home before the start is as delightful as it sounds and a nice perk of being affiliated with a team, program, or organization fortunate enough to commandeer a home on Marathon Monday.

- **Adaptive Program**—If you have a permanent visual, intellectual, or physical impairment (as defined by World Para Athletics Classification Rules and Regulations), can provide impairment documentation upon registration, and achieve the qualifying standard (currently 6:00:00 for men and women with physical or intellectual impairments and 5:00:00 for men and women with visual impairments), you can participate in the Boston Marathon's Adaptive Program.

Additionally, nonqualified runners with impairments may apply for the Adaptive Program via an invitational entry (i.e., raise money for a charity). Runners with visual impairments can run with one or two Guide Runners, and runners with physical or intellectual impairments are permitted a Support Runner.

- **Racial Disparity and Diversity**—The Boston Marathon maintains its foothold as the "Granddaddy of them all" by safeguarding its time-honored traditions while continuing to innovate and stay true to its vision that "all people can access and benefit from running." This is a tricky balancing act, particularly given the endurance sports' cultural shift from its predominantly White, male-dominated, upper-income heritage to its diverse, all-gender, all-income future.

  Sure, Narragansett Native American Tarzan Brown had to borrow a dollar at the start in Hopkinton in 1939 to afford the entry fee before winning the race and setting a new American record (2:28:51), but Tarzan was an anomaly among his White, less-impoverished competitors. And despite winning the Boston Marathon in 1936 and 1939 and competing in the 1936 Olympic Games, he faced extreme poverty and discrimination throughout his life.

  So, what does the future of the Boston Marathon look like? How does the Boston Marathon make amends for the shortcomings of its heritage? We've come a long way since 1939, but it's clear further changes are necessary.

  Some would argue the course itself needs to change. Boston Marathon purists might think altering the course is sacrilege, but, according to the US Census Bureau, each town and city on the course, with the exception of Framingham (63 percent White), is 70 percent White or more. It's fair for BIPOC (Black, Indigenous, and People of Color) runners to wonder why the course doesn't traverse Boston's neighboring Black and brown communities such as Mattapan, Dorchester, and Roxbury (82 percent, 70 percent, and 55 percent Black, respectively).

  Would changing the course bridge the racial divide? Not completely, at least not without addressing other inequities, too. For example, gaining an invitational entry into Boston requires raising significant funds (often $10,000 or more) for a charity. As a result, the majority of Boston Marathon charity runners are White, well-paid professionals. How can we amend the ways invitational entries are allocated to runners to improve the diversity of future Boston Marathons? Could a mandate requiring charity teams to distribute a certain percentage of bibs to BIPOC runners be a step in the right direction?

It will be exciting to see how these new divisions, rules, and policies evolve and what new advancements await us in the years to come. What actions will the B.A.A. take to advance distance running's cultural shift? Whether it's smartwatches, technical fabrics, or carbon-plated super shoes, Boston Marathon participants welcome innovation. Just because the race honors its storied past doesn't mean it can't embrace the changes required to brighten its future.

WORLDWIDE ALLURE

It's hard to believe the Boston Marathon was initially named the "American Marathon" in 1897. Not only were all 10 finishers American, but they were all from Massachusetts or New York. With the exception of several Canadians who crossed the border to run Boston in the first two decades of its existence, a runner from a foreign country didn't participate until 1919, when Peter Trivoulidas from Greece and Runar Ohman from Sweden finished seventh and eighth, respectively. Times have changed. Athletes from a remarkable 122 countries (63 percent of the more than 190 countries in the world) participated in the 2022 Boston Marathon.

The Boston Marathon has become a global phenomenon, attracting runners from Thailand to Qatar to Lithuania to Iceland to El Salvador and beyond. It's not uncommon for athletes who are complete strangers from a variety of countries to meet serendipitously at the Expo and bond over the event and sport that brought them together.

The running community and the Boston Marathon are truly borderless. And one of the understated joys of walking around the streets of Boston during Marathon Weekend is witnessing random acts of kindness among eclectic athletes who, if not for the Boston Marathon, would otherwise never have met.

In a city often criticized for its cold, New England demeanor and historically "siloed communities," Boston residents open their

Eliud Kipchoge greets fans after his sixth-place finish in his 2:09:23 Boston debut (2023).

arms to the diverse array of Boston Marathoners with a variety of races, genders, religions, ethnicities, impairments, and qualifying times. Skeptics would argue the generosity you see during the Boston Marathon is an anomaly, a blip on the screen for a traditionally austere, Puritanical caste. That seems a bit pessimistic.

The Boston Marathon is special to me not only because it is the oldest marathon and organized so well, but Boston is a unique course, and it's very exciting because of the fans on the course cheering us a lot with such good vibes.

Lonah Salpeter
3rd Place, Boston Marathon (2023)
Winner, Tokyo Marathon (2020)
2nd Place, New York City Marathon (2022)

Boston's good behavior during the weekend of the race is a hopeful harbinger of how the very best of a community of people resides innately inside each member, ready to emerge in unison if given the opportunity. And the Boston Marathon provides it with the perfect opportunity to bring out its best year after year.

PATRIOTS' DAY

Many things set Boston apart from other marathons, but one of the most significant is the festive, party-like atmosphere that takes over the city on race day and Marathon Weekend. Boston has a unique aura throughout the three-day weekend, and the catalyst is Patriots' Day, the statewide holiday held on the third Monday of April that commemorates the first battles of the American Revolutionary War.

Patriots' Day is often referred to as "Marathon Monday" because the Boston Marathon has been run on Patriots' Day every year since its inception in 1897 (with the exception of 2020 and 2021 due to the COVID-19 pandemic). Boston's Back Bay neighborhood, home to the finish line, Expo, and Newbury Street, is the spotlight of the running universe during race week. And Boston Marathon mania crescendos as the race approaches, reaching its zenith on race day.

Not only does the Monday holiday create a three-day weekend and begin a vacation week for local schools, colleges, and universities, Boston's beloved Red Sox join the fun by playing an 11 a.m. home game at Fenway Park, roughly Mile 25.25 on the course.

Much like the Boston Marathon can trace its name and roots to ancient Greece, Patriots' Day has intimate ties to the country, too. The Revolutionary War between the Americans and British is often compared to a deciding ancient

TJ's Food and Spirits (Mile 2 in Ashland) has a party vibe all year, but you'll see it and hear it at its best on Patriots' Day. Jill DellOrco

Greek battle (circa 490 BCE), the Battle of Marathon. Persians invaded Athens and, despite being outnumbered, the Athenians turned away the Persians and won their freedom. Because the Americans similarly defeated the British and the race's name, "Marathon," personifies a struggle against seemingly insurmountable odds, racing the Boston Marathon on Patriots' Day is a fitting way to pay tribute to both the patriots responsible for America's independence and the courageous originators of the marathon itself.

From a modern runner's perspective, Patriots' Day provides an opportunity to run a course that mimics the legendary route traversed by the ancient Greek foot soldier Pheidippides. But rather than run it alone without support or spectators, you can run it with thousands of like-minded type-A endurance junkies, ample support, and nearly one million cheering fans. And, live. There's that.

THE BOMBING

A tragedy that shook the world at large, and the running world in particular. Sure, the Rosie Ruiz incident in 1980 was a reminder that the Boston Marathon is not immune to evildoing. But the bombing in 2013 took evil to another level. The

Boston Marathon finish line is sacred ground, and an imposter crossing it and declaring victory was disgraceful, but unlike Rosie's short-lived "victory," the tragic desecration of hallowed ground and resulting bloodshed can never be reversed.

The events of that day felt like an emotional rollercoaster you didn't sign up to get on. Every marathon has highs and lows, but nothing quite as heart-wrenching as the day of the domestic terrorist attack on Marathon Monday, April 15, 2013. It began as a sunny, pleasant day, a welcome reprieve from 2012's sweltering 85 degree F heat-fest. Patriots' Day 2013 was blue-skied awesomeness, until it wasn't. Most elites, sub-elites, age-group contenders, and somewhat fast BQ'ers were finished and possibly showering before mayhem ensued. But when it ensued, everything changed, including the Boston Marathon itself.

Two bombs exploded 14 seconds apart near the finish line at approximately 2:49 ET, killing three innocent spectators and injuring more than 264 fans and participants, including 17 who lost limbs. Runners continued to cross the finish line until 2:57 ET when the race was officially halted, preventing more than 5,600 runners from finishing. The mood turned from festive to fearful, like a sprawling, citywide party transformed into a horrifying crime scene. Police officers, who were high-fiving runners and posing for pictures with fans minutes earlier, were now rescuing lives and drawing weapons as trucks of SWAT teams were deployed onto the scene.

The visceral memories of the bombing are recallable even if words can't adequately express how poignant the events were that afternoon. Smoke billowing above Copley Square. Spectators screaming and running in all directions. The look of fear in strangers' eyes. The smell of gunpowder. Sirens wailing. Armed forces with automatic weapons patrolling street corners. Feelings of joy replaced with dread.

But rather than glorify the terrorists responsible for the bombing or focus on the manhunt that brought them to justice, it's important to note that, despite the dreadfulness of the bombing, considerable good has come in the wake of this tragedy (including but not limited to the following):

- Boston University established a scholarship in honor of Lü Lingzi, a graduate student who died in the bombing.

- University of Massachusetts Boston established a scholarship in honor of Krystle Marie Campbell, an alumna who died in the bombing.

- The parents of Martin William Richard established the Martin W. Richard Charitable Foundation (dedicated to promoting education and sports in the community) in honor of Martin, their eight-year-old son who died in the bombing.

- The Massachusetts Institute of Technology (MIT) established a scholarship in memory of Sean Collier, the MIT police officer killed by the terrorists during the manhunt.

- One Fund Boston was established by then Massachusetts governor Deval Patrick and Boston mayor Thomas Menino, raising more than $70 million to make monetary distributions to bombing victims.

- One Boston Day was created on the second anniversary of the bombings by then Boston mayor Marty Walsh, establishing April 15 as an official and permanent holiday in the city of Boston, celebrating the resiliency, generosity, and strength of those in Boston and around the world in response to the tragedy of April 15, 2013.

Following the explosions, many heroes emerged. Emergency responders (police, fire, and EMS), B.A.A. medical volunteers, and numerous spectators and bystanders responded to the critically injured, triaging their injuries and facilitating their transport to area hospitals. The Boston hospitals that received patients rendered lifesaving medical care. Each patient treated at the scene who was transported to a local hospital survived. The city and the race emerged "Boston Strong."

HEARTBREAK HILL

The most (in)famous hill in road racing is a innocuous 88-foot rise in Newton, Massachusetts, that extends roughly 600 meters between Miles 20 and 21. Yep, 88 feet. That's not a misprint. A speed bump, really. And at its steepest, Heartbreak has a pedestrian 3.3 percent elevation grade. (***Note:*** A popular local training hill in neighboring Brookline, Summit Avenue, has an elevation grade that reaches 15 percent.) Yet marathoners from across the globe have their hearts broken year after year.

It'd be great if you could blame it on thin air, but Boston, from an altitude perspective, is as good as it gets; runners descend from 490 feet in Hopkinton at the start to 10 feet above sea level in downtown Boston's Copley Square at the finish. Heartbreak traverses an elevation of 148 feet to 236 feet. Oxygen is plentiful. Driveways in Colorado have more "vert" than Heartbreak.

So why is Heartbreak so darn mystifying? Well, first, there's the legend. Let's face it: If it didn't have the intimidating name and such history, the hill would just be a polite little climb to the forth-coming mayhem of Boston College. Fear is baked in its name, coined by *Boston Globe* reporter Jerry Nason. In 1936, Boston hero and defending champion Johnny "The Elder" Kelley overtook the leader, Ellison "Tarzan" Brown, and gave Brown a consolatory (or some would say patronizing) pat on the back before moving into the lead. Brown didn't take kindly to the gesture, rallied, and went on to win the race, famously breaking Kelley's heart. Ouch.

A sign in the window of Heartbreak Hill Running Company (Mile 20 in Newton) encourages athletes to take chances on Patriots' Day.

Johnny wasn't the first, and the notoriety of his blunder has opened the floodgates to generations of runners who have learned to fear Heartbreak Hill and fall victim to its curse. It doesn't help that Heartbreak is situated at Mile 20, the exact moment when scientists of running agree glycogen stores in your body (i.e., all the gels, bananas, waffles, pancakes, bagels, spaghetti, and pad thai you wolfed down while carb-loading) are finally depleted. So, not only do you "hit the wall" like you would at any other marathon, you have to run up Heartbreak Hill at the exact time you're bonking. Oh, and three hills precede Heartbreak. There's that, too.

The silver lining to Heartbreak is the enthusiastic fan support you'll experience from base to peak. When you cross Centre Street in Newton Centre, you'll be greeted by swarms of local families, many of whom have been encouraging runners on Marathon Monday for generations.

You'll pass Heartbreak Hill Running Company, where 2:20 marathoners who are a.) injured, b.) working a shift, or c.) both will be cheering outwardly while crying tears of jealousy on the inside. As you begin your ascent, friends and family of the MassGeneral Marathon Team will offer you Swedish fish and orange slices to catapult you up the hill. And, finally, screams from legions of fans lining the hill will prepare you for the cacophony of madness (i.e., deafening, beer-swilling students) awaiting you when you crest it, catch your first glimpse of the Boston skyline, and enter Boston College.

The bad news is your legs will feel pretty wrecked going up the hill. The good news is, once you reach the top, the remaining 5.2 miles are (mostly) downhill to the finish. Psychologically, it's a boost, even if your quads and feet are too angry to rejoice. But rejoice you should, because things are about to get more festive. Those screams that are getting louder in the distance belong to Boston College partiers, more than happy to hand you a celebratory beer to boost your spirits or drown your sorrows before you head downtown.

BANDITS

Boston's bandit-friendliness is as legendary as the bowls of beef stew that awaited finishers in the race's pre-running-boom years. If you see a runner with bloody nipples bleeding through a cotton T-shirt, basketball shorts, and tube socks, chances are strong you've spotted a bandit.

What's a "bandit"? A bandit is a participant who runs the race without paying its entry fees. Plain and simple. Unethical? Yep. Frowned upon? Sure. Illegal? Not quite. Banditing isn't a jailable offense. Is it a breach of B.A.A. policy? Yes. So, why bandit Boston? What's the appeal and why, historically, did race officials tolerate bandits for so long?

Running purists turn their noses up at bandits who run alongside paid entrants and indulge in plentiful, yet theoretically limited, race-day resources (water, Gatorade, gels, medical attention). Bandits would argue they are the running purists, choosing to run for the joy of running rather than stuffing the pockets of race organizers who orchestrate everything, including providing support, medals, T-shirts, and more in return for increasingly steep entry fees.

To be fair, banditing has changed over the years. In its heyday, hundreds of unapologetic bandits would flock to Hopkinton on Marathon Monday to run the historic 26.2 miles to Boston. Masochistic local college students, undertrained research analysts, egotistical (cost-cutting) corporate executives, and others intent on their slice of (free) fame found rides to Hopkinton and joined the herd heading east. But things changed in 2013.

Prior to the bombing, bandits were considered a nuisance, at worst, but never a "threat" to the race's honor or the safety of its runners, volunteers, and spectators. There was an unwritten, unspoken agreement between bandits and officials. Bandits could run the race relatively unimpeded and partake in any support they needed along the way. But they would not be honored as official race finishers, and they would not receive a medal at the finish line. In short, bandits got what they wanted, memorable life experiences, and officials got what they wanted, an uncorrupted race of the highest integrity with a bit of whimsy on the side.

Seven Tips for Modern Bandits

1. Bring some form of identification. Seriously. Official runners have bibs with their personal identification details printed on the back. You don't. So if something goes horribly wrong on the course, medical professionals will have no clue who you are, what you're allergic to, or anything else that might assist them in treating you.

2. Have a friend drive you to Hopkinton early (before 6:30 a.m.) to avoid the parade of buses carrying official runners, the ones who properly paid for entry.

3. Befriend a Hopkinton resident (or a charity team) beforehand so you can commandeer their house, or at least the parts that matter:

   a. Bathroom—"Dropping the kids off at the pool" feels better when the pool is filled with chlorine, not raw sewage.

   b. Kitchen—Coffee, bagels, bananas, peanut butter, and other gems (sponges!) will never be as magical as they are in someone else's kitchen on race morning.

   c. AC or heat—Even official runners in the Athletes' Village don't have the luxury of a climate-controlled respite on race morning.

   d. Living room—While official runners sprawl out on itchy grass, patches of dirt, or unforgiving mud, you can recline on throw rugs and cozy sofas.

   e. Yard—Years ago, you may have witnessed many runners "doing the unthinkable" on Hopkinton lawns. This still occurs, albeit less frequently (and when it does, it's captured on security or doorbell cameras). Instead, the yard is a great place to test the weather, chat with fellow nervous runners, and determine whether last-minute gear changes are warranted.

4. Avoid race officials at the start—easier said than done. Officials won't allow you in a corral if you don't have a bib. Your best bet is to wear many layers of shirts and fold your arms across your chest like you're shivering (yes, do this even if it's sunny and 84 degrees), hence disguising your bib-lessness.

5. Be courteous to everyone—You're crashing the most exclusive party in the distance running world, so be thankful you're inside the metal barricades. "Courtesy" includes but is not limited to the following:

   a. Do NOT wear a bib. You're a bandit, so this one should be easy. But sadly, some nefarious bandits have "borrowed" bibs from other runners and even stolen images of bibs posted online, printed them out, and worn them on their chests on race day. Be a bandit. Don't be a cheater (even though public opinion says you already are).

   b. Start in the way, way back—Being a human speed bump to faster, official runners is not fun for them and being passed by thousands of bibbed gazelles is both demoralizing and not fun for you.

   c. Obey race officials—If an official spots you in a corral without a bib and instructs you to exit the corral, do the right thing and exit the corral. Then attempt your chicanery in a different corral (until you succeed).

   d. Yield to official runners—Always. If you and a bibbed runner are reaching for the last cup of water held by a volunteer at a water station, don't be an ungrateful bandit and grab the cup. Technically, you didn't pay for that cup. So suppress your thirst for a hot second and wait for an uncontested one. Same goes for everything else available on the course.

   e. Do *not* take a medal at the finish—some would argue bandits should step off the course and shouldn't be allowed to cross the sacred finish line. Bandits feel the experience is incomplete without a finish, akin to skydiving and never touching the ground. By virtue of being a bandit, you're already pushing your luck. You don't want karma to find you with a medal around your neck.

6. Spend a lot of money—Buy merch, go out to big dinners, and make donations to nonprofit organizations, particularly ones affiliated with the Boston Marathon's Official Charity Program.

7. Don't do it—Seriously. Don't bandit. If you choose to ignore #7, look in the mirror and take stock of why you're making this poor decision. Better yet, plan in advance how you intend to atone for it.

Trust was at the heart of the relationship between bandits and officials. A bandit attempting to procure a medal at the finish would be "crossing the line," an act as egregious as a race official trying to remove a bandit from the course or a medical professional refusing to provide care to a bandit in a medical tent.

After the bombing, security heightened and the symbiotic relationship between bandits and officials was fractured. In fairness, the bandits weren't at fault. But innocence was lost, and it's safe to say bandits and officials will never enjoy the relationship they once shared.

Can you bandit Boston today? In theory, no. The official site of the B.A.A. states "no, please do NOT run." Yet, in practice, yes, you can. Is it as easy as it was in 1986? No, it isn't. Should you do it? No, you shouldn't. It's wrong. But many would argue that Boston without bandits is wrong, too.

If you're a runner and you're no stranger to blurring the boundaries separating ethical from unethical, legal from illegal, and upstanding citizen from complete charlatan, then the Seven Tips for Modern Bandits (pages 34–35) has the advice you need.

RED SOX

Every morning on Patriots' Day, the Boston Red Sox host something special, a rare morning game, an 11:10 a.m. ET start at the "cathedral of baseball," Fenway Park. On the only day of the year the Red Sox are second fiddle to anything in this town, the Boston Marathon is front and center and the star of the citywide party, relegating Red Sox Nation to an unfamiliar, but no less enthusiastic, supporting role.

The Boston Marathon wouldn't be the same without the vocal, "well-hydrated" Fenway crowd spilling over into the streets of Kenmore Square, the oft-rowdy section of real estate on game days that marries Boston University, Boston's Back Bay, and Fenway, a mile from the finish line in Copley Square. If you've ever experienced sharpened senses or spiritual elation (a "third wind" of heightened awareness) at the tail end of a marathon, you're in for a treat on Marathon Monday.

The potpourri of sensations begins for runners as they traverse the Mass Pike (I-90) overpass at Mile 25. You'll see Fenway Park on your right and the awesomeness that is the Citgo sign on your left. If the game is in progress, you'll hear the roar of the crowd whenever things are going the Red Sox's way, and a chorus of boos and jeers when they aren't. If the game is over by the time you pass by, then you'll be greeted by tens of thousands of fans, most in Red Sox gear of some variety, who are amped up to keep their party going, especially if the Red Sox win. (***Note:*** The Red Sox win 57 percent of the time on Patriots' Day.)

Have you really visited Boston if you haven't seen the Red Sox at Fenway Park?

Regardless of whether the game is over, you'll smell the heady scent of hops and hot dogs wafting over the Green Monster. Depending on how your stomach has handled your journey from Hopkinton, you'll either get increasingly nauseous or more hungry. Unlike high fives in Hopkinton (love taps administered by children or octogenarians), Fenway high fives pack enough force to rip your spindly, marathon-depleted arm from its socket. Just bear in mind that the person delivering it is fully fed, probably six beers deep, wicked angry (if the Sox lost) or jacked up (if the Sox won), and outweighs you by a factor of two.

By Kenmore Square (exactly one mile from the finish), everyone on the course is in the "pain cave," a cavern of discomfort where endurance athletes either lean into the pain or break down from the pain. The question is no longer "Are you willing to suffer?"—rather it's "How much are you willing to suffer?"

Before (or after) the race, if you arrive in town early (or leave late), swing by Fenway and rest your legs. There's so much to do and experience in Boston, but catching a Red Sox game at Fenway Park is a must if you want to enjoy the full Boston experience and stay, relatively, off your feet for three hours (bonus!). Go, Sawx!

TEAM HOYT

If any father and son were to be voted "least likely to participate in the Boston Marathon," Dick and Rick Hoyt would have made the short list. In 1977, Dick was a nonrunning 36-year-old father whose 15-year-old son, Rick, was quadriplegic and confined to a wheelchair, having been diagnosed with cerebral palsy at birth.

Everything changed when Rick asked his father to run with him in a local race that benefited a lacrosse player from his school who had been paralyzed. A photo capturing them racing showed Rick with, according to Dick, "the biggest smile he's ever seen in his life." That night, Rick spelled out on his computer, "Dad, when we're running, I don't even feel like I'm handicapped anymore."

What could have ended as a nice gesture for a good cause instead began an unlikely athletic career, totaling more than 1,130 events (including 72 marathons, 257 triathlons, and even six full-Ironman triathlons). The Boston Marathon was a pipe dream. When they expressed interest in running it, they were informed that Dick would need to qualify by running the time standard (2:50:00) for Rick's age (18). Dick and Rick BQ'd at the Marine Corps Marathon in 2:45:23, an average of 6:19/mile while pushing more than 125 pounds.

The ancient Chinese philosophy of yin and yang is a concept of dualism, the belief that opposite or contrary forces may actually be complementary, interconnected, and interdependent in the natural world, and how they may give rise to each other as they interrelate to one another. On April 21, 1980, the day of one of the Boston Marathon's greatest indignities, the Rosie Ruiz scandal, yin and yang produced a gem, the debut of one of the race's most honest blessings, the father and son team of Dick and Rick Hoyt.

Unlike Ruiz, whose name has been relegated to infamy, Dick and Rick Hoyt became instant fan-favorites, fixtures in the race for decades (completing 32 Boston Marathons together), and two-of-a-kind legends immortalized in bronze in a life-size statue near the Hopkinton starting line.

Despite their recent deaths, Dick and Rick continue to inspire runners and para athletes across the world, especially in Boston, home of Rick's self-professed favorite race. Each year, Team Hoyt fields a team of charity runners "who want to support the inclusion of people with disabilities," including many duos akin to the team's namesake. Don't be shy about offering encouragement to Team Hoyt athletes if you cross paths with them on race day. The race and the world are better because of them. The least we can do is pay our respects when we're fortunate enough to be in their midst.

CHARITY RUNNERS

The exact origins of charity running are a bit murky, but its beginnings seem to coincide with the running boom of the mid- to late 1970s. Walks for charity like the CROP Hunger Walk and March of Dimes' WalkAmerica began in the late 1960s and early 1970s, but it wasn't until road races increased in popularity that running and raising money for an established 501(c) organization became a thing.

Research has shown that people are willing to donate more when they believe a fundraising event will require pain or exertion than when the process is neutral or enjoyable. Coined "The Martyrdom Effect" by scholars, these findings help explain why running marathons for charity feels so right and has grown so prevalent. Pain and effort lead people to ascribe greater meaning to their contributions, thereby motivating higher prosocial contributions.

Official charity running began at the Boston Marathon in 1989. The American Liver Foundation became the first charity (followed by Dana-Farber and others) to receive official entries into the Boston Marathon. Many would argue that unofficial charity running at Boston began much earlier, most notably in 1946. Boston legend Johnny "The Elder" Kelley had befriended a Greek runner, Stylianos Kyriakides, at the 1936 Olympic Games in Berlin. After Kyriakides finished 11th and Kelly 18th, Kelley invited his new friend to join him at the Boston Marathon. Kyriakides traveled more than 5,000 miles by ship to run his first Boston in 1938, dropping out midway due to blisters. Kyriakides vowed to return to Boston to redeem himself and win, but World War II interrupted his plans.

It wasn't until 1946, after Greece had been decimated by war and famine, that Kyriakides not only ran Boston but made true on his promise to win for his native Greece. Kyriakides returned home to a parade, and soon thereafter shipments of

Leonardo da Vinci's Last Supper *is hardly as breathtaking as a charity team's "Last Suppah."* Norman Lang

clothes, food, medicine, and equipment arrived. He had fulfilled his promise to his country and, unbeknownst to the world, had pioneered charity running decades before the term was coined and its popularity ensued.

Charity running at Boston routinely raises more than $35 million per year for more than 40 official charities. Charity team members typically raise (depending on the charity's mandate) $7,500 to $12,500 (or more). Larger teams like ALS and Dana-Farber field teams of hundreds of runners. Smaller teams such as Project Hope and Best Buddies could have a handful of runners or a dozen or two depending on the year and availability of bibs.

The seven Boston Marathons I ran in a row were some of the most purposeful and meaningful events in my life, especially knowing that my fundraising efforts directly impacted so many people.

Richard Snyder
7 Consecutive Boston Marathons
The Fashion Director, Project Hope Marathon Team

If you don't have a BQ for your gender and age group, you can receive an invitational entry into the race, hence waiving the need to qualify. This is blasphemy to an ever-shrinking group of Boston Marathon purists, but it's nirvana to recipients of the charity funds. Beneficiaries include cancer survivors, ALS patients, suicide research programs, homeless shelters, children's museums, para athletes, Special Olympians, animal rescues, career training initiatives, and many other worthy charities. So, if you harbor animosity toward charity runners, remember that it's likely their efforts to gain entry to Boston helped discover treatments for incurable diseases, break the cycle of poverty for homeless women and children, fund the exhibit at the museum you just visited, and save lives.

Oh, and running for charity at Boston is fun, highly addictive, and (depending on your talent level and commitment to training) can lead to a BQ! Plenty of runners with BQ bibs between 2000 and 15,000 got their start as charity runners with bibs higher than 25,000.

There's camaraderie among charity runners, too. For those of you who weren't around for the Eliot Lounge or Crossroads Irish Pub eras, charity runners from across the Greater Boston area would convene after work at the Eliot (corner of Commonwealth Avenue and Massachusetts Avenue) or, after the Eliot's demise, Crossroads (495 Beacon Street) every Thursday from January 1 until the second week of April. Why? To change out of work clothes into running gear in a phone-booth-sized bathroom, take the D-line of the "T" to the Woodland station stop

(Mile 17) in a blizzard while everyone in a hat, scarf, long coat, gloves, and boots (like a reasonable human would wear in a nor'easter) looks at you as if you're insane, and run 9 miles on the marathon course to the bar for beer(s) and pizza, of course. It's marathon season, kid!

Charity teams are these dynamic, awesome conglomerations of characters, not dissimilar from fraternities or sororities, albeit a slight bit healthier. Team members are corporate executives, scientists, personal trainers, financial advisors, venture capitalists, bartenders, physical therapists, ne'er-do-wells, doctors, and a little bit of everything else. This variety and crucible of purpose and time create the magic you otherwise wouldn't experience if it weren't for the charity. Inevitably, teammates assume roles, many that are quite similar from team to team (see The 10 Charity Team Personas on page 42).

DAVE MCGILLIVRAY

If the B.A.A. is the backbone of the Boston Marathon and John "The Elder" Kelley is its heart and soul, then Dave McGillivray is its central nervous system, controlling its every move. McGillivray has worked with the Boston Marathon since 1988, starting as the technical director before becoming race director in 2001.

Race Director Dave McGillivray finishing his 50th consecutive Boston Marathon Dave McGillivray

The 10 Charity Team Personas

1. **The Cruise Director (TCD)**—The master organizer who serves as the hub of all team activity online and offline. Where and when do you meet for your final group long run? The Cruise Director's email will let you know. Who will arrange the house in Hopkinton you'll be headquartered at on race day? Yep. You guessed it.

   TCD gets things done. (*Note:* "Things" is shorthand for everything you can't do, everything you don't want to do, everything you're too lazy to do, and everything you weren't aware had to be done, but was done anyway.)

"The bus leaves at six. Not 6:05. Not 6:10. Six. No bus. No Boston." Marc Camm

2. **The Fashion Director (TFD)**—What color singlets are you wearing on race day? Fuchsia? Chartreuse? What should you write on your chest and arms? What about the Valentine's theme for your February 14th long run? Is it too much to wear lingerie on top of your tights? Do you even need tights?

   TFD has the final say on all team wardrobe choices on the roads (team swag, race kits, training gear) and off (team dinners, award banquets, fund-

"No photos, please, unless TFD is in the middle. Then, photos, please." Marc Camm

raisers). And you want TFD to make those choices. He or she has the best sense of style and, without TFD, the team would otherwise be a hodgepodge of ghastly fashion faux pas.

3. **The Connector**—Does the Connector raise the most money? Usually not. Does the Connector have a strong fashion sense? Doubtful. Is the Connector considered the leader of (or the fastest on) the team? No (and no). So, what makes the Connector so special? The Connector has a superpower; he or she seems to know everyone, and proceeds to connect them to one another as effortlessly as most humans breathe.

   The Connector is the teammate who says "meet me for a drink at Long Bar" (the newest iteration of the legendary Merry-Go-Round Bar and Oak Room at the Fairmont Copley Plaza Hotel), and when you arrive, he is surrounded by 35 friends. The diverse group is an assemblage of all walks of life that otherwise would never be in the same room. And you are all held together by one common thread; you are blessed to know the Connector.

"My cousin's sister's uncle's stepfather played lacrosse at Tufts with your dad. We'll be at Abe & Louie's at 8. Meet you there. Table for 30." Joe Findaro

This superpower is particularly invaluable on a charity team because 80 percent or more of your team can be linked (directly or indirectly) to the Connector. TCD may be the hub of the charity wheel operationally, but there wouldn't be a wheel without the Connector.

4. **The Comedian**—Just when you thought your team was a refined group of professionals intensely focused on training optimization, mission-driven fundraising, PR-chasing, and perhaps even BQing, enter the Comedian. It begins with an inadvertent f-bomb in an email, innuendo on a long run, bawdy banter in a group chat, or illicit anecdote from the previous weekend. The Comedian is often the teammate you would least expect to be so risqué. Keep your eye on the straight-laced patent attorney who orders a "filthy Grey Goose martini, Sam Winter back" at the team kickoff dinner.

The Comedian allows all team members to release their inhibitions. What started as a single stray comment morphs into a multi-month group email thread of one-upmanship the likes of which couldn't be matched at Boston's Improv Asylum.

The Comedian's exploits inevitably earn him (or her) a naughty nickname. It then becomes incumbent upon the Comedian to return the favor and create appropriate monikers for other prominent team members. Again, very fraternity-like, but the ritual, like each charity team initiative, is good-hearted at its core.

5. **The Ringer**—The Ringer is the one who drops the pack on the group long run and showers and foam rolls by the time the rest of the team finishes. When the team picks up their bibs at the expo, the Ringer's Wave 1 red 2840 bib looks out of place next to a sea of teammates with Wave 4 yellow 30000+ bibs.

   The Ringer is missing from the team picture in Hopkinton on race morning because Wave 1 starts more than an hour before Wave 4. On a positive note, teammates provide the Ringer with a champion's send-off worthy of an Olympian. The Ringer reciprocates by being the first to greet each teammate at the designated meeting place following the race (usually a gym or nearby hotel conference room), after showering and receiving a complimentary massage, of course.

"Just because I'm wearing a Hawaiian shirt and had four Bloodies at breakfast doesn't mean my 'A' goal isn't 2:55 tomorrow." Norman Lang

6. **The Legend**—Similar to the Veteran, the Legend has a reputation that precedes him- or herself. By definition, the Legend is the team member who raises the most money (typically 5x the team mean). He or she has earned the moniker. If a charity requires each member, at a minimum, to raise $10,000, the Legend raises $64,374. It's uncanny.

   How does the Legend do it? What sorcery or witchcraft is necessary? The Legend has a robust network of friends and colleagues, with an emphasis on the latter. It's not uncommon for the Legend to be a hedge fund manager, venture capitalist, founder of a post-IPO startup, or established executive at a Fortune 100 company who receives multiple $5,000 and $10,000 donations while the average charity runner is hard-pressed to find someone from his or her church or child's soccer team (or anyone) to donate $50.

   This isn't to cheapen the crown that rests firmly upon the Legend's head. The Legend's seemingly endless supply of influential connections and supernatural ability to raise donations from them are testaments to why he or she is so deserving of such a regal epithet. And not only does the Legend crush it once, he or she crushes it year after year, often in a surprisingly quiet fashion. That's real altruism. That's the stuff of legends.

"I'm excited to be a part of a team that benefits a cause so close to my heart."
Brett Gordon

"Meet me at Crossroads. We used to go to the Eliot. Tommy, Mike, Sam, and J.J. are family. This is 17 for me. How 'bout you?"
Rich Horgan

7. **The Veteran**—Much like the Ringer (bib number) and the Legend (funds raised), the Veteran assumes his or her role because the math says so. The Veteran is your teammate who has run the most Boston Marathons. On the majority of established charity teams, the Veteran has typically run more than 20, but totals in the 30s and beyond are not uncommon.

   Best to catch the Veteran one-on-one. Just spit out a year (especially 2013 [the bombing] or 2018 ["Perfect Chaos"] or, even better, one from the 20th century), and the stories will flood forth like a local ale at the Green Dragon, the tavern where the Boston Tea Party was planned. Savor the good stuff while the tap is flowing. You never know when you'll have your last pour.

8. **The Rookie**—Remember when your inquisitive kindergartner was in the back seat of the minivan on a road trip interrogating you like you were a double agent? Are we there yet? How old's grandma? When do fish sleep? Well, that meddlesome tenderfoot is all grown up, just started to run, and joined your charity team to attempt her first marathon. Say "hello" to the Rookie.

There's a lot to learn about the Boston Marathon, and the Rookie intends to hack the system and learn everything before Patriots' Day. But, much like a toddler, who isn't reading chapter books yet, the Rookie relies on conversations with her team to glean as much information as possible. These "conversations" feel like a litigator's cross-examination at a murder trial. Oh, and just wait until the questions turn to fundraising. She has plenty of those, too. The more questions she asks, the more you realize, despite having run eight consecutive Boston Marathons, you really don't have all the answers she thinks you do.

9. **The Checkmate**—It's easy to spot the Checkmate among your teammates. Go to the team's fundraising website in early April and take a look at the amount each team member has raised. Scroll down to the bottom of the list where there's a $0. The Checkmate's name will be adjacent to the zero. Why? It's because the Checkmate "pays to play." While team members claw and scratch to raise the $10,000 minimum the hard way (i.e., procuring donations from their social networks), the Checkmate has pockets deep enough to cover the entire amount with one personal check. Checkmate!

10. **The Out-of-Towner**—Most charity runners are locals, but it's common for teams to recruit and welcome runners from afar. When your team posts a photo on Instagram after a long run in a nor'easter, the Out-of-Towner posts a tan selfie in split shorts from subtropical Naples, Florida, or New Zealand. The caption will read "Took a ride on the struggle bus today." Cough.

You can spot the Out-of-Towner on race day, too. He or she shivers beneath multiple layers in Hopkinton while you and your pale teammates are sprawled out on the lawn in 48 degrees F like it's late July on Nantucket.

Oh, and lest we forget the Out-of-Towner's pièce de résistance, the post-race party request. Most locals are wiped out after the race and just want to get home and collapse in the comfort of their beds. By contrast, the Out-of-Towner has a Tuesday afternoon flight and wants to celebrate, baby! That leads to a Marathon Monday quandary. Do you raise a glass (or two, or three) at Contessa (on the roof of The Newbury) with your teammate, or do you swaddle your angry legs in your comforter and close your eyes? Tough call.

McGillivray's success as race director has been earned. The Boston Marathon race director needs to protect the traditions that make Boston special while overseeing the modernization it needs to keep it relevant. The constituents (e.g., elites, sponsors, charities, volunteers, communities, para athletes, charity runners, and DEI advocates) on all sides of that juggling act don't often see eye to eye, making it difficult for McGillivray (or anyone in his role) to please everyone when decisions need to be made (field sizes, start times, pandemic restrictions, and everything else).

But McGillivray has navigated the challenging waters with the focus and determination of a talented endurance athlete, which, oh, by the way, he is. In 1978, McGillivray ran across the United States from Medford, Oregon, to Medford, Massachusetts (3,452 miles), in 80 days, averaging 42 miles a day. And that's just the tip of McGillivray's iceberg of accomplishments, which include:

- Running 120 miles in 24 hours

- Running 1,520 miles from Winter Haven, Florida, to Boston, Massachusetts, with Ron Hall, a pioneer of wheelchair racing

- Running, cycling, and swimming 1,522 miles in the annual New England Run

- Winning a marathon against inmates at Walpole State Prison

- Swimming for 24 consecutive hours in the Jimmy Fund 24-hour swim (26.2 miles)

- Cycling 385 miles in 24 hours while directing the Bay State Triathlon

- Running his age in miles on his birthday every year from the age of 12 to 64 (**Note:** McGillivray had triple-bypass open-heart surgery in 2018 and now runs a marathon and bikes the remaining miles each birthday)

- Running more than 165 marathons (with a 2:29 PR), including 51 straight Boston Marathons (and counting)

- Running the World Marathon Challenge (seven marathons/seven continents/seven days)

Even better, McGillivray's athletic achievements are often vehicles for generous philanthropy. Perhaps the only things more impressive than McGillivray's benevolence and exploits by land and sea are his professional credentials, accumulated by organizing more than 1,000 mass-participation endurance events over a career spanning more than 40 years.

McGillivray's prolific body of work appears as if dozens of extremely talented athletes, businessmen, and philanthropists conspired to combine their résumés into one hyperbolic, Frankenstein-like masterpiece. But to be clear, McGillivray's magnum opus is and always will be embodied in one work of art, the Boston Marathon.

It's comforting to know a living legend is at the wheel and there is a legacy of success to leverage when it's time for McGillivray to hand the keys to his successor.

SWAG AND MERCH

There's nothing in the running community that screams "I'm a runner, not a jogger" quite like the yearly official Adidas Boston Marathon jacket. Wearing the 2013 Boston Marathon jacket communicates something very different from the 2004 jacket, just like a Woodstock '99 concert T-shirt tells a far different story from Woodstock '69.

If you want to raise eyebrows on the streets of Boston, wear merch from a bygone era. Heather Schulz

The jacket "screams," in part, because the colors are often quite garish (electric yellow, neon orange). If you're a streaker with a collection of jackets, sunglasses are advisable when admiring the kaleidoscopic rainbow inside your closet.

Many feel it's an unwritten rule that jackets should be worn only by official Boston Marathon finishers, particularly *after* they've crossed the finish line (wearing the jacket in advance is considered by some to be bad luck). Similar to what a townie in a Harvard sweatshirt would dread if an alumnus asked what he thought of Classics professor Richard Thomas's "Bob Dylan 101" seminar, nonrunners would feel awkward having to explain they didn't run the race while wearing a fluorescent purple Boston Marathon jacket that shouts they did.

On a positive note, a Boston Marathon jacket is a keepsake: tacky to some who feel it's akin to a high schooler wearing a letterman's jacket, aspirational to others who believe one day they'll BQ and be able to wear one. The finisher's medal is the best race memento, but as far as Boston merch goes, the jacket is most coveted.

CHAPTER 3

Getting In

You've probably heard there are just two ways to gain entry into the Boston Marathon: qualify (80 percent of the field) or run with a charity (20 percent of the field). And, yes, nearly the entire field enters through these two well-known doors. But there are some side doors and windows available to you.

10 Ways to Run the Boston Marathon

1. Qualify—perhaps the biggest reason Boston is so special is because it's so darn hard to get in. Unlike the other five World Marathon Majors, Boston doesn't have a lottery. Hence, roughly 80 percent of participants qualify to gain entry, resulting in the fastest field assembled for a marathon other than the Olympic Trials and Games.

2. Invitational entry via charity

3. Invitational entry via international tour company

4. Adaptive program

5. Duo Team

6. Guide or Support Runner

7. Elite athlete

8. Sub-elite athlete

9. Invitational entry via influential Bostonian or sponsor (or some person or entity that knows one)

10. Bandit (if you dare)

BQ

Prior to 1970, Boston was a come one, come all event. When women began to run marathons and the running boom of the 1970s hit its stride, field sizes swelled into the thousands. With a mass start at noon (before waves were introduced in 2006), field sizes were too large to fit on the narrow roads.

The Boston Marathon's introduction of time standards gave rise to its most renowned acronym, "BQ." As B.A.A. president and CEO Jack Fleming said best, "Qualifying standards have become a cornerstone of the Boston Marathon, helping differentiate Boston from other races." Runners need to BQ (Boston Qualify) by running a marathon faster than the time standard corresponding to their gender and age within the qualifying window to submit a registration application. A BQ does not guarantee entry into the race.

That's like telling you the driver's license you earned doesn't guarantee you'll drive a car, it simply represents an opportunity to submit an application to drive a car. But the B.A.A. is looking through a different lens, akin to a college admissions officer's point of view.

It can be argued Boston is the "Harvard" of marathons. Like Harvard is to US colleges, Boston is the oldest and most prestigious marathon. It's also the most difficult to gain entry into, and just because you achieve a perfect 1600 on your SAT doesn't guarantee you'll be offered admission to Harvard. Sure, a solid SAT, much like a solid BQ, puts you in the realm of being considered. But, much like Harvard and alternative colleges, if you don't get into Boston, there are many other marathons to choose from, so it's best not to put all your eggs in one basket. Apply to some "safety" spring marathons just in case.

On a positive note, qualifying times for men and women are specific to age divisions (e.g., 40–44, 45–49, 50–54) so older runners can qualify with slower times. While the general population often dreads aging up, especially to round numbers such as 50 or 60 and beyond, runners hoping to BQ rejoice because they gain additional time, making it, theoretically, easier to qualify. If you're a 64-year-old male who can't quite crack the current 3:55:00 standard, you'll be happy to know the 65–69 age group standard is a more pedestrian 4:10:00. So blow out those candles with a smile.

For those fortunate enough to achieve a BQ, you never forget your first. It's like the velvet rope has been lifted to a previously impenetrable club. And unlike the charity runners who randomly receive all of the highest bib numbers, your BQ seeds you in the field. If your 3:16:52 at Hartford qualifies you as the 7,542nd fastest entrant, you'll receive bib 7542. You know that everyone with a lower bib is faster and everyone with a higher bib is slower.

Speaking of BQs and bib numbers, every photo ever taken at the Boston Marathon tells a story. All you have to do is look at the bib numbers of the runners to discern who is crushing it and who's being crushed by it. If the gentleman with bib 7542 crosses the finish line surrounded by bibs in the 10000s, you know he had a rough day. But if he has his hands above his head next to a mustachioed runner sporting bib 2563, chances are that mustache caught some tears.

No matter how much pain or glory can be captured in a photo, it's tame compared to what's felt by runners on either side of the cutoff. In 2012, the Boston Marathon instituted a cutoff for the first time. Prior to 2012, you just needed to BQ and register and you'd be granted a Boston bib. Simple. If you're fast enough to BQ, of course. But runners not only had to BQ in 2012, they had to run 1:14 faster than their BQ to gain entry into the field. Anything slower, and runners were rejected.

Subsequent years have proven to be even more difficult for prospective applicants, similar to top-tier students awaiting Harvard's decision in the face of ever more stringent acceptance rates. Boston's 2021 field (reduced to 20,000 entrants due to COVID) had the most severe cutoff ever, 7:47 below BQ. Boston's 2024 field turned away 11,039 qualified runners. Yowza.

The Boston registration process is nerve-racking to say the least, especially for runners who qualify with times marginally faster than necessary to BQ. Until the process changes, the only answer for runners is to run so fast that you're no longer on the bubble. And because the exact cutoff is an annual mystery and the bubble seems to randomly expand and shrink, the faster you run, the better chance you have to gain entry. A new "BQ minus" vernacular has emerged to quantify your chances of gaining entry: A BQ means you qualified, a BQ-5 denotes you qualified by more than five minutes, a BQ-10 signifies you qualified by more than 10 minutes, etc.

If you register for the Boston Marathon and your BQ isn't a BQ-10 or greater, you are in jeopardy of finding yourself on the wrong side of the velvet rope in September. Depending on the cutoff, it's entirely possible to run the race of your life, BQ, and still be left out of a given year's field. That's a sobering reality.

Now that a simple BQ is often insufficient to gain entry, runners need to be mindful of more than one magic number when they toe the line at their qualifying races. For example, if you're a 37-year-old female hoping to gain entry into Boston, you need to be aware of not only the qualifying standard, 3:35:00, but also each variation (e.g., BQ-5, 3:30:00; BQ-10, 3:25:00, and BQ-20, 3:15:00). If your "A" goal isn't sub-3:25:00, you're rolling the dice during Boston Marathon registration week.

BOSTON MARATHON QUALIFYING STANDARDS*

Age Group	MEN	WOMEN
18–34	3hrs 00min 00sec	3hrs 30min 00sec
35–39	3hrs 05min 00sec	3hrs 35min 00sec
40–44	3hrs 10min 00sec	3hrs 40min 00sec
45–49	3hrs 20min 00sec	3hrs 50min 00sec
50–54	3hrs 25min 00sec	3hrs 55min 00sec
55–59	3hrs 35min 00sec	4hrs 05min 00sec
60–64	3hrs 50min 00sec	4hrs 20min 00sec
65–69	4hrs 05min 00sec	4hrs 35min 00sec
70–74	4hrs 20min 00sec	4hrs 50min 00sec
75–79	4hrs 35min 00sec	5hrs 05min 00sec
80 and over	4hrs 50min 00sec	5hrs 20min 00sec

*These standards are subject to change as the B.A.A. deems necessary.

Since it's difficult to earn a Boston bib, what, pray tell, can you do to stack the odds in your favor?

PUTTING YOUR BEST FOOT FORWARD (THE FASTEST QUALIFIERS)

Can you run Boston each year by using your qualifying time from the previous year? Sure. But, given the difficulties we discuss (spring marathon, tough course, unpredictable bubble, lack of pace groups, extreme weather), you're bound to run into a buzz saw one year and fail to BQ. Then what? Well, don't fret. Here's a one-word answer: REVEL.

What if you could find a marathon that was straight downhill? Would you run it? Well, that's REVEL. To be clear, REVEL isn't shy about the runner-friendliness of its courses, stating "the downhill nature of REVEL races provides a unique opportunity for runners to achieve personal best times and qualify for exclusive events." That's a polite way of saying a decently inflated basketball could roll down the course and BQ. For example, REVEL Big Cottonwood (Salt Lake City, Utah) loses more than 5,255 feet of elevation from start to finish.

To be fair, there are other downhill marathons that aren't REVEL races. But, REVEL or not, times from these marathons are surprisingly still allowed to be submitted as qualifying times for Boston. So if you're on the cusp of a BQ, go west and run down a mountain, stat. Heartbreak Hill is an 88-foot incline, and REVEL races typically decline more than 5,000 feet. Let that sink in.

REVEL Big Bear Elevation Profile

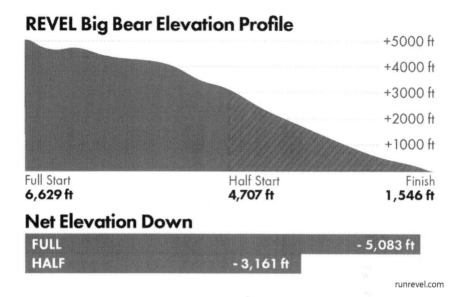

Full Start	Half Start	Finish
6,629 ft	**4,707 ft**	**1,546 ft**

Net Elevation Down

FULL	**- 5,083 ft**
HALF	**- 3,161 ft**

runrevel.com

Which begs the question, "Are races like REVEL fair?" Arguably, anyone touting a PR from a REVEL race should have difficulty saying it with a straight face. Perhaps those with PRs on downhill courses could at least put an asterisk next to the time, particularly if it is markedly faster than any previous marathon they ran on a flatter course. Could Eliud Kipchoge and Kelvin Kiptum run sub-2 at REVEL Big Cottonwood? Please. They would be showered and fielding questions from journalists before a "2" appeared on the clock.

CHARITY

Depending on who you talk to, charity runners are either the best thing that ever happened to the Boston Marathon or the worst thing that ever happened. There's little gray area between the two.

Why the animosity? Ask a 42-year-old female runner with a 3:37:12 BQ (2:48 below the 3:40:00 age-group standard) who missed the cut in 2021 because the cutoff for entry required 3:32:13 or better, and she'll have a very different opinion than the Massachusetts General Hospital pediatric oncology employee whose salary was paid by charity team fundraising. The feeling is that the aforementioned qualified female didn't make the cut because charity runners represent 20 percent of each year's field. Due to field size limitations, race officials turn away qualified runners to accommodate charity runners.

Recent tightening of the BQ time standards has helped, but it's likely REVEL-like races allowing marginal qualifiers to run faster times downhill and ever-faster super shoes have increased the pool of qualified applicants in lockstep with whatever decrease can be attributed to more stringent time standards. Both sides of this contentious debate have a solid argument. Charity programs at Boston have raised more than $400 million since the inception of running for charity at Boston in 1989. And that's a light number, because many charities that aren't recognized as official charities by the program field teams and raise significant funds, too.

So, how can something that does so much good be perceived to be so bad? It can be argued that charity running goes against the spirit of the race. In 1970 (the first year Boston required a qualifying time) the race application stated entrants must have trained sufficiently to finish the course in less than four hours, and added "this is not a jogging race." The reason for implementing a time standard was to curb the number of entrants, which had swollen to 1,342 the previous year. Officials felt a congested course would compromise the overall quality of the Boston Marathon race experience.

Perhaps we're ready for a new definition of "race experience." If "the overall quality of the Boston Marathon" is measured by speed alone, then, yes, unqualified charity running and banditing compromise the race experience. But speed is one of so many attributes that have come to characterize the race that it seems unjust to shortchange it with such a limited definition.

It's time for qualified runners and charity runners to reach a détente and embrace what Boston has become, three races in one: elites and sub-elites racing for prize money, qualifiers racing for PRs and BQs, and charity runners running to raise money for great causes. B.A.A. officials have done a great job of separating the three; qualified runners are seeded fastest to slowest in waves and corrals from front to back, and charity runners are relegated to the last waves and corrals. The three races play out nearly separate from one another.

The peskiest unresolved issue is the ire of runners who BQ, register, and are cut off and denied a bib. That's a tough one, but not insurmountable. In 2021, more than 9,000 qualifiers were denied entry due to "field size limitations." That's a COVID-inflated number due in large part to the registration window being widened considerably.

The good news is a possible solution appeared in 2021, the rolling start. Could the B.A.A. continue assigning specific start times to runners, allowing more runners to participate and be more evenly spaced along the course? It's imperfect (critics feel a rolling start feels less like a race and more like a time trial). But it's possible. Without a doubt, a race where charity runners and qualifiers can coexist and even root for one another would be in Boston's best interest. Finding a solution that satisfies all parties remains the challenge.

IS THERE ANOTHER WAY?

Well, let's keep this among us, but yes, there are a few secret doors into Boston. You always hear that you need to BQ or raise five figures for a charity to run Boston, but that's not completely true. There are hundreds of official bibs (often referred to as "invitational bibs") available to athletes. And, yes, they are legitimate. You just need to know how to get them. Or, to be precise, you need to know someone who knows how to (and is able to) get them.

So, who are these people that hold the golden tickets? The short answer is they typically fall into one of two camps: either a.) they wield some power within the government in the city of Boston, or b.) they are executives at companies or entities that sponsor the race or have a close affiliation with the race, its officials, or athletes.

For example, if you happen to know a city councilor or the commissioner or a superintendent of the Boston Police Department, you, whether you know it or not, have an opportunity to procure a Boston Marathon bib. No guarantee, of course. But high-ranking government officials are no strangers to imparting favors of a wide variety, and one such perk is access to a limited number of official Boston Marathon bibs that they can distribute per their wishes. Many of these bibs are bequeathed to smaller local charities that require the bib recipients to raise funds, but others find their way into the hands of very fortunate souls with no such qualifying time or fundraising requirements.

Similarly, entities that sponsor the Boston Marathon have access to bibs, too. Again, the number of bibs isn't large, making these golden tickets all the more precious. If you're unable to BQ and don't have a sufficient network with pockets deep enough to raise high-four or low-five figures, then it will behoove you to befriend an influential executive or two at one of the Boston Marathon's ever-growing list of sponsors.

Again, there's no guarantee the velvet rope will be lifted, but nothing ventured, nothing gained. Oh, and your chances will improve if you bring something to the table to help your cause. For example, if you have a "platform" (social media or otherwise) to sell into or influential audience to communicate with, your golden-ticket contact will have a much easier time justifying why the bib was given to you and not someone else. So, figure out why you are deserving, articulate your reasons, and give it a go. Happy hunting!

CHAPTER 4

Training

If you thought BQing wasn't challenging enough, you'll be pleased to know that training for the intricacies of the Boston Marathon (irrational weather, over-whelming gear choices, injury triage) will test you far further.

WEATHER

As if the Boston Marathon (with its oh-so-tempting downhill start, infamous hills, and quad-busting finish) isn't difficult enough, perhaps the cruelest training challenge is preparing for a mid-April race (for most participants) in the heart of winter. An added wrinkle of complexity is the weather on race day. Will it be 85 degrees F and sunny like 2012? Or will it be 37 degrees F with driving rain and 25 mph headwinds like 2018? How can you acclimate to race-day conditions that are so random and often severe?

Most runners have a nice base of mileage heading into the New Year, so it's common to begin ramping up training on New Year's Day. Your taper typically begins at the tail end of March or early April, so that means your heaviest train-ing will be from January 1 to April 1, guaranteeing you'll experience some pretty gnarly winter conditions. For locals in Boston, winter provides a smorgasbord of wickedness that includes freezing rain, black ice, snow, blizzards, sleet, nor'eas-ters, bomb cyclones, slush, "wintry mix," and subzero windchills.

In 2015, the year Boston set a new all-time record for snow in one season (110.3 inches), runners may recall an entire winter where pavement wasn't visible. Try training on snow and ice for three months before running 26.2 miles on pave-ment on race day. The equivalent would be a figure skater practicing her routine in a gravel parking lot before hitting the ice for the first time at the Olympics. Neither prepares you very well for what's coming.

But the craziness and unpredictability of the weather, oddly enough, are what make Boston special, too. You're going to hear all kinds of horror stories about the Boston weather. And, to be fair, weather for the Boston Marathon on the third Monday in April is a little all over the place and difficult to predict. But, as bad as it gets (1976, 2004, 2007, 2012, 2018), you need to understand that it isn't horrifically extreme, at least as measured relative to races prone to more rapid

Winter miles bring April smiles.

and violent changes in conditions. The B.A.A., Dave McGillivray and his team, volunteers, and medical staff make it very clear that each year, every year, safety is their top priority.

The tragedy that befell the 2021 Yellow River Stone Forest Ultramarathon (100km) in Gansu province, China, that resulted in 21 runner deaths from hypothermia, including many of China's legendary and rising ultra stars, shook the endurance event world. By contrast, the Boston weather is difficult, but let's not exaggerate its severity. Since its beginning in 1897, the Boston Marathon has never been canceled due to inclement weather. And the incredible organization of the Boston Marathon and the abundance of medical professionals on the course (and within close proximity at neighboring top-tier Boston hospitals) provide a good measure of assurance that regardless of what Mother Nature doles out on race day, participants will have the care and resources they need when they need them.

So, how do you train for Boston's unknown conditions? It behooves you to train in unpleasant conditions. Des Linden, Yuki Kawauchi, Marcel Hug, and Tatyana McFadden are prime examples of gritty Boston champions who handled the "Perfect Chaos" of 2018 better than their competition. Jack Fultz and Kim Merritt persevered through a heat index registering more than 100 degrees F in 1976's "Run for the Hoses."

If you live in the Northeast (Boston, Syracuse, Bangor, or anyplace similar), you're in luck. Winters will subject you to pretty much everything evil, and you can always overdress to heat acclimate as race day approaches. If the winter is especially awful, figure out a way to gain access to an indoor track, especially if you're racing Boston and not just "running" Boston. It's tough to PR without speedwork. Sessions on an indoor track once a week (or even once every two weeks) will help you inject some pace in your workouts that would otherwise be impossible to perform outside.

If you're from a warmer climate, you'll be as prepared as you possibly can be for a surprise heat-fest à la 2004 or 2012. Your biggest concern might be the rogue nor'easter that crops up on Marathon Monday like it did in 2007 or 2018. Setting up a treadmill in a commercial-grade walk-in cooler like you'd find at a restaurant or hotel would be ideal. A close second might be cranking a window-unit air conditioner down to its chilliest setting in a small room in your house that just so happens to fit your treadmill. If those aren't doable, you may have to resort to a more expensive option, a run-cation.

A well planned run-cation during your training cycle can rejuvenate you and help you acclimate to whatever Boston has in store for you. If you live in Tampa, Florida, hop on a flight to Maine and run in the frigid air and rolling hills of Freeport that helped Joan Benoit Samuelson become an Olympic and two-time Boston Marathon champion. Do a little shopping and prop your legs up by the fire at your cozy B&B while you're there, too. If you're used to running on Tampa's Bayshore Boulevard in shorts and a singlet, there's nothing quite like a pre-dawn, subzero 20-miler from Freeport to Brunswick and back to build the character you'll need to PR in Boston on race day.

John Young smiles his way to a 5:58:45 finish in some of the worst weather in Boston Marathon history (2018). John Young

The last word on Boston weather is don't shy away from the gruesome conditions when you're training. Seriously. If it's 7 degrees F with a feels-like temperature of -5 degrees F and it's snowing sideways, don't wrap yourself in a warm blanket and wait for a better day tomorrow. Get out the door and go. The more "character-building" runs you have under your belt, the better. When it's 35 degrees F on race day and everyone in your corral is shivering in garbage bags, channel the zen you experienced on that early-March run when you sucked in snowflakes in a blizzard. Like Linden and Kawauchi in 2018, the more your training has hardened you, the better off you'll be when Mother Nature throws everyone a wicked top-shelf curve on race day.

Oh, and expect the worst. That's the proper Boston Marathon weekend mindset. If the forecast keeps shifting as race day nears, assume the absolute nastiest scenario. Only then will you be pleasantly surprised in Hopkinton. In 2007, Weather Channel meteorologist Jim Cantore (known as "The Hurricane King" or "Dr. Doom") was reporting in Hopkinton at 7 a.m. on race day as heavy rain and winds greater than 60 mph blew signs and festive marathon banners off buildings. Officials had earlier considered canceling the race for the first time in history. But just as Cantore braced himself against the side of a house and it looked like officials had made the wrong decision, the weather began to improve. By 10 a.m. when Wave 1 started, rain was minimal and winds had backed off from gale-force to manageable.

This "expect the worst" strategy isn't foolproof, of course. Every once in a great while, an anomalous year like 2018 comes along. That's when the image in your head is adequately horrible, but Mother Nature one-ups your dark imagination and delivers something far gnarlier. And then all you can do is lean on the memories of your character-building runs and trust the support of the B.A.A., Dave McGillivray and his team, spectators, volunteers, and medical professionals to get you through.

HEAD-TO-TOE BOSTON MARATHON GEAR GUIDE

In 1897, John McDermott, a lithographer from New York representing the Pastime Athletic Club, breasted the tape at the inaugural Boston Marathon in knee-length shorts and leather lace-up shoes with a winning time of 2:55:10. You might think "okay, that makes sense because it was the 1800s," but in 1954, Finland's Veikko Karvonen won by more than two minutes with a time of 2:20:39 wearing leather shoes "found in a men's room somewhere in Massachusetts." The innovation that was clearly lacking in the sport in its earliest decades has been made up for in spades in its most recent years. We've come a long way. Shoes. Fabrics.

Electronics. Analytics. Improvements aplenty, but, with so many choices available, how do you possibly choose what's best for you? Fear not. Top to bottom, here's everything you need to know.

Head Gear

Your head is the radiator valve for your body. Hats, caps, balaclavas, shower caps, sunglasses, headbands, visors, hair-ties, bandanas, and headlamps can make or break a training run or race. Get it right, and you're the perfect temperature. Get it wrong, and your janky thermostat can dash your PR attempt.

> **Hot (greater than 75 degrees F)**—It seems counterintuitive to think that a hat can keep you cool, but modern technology, especially moisture-wicking fabrics, draw moisture away from your head while simultaneously permitting air in through the fabric, allowing your head to breathe. Dick Beardsley had the right idea in Boston in 1982 when he wore a white, paper-thin painter's cap to shield himself from the elements in his Duel in the Sun with Alberto Salazar.
>
> On shockingly hot days, place ice inside your hat and let it melt as you run. In 2004 and 2012 at Boston, the most awesome spectators handed runners ice, allowing those with hats to replenish the ice as they made their way

If you're ever in doubt about what to wear on a charity team, follow the lead of The Fashion Director.
Marc Camm

to Boston. Heat-related illness is a huge safety concern. In 1976's "Run for the Hoses" more than 40 percent of the marathon field dropped out (i.e., DNF'd). If you see ice on the course, grab it. Don't even think twice.

Oh, and if it's sunny, don't forget some sporty, nonslip sunglasses. Because Boston is a spring marathon, trees aren't laden with leaves yet, so there's not a lot of shade on the course on bluebird days. Plus, all that squinting takes up valuable energy you'll need in Brookline. As a bonus, those reflective shades in your race photos will hide your RBF and evoke a *Terminator 2*, robo-runner vibe. Nice.

Warm (between 50 and 75 degrees F)—Wearing nothing on your head is liberating and often the right choice when it's warm. But runners with long hair know what a relief it is when scrunchies or hair bands (or man-buns) take the weight (and heat) of hair off their shoulders. And because Boston's weather is tricky (sometimes the feels-like temperature can swing 20 degrees or more from Hopkinton to Boston), what seems warmish at the start can be limb-numbing at the finish (or vice versa, depending on the year).

With winds from the west, what feels "warm" in Hopkinton can turn downright sweltering by the time you make it to Copley Square. Conversely, it's not uncommon, with winds from the northeast, for it to be warm at the start and be quite chilly when those northeasterly winds you were shielded from in Hopkinton whip across the 43 degrees F waters of Boston Harbor.

Wet—If it's warm and raining (and not too windy), a moisture-wicking baseball cap with a bill keeps your eyes shielded from the aggressive drops. If the wind is too unwieldy, thereby threatening to send your cap flying into a neighboring body of water (like Lake Cochituate at Mile 9), either a.) turn your cap backwards until the wind settles down, or b.) push your hat down low (just above eye level) in serial killer, hiding-from-paparazzi position.

If it's like 2007 and both windy and raining cold buckets, a moisture-wicking cap with a bill beneath a wool hat pulled over your ears (or, alternatively, a wool ear-warmer headband) works pretty well. If it's like the monsoon of 2018, a shower cap can be worn over the aforementioned items to stave off immediate saturation.

Hats made of technical fabrics or fleece tend to get waterlogged quickly and don't do a very good job of insulating you from cold winds once they're wet. Your best bet in cold weather is to stick to wool. Wool is a smart insulator that can soak up to 30 percent of its own weight in moisture without feeling wet.

Cool (between 36 and 50 degrees F)—Most Boston Marathon participants would likely choose race day (and optimum training) temperatures to be in the upper end of this range. Two caveats: 1.) How aggressive is the wind? and 2.) what direction is the wind blowing?

If temperatures are above 50 degrees F, wind is a bit of a nonfactor from a climate control perspective. Sure, wind can be annoying, especially if it's a northeast headwind on race day. But in general, wind is pleasant, until the temperature drops below 50 degrees F. Then you have to factor in winter runners' greatest bane, the windchill factor.

A good way to think of the windchill factor is to multiply the speed of the wind in miles per hour by 0.7 and then subtract that value from the air temperature. So, for Boston Marathoners in 2018, the 41 degrees F start in Hopkinton with a 25 mph northeast (head) wind resulted in a windchill of 23.5 degrees F. That might explain your numb hands and inability to tie your shoelaces.

Your head accounts for 7 percent of the surface area of your body. On average, runners lose 7–10 percent of body heat through their heads. If it's in the 40 degrees F range without much wind, no hat or a very light technical hat or beanie will suffice. For the headband fans, a light headband or bandana will do the trick, too.

As temperatures drop and winds intensify, you'll need an actual winter hat. A technical-fabric hat will be fine unless there's precipitation (rain, sleet, freezing rain, snow, wintry mix), in which case a wool-blend hat will retain heat despite the moisture.

The tricky thing about dressing for cool temperatures is the tendency to get too aggressive and end up overheating. It's not a good feeling when you're overheated in a wool hat and your only option is to take off the hat or keep the stifling hat in place. Neither is the optimum solution, so it's best to get your gear choice right from the get-go rather than face an uncomfortable dilemma mid-run or, even worse, mid-race.

Cold (between 20 and 35 degrees F)—In New England, the Northeast, or any chilly winter locale, runners log most of their training miles in this temperature range. Those of you in Houston are cringing at the thought, but decades (or, in some cases, a lifetime) of cold winters makes this temperature pretty comfortable for training. It's certainly less than ideal for racing, but a technical or wool blend hat is pretty much all you need up top, and you're good for a recovery run, tempo, long run, or whatever your heart desires.

Wicked cold (less than 20 degrees F)—If the windchill is subzero degrees F, you might want to ditch the wool hat in favor of a balaclava that covers the head and neck. Balaclavas have long been used by the military and police as well as race car drivers, skiers, and snowmobilers. Runners are beginning to pick up on its awesomeness, too.

The beauty of the balaclava is it exposes just the eyes (and occasionally the nose), providing maximum protection from brutal windchills and the dangers of frostbite. Add sunglasses or ski goggles to the mix and voila! You have a toasty, happy noggin. Skin and tissue surrounding the ears, nose, and mouth (and extremities) are most susceptible to frostbite, so the balaclava is a godsend for winter runners in unforgiving climates. Modern versions are made of water-repellant fabric, have perforations near the mouth for enhanced breathability, reflective logos and designs, and even have openings for ponytails.

The coldest Boston Marathons on record have been in the 30 degrees F range (with windchills even colder), and snow has greeted runners on many occasions (1907, 1908, 1925, 1961, and 1967 to name a few). That's not quite balaclava weather, but remember you have a friend who's willing to lend a hand if you do.

Neck Wear

Runners fall into one of two categories: 1.) The neck is a sensitive area that needs attention to regulate body temperature (mostly when it's cold, but sometimes when it's hot, too), or 2.) don't you dare put anything on my neck, ever.

No matter the camp you're in, here are some tips for a happy throat and nape.

Hot (greater than 75 degrees F)—It's natural to say a free neck is a happy neck when the weather is sizzling, but innovation in running hasn't stopped at the feet. Neck gaiters (aka buffs) aren't just for winter anymore. Modern technology has birthed cooling neck gaiters and towels that are made of breathable, spongelike materials, allowing you to stay cooler for longer.

For those among you who are comforted by neck coverings, grab some ice from spectators in Wellesley and Newton to rejuvenate your neck covering and those unfriendly running temperatures will be a little more bearable.

A great alternative to neck gaiters and towels is the common household sponge. Just stuff a sponge in your shorts in Hopkinton, then remove it, douse it with water and ice whenever your heart desires, and apply it to your face, neck, and throat and any other pressure points that could use some refreshment along the way to Boston. (**Pro Tip:** If the sponge is thick enough, slice an opening in the side so it retains the ice when you stuff it in. Absolute bliss. You're welcome.)

Warm (between 51 and 75 degrees F)—These are the temperatures when a free neck is your best bet. The human body is a remarkably sophisticated heating and cooling machine, and sometimes it's appropriate to let it do its thing and not intervene.

When the air is cooler than your body temperature, heat is lost by radiating from your skin into the cooler air. A free neck also cools itself when perspiration evaporates from the skin. Your blood vessels work hard to keep you cool, too. If you've ever overheated and you notice your skin is flush, it's your blood vessels nearest to the surface of your skin dilating, allowing cool air to reduce their temperature.

Grab some ice from the outstretched hands of Framingham children or Brookline octogenarians and refresh your pressure points with your sponge, especially if it's muggy. High humidity means there's a lot of moisture in the air, preventing your sweat from evaporating as efficiently as it otherwise might. A little ice goes a long way in regulating your temperature on a sneaky-hot, sticky day.

Cool (between 36 and 50 degrees F)—If the windchill is minimal, these temperatures are usually, depending on your sensitivity to cold, perfect for neck wear–free running. However, throw in a decent wind with temperatures in the lower end of the range, and it's perfectly understandable to wear a light, moisture-wicking neck gaiter. And, hey, it's Boston, so what might feel temperate in Hopkinton could turn ornery by the time you crest Heartbreak Hill. So a crafty tactic is to carry the neck gaiter in the waistband of your shorts or around your wrist and use it as an all-purpose cloth until increasingly adverse weather requires it to be summoned to neck duty later in the day.

Oh, and if the wind is brutal and the "feels-like" temperature is in the 20 degrees F range (or lower), a fleece or wool-blend neck gaiter will preserve heat far better than a light piece of cloth. On race day, wind speed is good to know, but wind direction is most important. If the wind is at your back (i.e., west, southwest, or south-southwest), the impact on temperature will be negligible. But if the wind is in your face (i.e., east, northeast, or north-northeast), you'll need to factor in the windchill as you make your gear decisions, neck or otherwise.

Cold (between 20 and 35 degrees F)—Again, personal preference and wind speed and direction rule here, but, in general, temperatures in this range will require some sort of neck coverage. Heartier souls will be fine with a mock turtleneck or turtleneck, but others, especially those from warmer climates who are less accustomed, will find comfort in a technical fabric neck gaiter. If windchills reach the teens or single digits, the warmth of a fleece or wool-blend neck gaiter will help you retain body heat more readily.

The beauty of a neck gaiter is if you guess wrong and start overheating, it's not too difficult to remove it and either stuff it in your waistband on a training run or, if you're racing and concerned about every precious ounce you're carrying, simply discard it. No biggie.

Wicked cold (less than 20 degrees F)—If you're one of those who's averse to neck coverings, you may be tempted to bite the bullet and find some coverage once temperatures dive below 20 degrees F, even more so when the wind is howling. And if temperatures above freezing don't persuade you, your resolve will be tested further once temperatures or windchills go below zero.

The Boston Marathon is a storied race with a long tradition behind it, a pinnacle of the sport of running that normal people can strive to achieve; it is a challenge in every way you look at it, from qualifying or fundraising for a bib to racing in the unpredictable weather up and down the hills—a combination of hurdles and history that makes Boston special to me.

Huy Son
9 Marathons
2 Boston Marathons

Frostbite is no joke. And, yes, your neck is slightly less susceptible because heat from your well-covered skin atop your neighboring vital organs rises toward your neck. But uncovered neck skin is at risk. And the colder it gets, the faster you can get frostbite.

How fast? Faster than you think. Within 30 minutes if the temperature is 0 degrees F and winds are 15 mph. So, don't be the runner who is too proud to throw on a balaclava for your subzero long run. It's better to look like you want to rob a hospital than to be wheeled into the emergency room of one.

Tops

Things were so simple in 1973. Just throw on your favorite cotton T-shirt, step out the door, and go. Boom. You're a runner. You're running. Stop Pre!

Well, those carefree, innocent times are gone. Step outside in a T-shirt today and you might as well have a neon-pulsing sign over your head that reads "jogger." Fashion is real now in the running community. Should you wear a perforated singlet, moisture-wicking tee, or compression mock? What about a vest? Or, for you guys out there, why even wear a shirt? And, you girls? Ditto. Just throw on a sports bra.

Welcome to the future. And we're just getting started. If you're curious what to wear up top on your next Boston Marathon training run, get off the internet and pay attention to the following:

Hot (greater than 75 degrees F)—If you're a guy, and it's more than 75 degrees F and the sun is blaring, take off your shirt and throw on a little sunscreen. Sun's out, guns out. If you're a girl, we've come a long way, but you'll still have to be a bit more discreet. A sports bra is the answer to your summer prayers.

It's important to note that racing without a shirt is prohibited at certain races. The Boston Marathon does not forbid shirtless running, but it doesn't go out of its way to encourage it either. If you're wondering why you don't see elite male runners going shirtless, they are paid by companies who sponsor them to wear brands front and center all over their bodies, including their shirts. Would you wear a shirt when it's 85 degrees if someone handed you a $100,000 check? Exactly.

Running purists either a.) feel running shirtless is disrespectful to the sport (akin to a baseball player not wearing a hat), or b.) believe running shirtless is natural and necessary, especially when temperatures are in a dangerous range.

There are alternatives to shirtlessness and sports bras, of course. A moisture-wicking singlet is a good answer, as is your favorite technical fabric singlet with homemade perforations (as pioneered by Alberto Salazar at the 1984 Olympics in Los Angeles and sported by Salazar protégé Galen Rupp at the US Olympic Trials Marathon in 2016).

On race day, you'll have to pin your bib somewhere. At Boston, your timing chip resides in your bib, so you better be sure your number is visible (your cache of race photos depends on the visibility of your bib), and you better be certain your chip is able to register at each checkpoint. That said, it's proven that a bib on your chest or torso works best. Yes, you can pin it to your shorts, but do so at your own risk.

With temperatures at these levels, remember your goal is to stay cool, not "look hot." Running a marathon in temperatures above 75 degrees F is challenging for everyone, and can be dangerous if proper precautions aren't taken. Put safety first. Save the fashion for the post-race party.

Warm (between 51 and 75 degrees F)—A simple race singlet is suitable at every temperature, especially if wind is minimal and you're racing Boston or running an up-tempo long run, thereby revving your engine at high rpms for an extended length of time.

If temperatures are near 50 degrees F and you're "running" Boston (i.e., running for fun vs. racing for a PR), compression arm sleeves are a good way to retain some warmth when needed but also provide optionality, allowing you to push them down to your wrists or take them off if you start feeling too toasty as you navigate your way downtown.

Wind could be aggressive enough to warrant a long-sleeve technical shirt, but, more often than not, you'll end up constantly (i.e., annoyingly) pushing up your sleeves (an inconvenience in a 5k, but a bit more maddening in a marathon).

A strong fail-safe plan for women is to wear a technical T-shirt or singlet on top of a sports bra. If temperatures rise as you're running and your core temperature redlines, just take off your shirt and wrap it around your waist or tuck it in the back of your sports bra straps like the trendy female runners along the Charles do. And if things cool back down after you summit Heartbreak Hill, just throw your shirt back on and you're all set.

Well, one caveat: Pin your bib on your shorts to avoid having to de-fasten and refasten your bib. Running at a decent clip while attempting to pin a bib on your chest is a recipe for disaster. There will be blood.

Cool (between 36 and 50 degrees F)—The variety of what you wear up top opens up dramatically once the temperature drops beneath 50 degrees F, even more so if you throw a little wind into the mix. A good rule of thumb when training is to dress for weather that is 5–10 degrees warmer than the actual temperature. When racing, you could even dress 10–15 degrees warmer, but that's only if you're going all-out and gunning for a PR. For example, if it's 45 degrees F and you're going on a training run, dress like it's 50 or

55 degrees F. Your body will heat up nicely during your run, and you don't want to overheat and be too sweaty to remove layers.

A race singlet is still doable if temperatures are in the upper end of the range, and the addition of arm sleeves, depending on your tolerance for cold, should work if temperatures are relatively windless in the lower end of the range.

If you race a lot, especially in the fall and winter, your closet and drawers are teeming with long-sleeve technical race shirts. Throw on your fave shirt from races gone by and you're good to go. Some runners find these shirts are too often incorrectly sized, especially when shirts are unisex (which is just code for "this shirt won't fit any human on Earth properly").

An excellent alternative to the poor-fitting race shirt is a snug compression mock turtleneck. There's something comforting about being swaddled in compression gear. It's like a second skin. Plus, compression shirts just look and feel like you should be running fast when you wear them. As a bonus, long-sleeve compression shirts come in an assortment of thicknesses, so you can pick just the right one to match race-day weather.

Another must-have for the training wardrobe in this temperature range is a zip-up vest. The vest would be a bit too sloppy for a race, but it's perfect for training runs, particularly the ones when you're running an easy recovery run and you want to keep your core toasty the whole way.

Race-day weather in Boston has been described as "three seasons in one race." It's not uncommon for it to be 42 degrees F and overcast with a windchill of 31 degrees F and feel like fall in Hopkinton before the weather morphs into a more spring-like 50 degrees F at the half in Wellesley. Then, just when you thought you dressed perfectly in your long sleeves, the sun comes out, the wind dies down, and the heat index is summer-like.

Or you could traverse all aforementioned seasons in reverse. Welcome to Boston.

Cold (between 20 and 35 degrees F)—It's not often that the Boston Marathon has race-day temperatures (or windchills) in this range, but, when it occurs, you're in for a doozy, especially runners arriving from more temperate locales. And since it hasn't snowed since 1967, Boston is overdue for a snow event on Marathon Monday. You heard it here first. So what do you wear? Will you need a jacket? Or is a jacket too cumbersome? The first rule of thumb is to determine your purpose: Will you be merely running or will you be racing for a PR? If you're racing, avoid a jacket at all costs.

In addition to its unwieldiness, a jacket has a tendency to cause you to sweat within its confines. This can be problematic if your race goes south (due to injury or otherwise) and your pace falls off dramatically. The once-warm moisture retained within your jacket will soon turn far cooler and could contribute to hypothermia.

Now, I know what you're thinking: Didn't Des Linden win with a jacket in 2018? Yes, she did. But she's the only runner in modern history to win while wearing a jacket. Save the jacket for training runs, and HTFU like Yuki Kawauchi.

If you're running (vs. racing), a jacket is perfectly understandable. The bulk won't be as much of a nuisance, and your core temperature should remain, relative to those racing for prize money and age-group podiums, fairly constant as you make your way from town to town (if you're not stopping and starting along the way).

So, what should you wear if you want to PR and it's (heaven forbid) 24 degrees F on race day? First, there is no magic race kit. That said, it's best to play offense, not defense. Visualize yourself making a left on Boylston with your PR in the bag. Despite the rough weather, the crowd is thick and going nuts. You may have been wearing a jacket and trash bag before the start in Hopkinton, but you sure as heck aren't now. Sure, it's cold. But your engine is revving hot. You've been running PR pace for more than 26 miles. Your Mylar blanket and warm clothes will be your reward when you finish.

Wicked cold (less than 20 degrees F)—The good Lord willing, you'll never see a Boston Marathon this cold. But if you live in northern climes, you'll be training in this wintry goodness quite a bit. So, what do you do when the wind is angry and the thermometer is covered in ice?

First, if you're in the wrong frame of mind, you'll never get out of your house. How easy is it to silence your 5 a.m. alarm when you see snow falling diagonally outside your window? Too easy.

Extreme temperatures require an extreme reframing of your mindset. "There's no such thing as bad weather, only unsuitable clothing," said British fellwalker and author Alfred Wainwright. Running year-round becomes enjoyable if, and only if, you channel Alfred Wainwright. Got it? Good.

With your head in the right place, you're ready to consider suitable clothing. A compression mock-turtle or turtleneck is a great place to start. Again, the snug fit is just too darn comforting to begin with anything else. A technical, long-sleeve race shirt is a strong second layer. The material is looser, but it provides a much-needed second buffer from the cold.

If the wind is calm and you're racing (or running an up-tempo training run), you might be able to get by with a technical-fabric vest as a third layer. The vest will do a nice job of keeping your core warm, but it won't be too bulky and aggravating like a jacket can be, especially if you're grinding away at PR pace.

When Mother Nature is irritated, winds are gnarly, and/or the temperatures are just too chilly, a jacket (or, alternatively, a jacket over a vest) is the way to go. Jacket technology keeps getting better and better, so just because your official Adidas Boston Marathon jacket has a special place in your heart doesn't mean it's always the right choice given the ever-variable winter running conditions. An exterior wind-resistant shell with a low-profile fleece interior makes a great combo of features. And since daylight is scarce and you'll be logging a lot of your winter miles in the dark, reflective tape in strategic locations is key for safety, too.

If your training runs are early in the morning or at night and your top isn't reflective, please, for everyone's safety (yours included), wear a reflective vest. Some vests have blinking lights, some just reflect light, but, either way, they save lives. More than 120,000 runners get hit by cars in the United States annually, and more than 4,000 runners, joggers, hikers, and pedestrians die in traffic accidents each year (70 percent of whom are killed at night). You won't have to worry about this on race day, but you would like to make it to race day, right?

Hands

Running is leg-intensive, but if your hands aren't happy, your run will be proportionately unpleasant, too. When you're gearing up for a run or race, hands are often an afterthought. And it's that reactive mentality (or simply the fact that you forgot to pack gloves) that can come back to haunt you.

Rather than anguish over an oft-neglected body part, here's a temperature-by-temperature guide to hand happiness.

Hot (greater than 75 degrees F)—Your first inclination is to think bare hands are the best you can do when the heat is on and the sun is blazing. That's logical. But what those bare hands are doing in the heat could make or break your race. Did you remember your sponge? If so, douse that sponge in water every aid station and refresh all the pressure points you can reach (without breaking stride). Wiping away your sweat and replacing it with cool(-ish) water feels oh-so-good, especially if there's a gentle breeze to help it evaporate.

Should you carry a water bottle with you on Marathon Monday? Have you trained with holding a water bottle on your long runs? If yes, then the answer is a strong maybe. There's ample water and Gatorade on the course, but if your stomach can't handle Gatorade, then carrying your electrolytes with you is a good idea. Also, it can get a bit congested at the aid stations (most notably in the early miles), so you can steer clear of the masses and avoid the chaos.

The drawback to carrying water (or an electrolyte beverage) is you can only carry so much and will likely need to refill at some point. Plus, the liquid you're carrying adds extra weight, which won't help your PR efforts. Elite American marathoner Ryan Hall, owner of the fastest American time in Boston Marathon history (2:04:58 in 2011), weighed his shoelaces before races. Yep, shoelaces. Let that sink in.

You may not be dialed in to your race as maniacally as Hall, but water sloshing around in your hand (and possibly around your waist) isn't ideal if you're racing. If you're "running" Boston or simply training, yes, carry that water, especially in the winter when water fountains ("bubblers" in Boston) in parks and along running routes are turned off (so as not to freeze).

Warm (between 51 and 75 degrees F)—Many Boston Marathons are "sneaky hot." Back in the old days when the race started at noon (any year before 2007), there wasn't anything sneaky about the heat. If it was warmish by noon, you could bank on it getting more uncomfortable as the afternoon progressed. But the advent of the morning start (10 a.m. ET in 2007, and increasingly earlier [before 9 a.m. in 2021]) has added a bit more complexity to gearing up.

The good news is not even the most sensitive among you (who are the first to put gloves on in the fall and the last to take them off in the spring) will be tempted to wear gloves in this range of temperatures. The bad news is you could be shivering in your corral in Hopkinton at 9:27 a.m. ET in cold rain, and then the skies can part, the sun can blare, and you can roast like a s'more atop a fire pit in Chatham.

If your hands are cold in Hopkinton and the forecast is calling for temperatures to increase throughout the day, slip your oldest, ugliest, most threadbare (but clean!) pair of socks over your hands. You'll have no qualms discarding them when the time is right.

Cool (between 36 and 50 degrees F)—This is the temperature range where gloves on race day begin to make the most sense. In three of Bill Rodgers's Boston Marathon victories (1975, 1978, and 1979), he is pictured breasting the tape in Copley Square either wearing or holding his signature white gardeners' gloves. With his lean sub-2:10 marathoner frame, the white gloves look oversized, akin to Mickey Mouse's iconic four-fingered variety.

If you'd like to channel a little "Boston Billy" mojo, Rodgers's iconic white gloves have inspired numerous knock-offs, albeit with runner-friendly modern fabrics, unlike their cotton ancestors.

Alternatively, many lightweight contemporary running gloves are less bulky, reflective, provide maximum thermal protection, have touchscreen-friendly fingertips, and anti-slip surfaces. You may not want to throw them out if temperatures heat up, but they're sleek enough to tuck into your waistband, so no worries.

Cold (between 20 and 35 degrees F)—The variety of glove choices grows as temperatures drop. Technical fabrics, fleece, wool, and fabric blends provide a spectrum of options.

To further complicate your decision-making, gloves can be layered over glove liners and mittens can be layered over gloves. And let's not even get started on what temperature hand warmers become necessary (or whether they're ever necessary). Madness, right?

The good news is that, pretty much no matter what you wear, you'll be warmer than all those runners in the 70s who sported cotton gardeners' gloves. Don't overthink your decision. Experiment with different combinations of gloves, layers, and mittens while you're training. Just know that if you're racing (i.e., not merely running) on Marathon Monday, the heat you generate at max rpms will more than likely result in you shedding more layers of clothes than you anticipated, including what's on your hands.

Wicked cold (less than 20 degrees F)—If Mother Nature spins her wheel of weather on race day and it lands on "bitter cold," it's safe to say very few PRs will be chased and attained. It's really all about keeping warm and saving yourself for another day.

That said, your best bet to ensure maximum warmth is to find a hybrid glove made of technical fabric (nylon, elastane) and wool. The wool will keep your hands toasty, and the wicking fabrics will keep moisture at bay. If it's particularly windy, be sure to find a pair with windproof fabric.

A strong alternative is wearing convertible gloves that have a mitten that can be pulled out and extended over your fingers for added warmth. The mittens in most of these convertible models have windproof and water-resistant covers that can be tucked and untucked as needed.

Bottoms

When it comes to runners' personal preferences, what you choose to wear below the waist ranks a close second to favorites you play when picking shoes. Again, it used to be so easy in the mid-70s when there was really only one cold weather choice, gray sweatpants, and one warm weather choice, Dolfin shorts. Remember them? Short. Really short. Nylon. Neon yellow. Side slits. Unlined. Yes, unlined. Hard to believe.

We've made great strides since those days, opening up a whole new world of options in every temperature range. The hardest part is choosing what to wear, especially when getting it wrong can cost you a good workout or, even worse, a PR or podium (age-group or otherwise). Here's a closer look at how to get it right, no matter the conditions.

The heart of one's bottom should be chosen from the bottom of one's heart. Marc Camm

The Men's Shorts Dilemma: Split Shorts vs. V-Notch Shorts vs. Half-Tights

What's the proper length of shorts to run your fastest? The debate rages on. In the late 19th and early 20th centuries, long shorts were in vogue. Who can forget Dorando Pietri in knee-length shorts staggering around the track like a drunken sailor in the final 400 meters of the 1908 Olympic Marathon in London? Or what about The Flying Finn, Paavo Nurmi, in thigh-length white shorts dominating the world and winning Olympic gold in Antwerp (1920), Paris (1924), and Amsterdam (1928)? Long shorts (by today's standards) didn't slow Nurmi down.

But the length of men's running shorts kept getting shorter and shorter, especially during the 1970s when the running boom was taking hold and long-distance icons such as Frank Shorter, Steve Prefontaine, and Bill Rodgers graced the covers of *Sports Illustrated*. Running was finally cool. And the fastest in the world (and heroes of the sport) wore split shorts. It felt like a natural progression; runners got faster and shorts got shorter.

But just when it looked like split shorts would rule the day in perpetuity, a funny thing happened; half-tights popularized by 100m and 200m sprinters started to creep up in distance. Soon, half-tights were spotted at 5000 and 10,000 meters on the track. And then the unthinkable happened: Half-tights made their way to the roads, eventually becoming common with elite half marathoners and marathoners.

So, now what? What should you wear for your Boston Marathon debut? Fear not. We'll make the case for each of your choices. Then, it's up to you to decide.

Split Shorts

1. When you think of speed, you summon the memory of Eamonn Coghlan, the "Chairman of the Boards," crushing souls indoors on the wooden boards at the Millrose Games at Madison Square Garden or Sebastian Coe shifting into an unmatched gear at The Golden Mile in the homestretch at Bislett Stadium in Oslo.

2. You play lacrosse in long shorts, basketball in a tank top, baseball with stirrups, and tennis in whites. Each sport has its traditions and uniform. You respect and honor them all, including running. You wouldn't be caught dead in V-notch shorts or half-tights in Hopkinton. You harbor a bit of animosity for those who do.

3. When someone in V-notch shorts passes you in Brookline, you feel an overwhelming sense of dread, less because he's faster than you and more because you feel he should be playing point guard in a rec-league basketball game.

4. Your dog-eared copy of Jim Fixx's *The Complete Book of Running* occupies a special slot on your bookshelf next to Pete Pfitzinger's *Advanced Marathoning* and Jack Daniels's *Daniels' Running Formula*.

5. You long to grow a mustache like Frank Shorter when he won gold in Munich or the droopy handlebar Steve Prefontaine sported at Oregon.

V-Notch Shorts

1. You're a reformed soccer player and the idea of running or playing a sport (nay, any sport) in short shorts is a nonstarter.

2. When you're off the roads, you wear loose-fitting boxer shorts. Not tighty-whities. Not boxer briefs. Boxer shorts.

3. Remember when kids wore Speedos to go swimming? Yeah, you never did that.

4. Half-tights are what you wore underneath your soccer shorts. Underneath. Which is where you feel they belong.

5. Unless you're in court, someone died, or someone's getting married, you don't tuck in your shirt.

Half-Tights

1. You ran the 200m and 400m in high school. You proceeded not to run for a decade or two. Now, you'd rather wedge your adult self back in half-tights than be caught dead in the short shorts you mercilessly belittled in your youth.

2. Remember when kids wore Speedos to go swimming? Yeah, you wore them. And nowadays, when you swim laps at the YMCA, you still do.

3. You wear spandex tights in the winter, and you harbor an unspoken desire to make Capri tights more acceptable for men. You'd start the movement yourself, but you're already hearing comments behind your back at the pool about those Speedos.

4. When you were a newborn, you were the baby in the nursery who screamed like a banshee until you were swaddled perfectly in your crib.

5. You believe the inventor of shrink-wrap deserved a Nobel Prize, and you get a little jealous when you see a marina filled with winterized boats perfectly weatherproofed in the offseason.

The Women's Shorts Dilemma: Buns vs. Booties vs. Split Shorts vs. V-Notch Shorts vs. Skorts

As with most matters related to women's fashion, running styles and choices are more diverse than men's options, and decision-making is a touch more complicated.

When marathon legend, two-time Boston Marathon champion, and gold medalist in the first-ever Olympic marathon for women (1984 Los Angeles) Joan Benoit Samuelson first started running, she was so embarrassed to run in public that she would "slow to a walk and pretend to look at flowers as cars passed." Women's running apparel had a similar inauspicious beginning: Women running pioneers crafted makeshift outfits of their own or ran in men's apparel that, at best, may have been colored pink or pastel (the "shrink it and pink it" era of women's athletic apparel).

As more and more women began to run, sports apparel manufacturers started to warm up to the idea of creating lines of clothes specifically for women. Shorts were a no-brainer, but concepts unique to women (buns, booties, skorts) began to gain appeal, too. Marathon legends like Samuelson, Grete Waitz, and Uta Pippig rocked split shorts, but soon Rosa Mota, a three-time Boston Marathon Champion (1987, 1988, 1990) and two-time Olympic medalist (Bronze, 1984 Los Angeles; Gold, 1988 Seoul), burst onto the scene in buns. Much like half-tights for men, buns were more commonly associated with the track oval before they started making appearances on the roads.

Booties, the close cousins of buns, emerged on the long-distance running scene from multiple directions: the track, the gym, dance floors, cheerleading, and the entertainment industry. Much like buns, booties trace their roots to sprint events like the 100m and 200m as well as the long jump and triple jump. But booties differ from buns in that they first gained popularity among a diverse set of women in ballet studios, on club dance floors, in the gym, being thrown in the air at football games, and earning a living performing (at Caesar's Palace or otherwise).

A more modern wardrobe addition is the hybrid half-skirt, half-short or, aptly named portmanteau, "skort." You'd think the skort lived first as a favorite of women's tennis players, but its origins begin much earlier, in a fad of the late-1900s, bicycling. Before the hyper-cool moniker "skort" came to be, "trouser skirts" were a thing, And this skorting happened nearly a century before Serena Williams was born or a runner had even the seed of an idea to wear such a thing.

So many choices, right? What do you wear if you want to run your fastest Boston Marathon? Don't fret. Read. Listen. Discern. And feel in your heart what needs to be on your body on race day.

Buns

1. Sun's out. Buns out. 'Nuff said. Let's PR this bitch.

2. You're convinced the girl standing next to you in a skort in your corral in Hopkinton is the same girl who would sit, fully clothed, under an umbrella at the beach. And there's not an inconsequential part of you that feels sickened that she ran a qualifying time similar to yours that gives her the right to stand next to you.

3. Remember the only girl in your school who wore a thong to Spring Break at Daytona Beach? Of course you do. That was you. Shots!

4. Not only do you know who Mary Decker and Suzy Favor Hamilton are, but you're disheartened they never moved up to the marathon so they could rock their buns on the roads.

5. Buns don't sexualize you and they aren't a statement to anyone. The only judge you answer to is the clock.

Booties

1. If someone told you that you could jump in a hot tub and go back to the 80s, you would cannonball your crimped-haired awesomeness into the bubbles so fast you might even forget to take off your Sony Walkman.

2. You're as comfortable on the starting line in Hopkinton as you are flipping tractor tires, squatting more than you weigh, climbing walls, hammering burpees, and puking in CrossFit garbage cans.

3. Remember that kid in grade school who scared the bejesus out of the opposing team in Red Rover and sent classmates to the nurse during dodgeball? Sure you do. That was you.

4. How did you BQ? Did you run one of those downhill REVEL races? Ha. You ran a net-uphill trail marathon at 7,000 feet with 2,500 feet of vert, choked out a rabid mountain lion with your bare hands to save a competitor's life at Mile 24, and still BQ'd.

5. "Why do you wear those when you run?" You get asked that a lot. And you've learned not to say a word. You stare into the eyes of the person asking the question uncomfortably for however long it takes until you feel their life force melting onto the floor into a puddle that occupies the space between you.

Split Shorts

1. When Des Linden was asked by a reporter whether her post-race celebration would involve bourbon or whiskey and she replied, "Bourbon is whiskey, Larry," you raised your Perfect Manhattan in solidarity.

2. Remember when Lynn Jennings wore split shorts on the roads and buns on the track, never commingling the two? Of course you do. And you feel the same.

3. There was only one girl in your gym class who didn't complain about the standard-issue blue shorts with the white piping. That girl was you.

4. You're a firm believer that yoga moms in their split shorts who sip foam lattes at Starbucks are misusing sacrosanct athletic gear.

5. When you survey your corral in Hopkinton, you feel like a runner among retired cheerleaders (skirts), former roller derby queens (booties), and misplaced, bikini-clad beachgoers (buns). You can't help but think to yourself, "Am I the only one taking this race seriously?"

Skorts

1. Remember the disheveled girl in third grade who wore gray sweats to school every day? That wasn't you. You were sitting next to her in a knee-length floral dress with ribbons in your perfectly braided hair, taking notes in your color-coordinated binder with a pink pencil.

2. The debate over whether cheerleading should be a sport or not rages on, but there was never a doubt when you were flipping and back-handspringing your way across a field or court.

3. You either a.) went to prep school and wore a skirt as part of your school uniform, b.) played field hockey, lacrosse, or tennis, c.) retired from figure skating, or d.) all of the above.

4. Your average Bloody Mary tab at the country club is roughly equivalent to the entry fee for the Boston Marathon.

5. You know the runner in your corral in Hopkinton who matches completely from head to toe, including eye shadow and nail color? That's the reflection you see in the mirror.

Hot (greater than 75 degrees F)—Buckle up. "Shorts" is a great answer, but it's like walking into a bar and when the bartender asks what you'd like, you respond with "a cocktail." Great. Much like "cocktail," "shorts" is less of an answer and more of a gateway to more questions. Welcome to the modern era of shorts.

Men, wear what makes you comfortable. Sincerely. Wear what makes you happy. But if you're fast (i.e., elite, sub-elite, or "I'm chasing my PR at all-costs-fast"), then you really have two choices: 1.) compression half-tights, or 2.) split shorts. Can you PR in basketball-style, 9-inch, V-notch shorts that look like you're ready to shred The Wedge in Newport Beach? Sure. But once you PR looking like the forgotten sixth member of Michigan's Fab Five, you're bound to get faster, which leads you to half-tights and split shorts.

Are you "running" Boston and not racing? Okay. Wear the long shorts, if that's your preference. Just make sure they're not cotton. Please. You really can't put enough Body-Glide or Vaseline on your body to prevent the chafing from cotton in temperatures above 75 degrees.

Women, it's more complicated. Are you wicked fast? If so, wear buns, booties, or split shorts. Do you hope to one day be wicked fast? Consider the aforementioned items, but also think about skorts, V-notch shorts, shorts with liners, high-rise shorts, and high-waist biker-style shorts with pockets. Can you wear Capri pants in temperatures exceeding 75 degrees? If the fabric is light enough, absolutely.

On a related note, male or female, you're going to want to store some fuel (GUs, gels, bloks, sodium tablets, Gummi bears, licorice, jelly beans, or anything else you deem appropriate) in whatever you wear. So make sure you have some pockets that provide ready-access to what you need. If not, a good trick is to use safety pins to secure your fuel to your bottoms. Or wear a running belt (aka waist pack, fanny pack, or flip belt) to help carry the load.

Warm (between 51 and 75 degrees F)—Temperatures in the lower end of the range introduce some new alternatives. If it's 55 degrees F with a pretty aggressive wind, you're not quite in tights territory yet, but you do have an opportunity to sport the perfect bridge between bare legs and covered legs, calf sleeves.

Calf sleeves are to aging runners what the philosopher's stone was to medieval alchemists. Designed to improve blood flow and increase oxygenation of the muscles and the removal of waste products, calf sleeves are compression stockings that support muscles and protect them from stress effects.

Paula Radcliffe single-handedly turned a garment previously worn primarily in hospitals (i.e., anti-embolism socks) into a running sensation when she was sporting compression socks whilst demolishing the world record (2:15:25) at the 2003 London Marathon. Technically, Radcliffe wore socks, not sleeves, but she set the wheels of compression mania in motion, passing the torch to the likes of Meb Keflezighi, who won the 2014 Boston Marathon in compression gear.

Aging runners (especially men over 40) are at higher risk of calf injuries, so much so that a "disease," "Old Man's Calf Disease," has been coined. But beyond calf sleeves' debatable power to cure, they serve another great purpose, providing just the right amount of protection from the cold and wind when the weather is in its transitional stages (namely spring and fall).

So when the weather gets crisp, rather than throwing on tights and potentially overheating, just add calf sleeves to your fave pair of shorts. Boom. Oh, and you fashionmongers will be happy to know calf sleeves come in different compression levels, colors, and fabrics. They're not just for hospitals and old men anymore.

Cool (between 36 and 50 degrees F)—Wind speed and direction and whether you're training for or "running" a race vs. redlining your effort and "racing" a race will influence your decision-making.

If you're racing, let it rip in your shorts of choice and calf sleeves if you're concerned the cool air will be too much for your legs. If you're not racing, you can be a bit more conservative with your race kit. Why take risks when you'll be high-fiving toddlers in Ashland, kissing students in Wellesley, and taking sips from Solo cups at Boston College. Wear whatever makes you comfortable.

Speaking of safety, it's important to note that hypothermia in this temperature range is a real concern no matter how fast you run. In the epic mess that was 2018, more than 2,500 runners received medical attention at the finish line. And if you think elites run so fast that they're immune to such afflictions, think again. More than half of the elite runners (23 to be precise) dropped out of (i.e., DNF'd) the 2018 race, most all due to hypothermia.

Even the elites who finished struggled. Kenyan Geoffrey Kirui, the 2017 Boston Marathon champion, seemed destined to repeat in 2018 before hypothermic symptoms relegated him to zigging and zagging at a pedestrian pace in Kenmore Square before being passed by eventual winner Yuki Kawauchi.

American Shalane Flanagan, a pre-race favorite after her win at the 2017 New York City Marathon, finished seventh in 2:46:31, calling the 2018 Boston conditions "the most brutal conditions she's run in." Interviewed after the finish, Flanagan expressed that at one point late in the race, she was so delirious from the cold she actually thought she was winning.

Extreme weather years like 1976, 2004, 2012, and 2018 serve as reminders to look beyond the temperature on your thermometer. Gear up for fluctuating conditions and lean on the generous support from dedicated race officials, volunteers, and medical personnel.

Cold (between 20 and 35 degrees F)—Spring PRs are made in the winter. The upper end of this range of temperatures is still conducive to shorts and full-on racing for PRs, especially if the winds on Marathon Monday are forever in your favor (e.g., calm, west, southwest, or even west-southwest). But add a little (or a lot of) wind to the mix, especially headwinds (i.e., anything from the east or northeast), and then shorts won't provide enough coverage to keep your finely tuned leg muscles warm.

During a marathon, the body's core temperature rises from normal levels (98.6 degrees F) to as high as 102–103 degrees F. This is natural and healthy, but what's healthy becomes unhealthy when a variety of factors (physical depletion, slower pace, decreasing air temperature, increasing wind) conspire to drop your body temperature below normal levels.

One of the real dangers indigenous to Boston is post-bonk distress, which can lead to hypothermia. Can you bonk in New York, Chicago, London, Tokyo, or Berlin? Sure. But, there are two big reasons why Boston is more treacherous: 1.) Boston weather is a bit more erratic ("erratic" being a gentle euphemism for batshit crazy), and 2.) Boston's hills occur just when your glycogen stores are depleted, so it's far easier to hit the wall mentally, physically, and emotionally in Boston. Unlike the other World Major Marathons' less harrowing courses, Boston's undulations have a way of ripping your heart out, throwing it in the Cemetery of Lost Hope (Mile 21.5), and relegating you to a zombie march through Brookline toward the finish downtown.

To add insult to injury, the weather is known to shift considerably once you head down the back side of Heartbreak Hill (Mile 21) and leave the exuberant madness of Boston College behind you. Things get eerily quiet as you run past the aforementioned cemetery, and just as your spirits are feeling as wobbly as your legs, a cold New England wind whips in from the east (off the chilly 40-something-degree-F waters of Boston Harbor). Mild hypothermia occurs when your body temperature drops to 96–97 degrees F, and that's something that can happen pretty quickly when you're not layered properly and your core temperature is dropping in lockstep with the air temperature.

Wicked cold (less than 20 degrees F)—Can you run a marathon with bare legs in temperatures below 20 degrees F? Yes. Is it wise to do so? No. The faster you run and the faster you finish, the better, of course. But it's just too darn risky to expose your legs to freezing temperatures for a sustained period no matter how fast you're running.

Half-tights (or booties for women) under full tights is a strong combo in these conditions. If that doesn't provide enough warmth, add calf sleeves to the mix. Alternatively, you can wear two pair of tights or wear a thermal, fleece-lined pair of tights as your outer layer to ensure you're even more protected. Be sure to remember your favorite anti-chafing substance (Vaseline, Body Glide, Nutt Butter, or otherwise) because extra layers could result in wet underlayers, more friction, and potential discomfort if not lubricated properly or worn frequently prior to race day. (**Pro Tip:** Slather a layer of Vaseline on all areas of skin that are exposed to buffer them from the wind and cold.)

Socks

Remember shapeless, unisex, one-size-fits-all tube socks? Alas, times have changed. The downside is the wide variety of choices makes your decision-making more difficult. The upside is tube socks really weren't that great for running after all, and the alternatives are pretty darn fantastic, especially if you train and race year-round in all manner of wickedness.

Before I was inspired to run the Boston Marathon, I didn't consider myself a runner; the race changed my life and my relationship with the sport, sparking my passion for running and transforming me from a "lacrosse player who ran" into a runner for life.

Mike Wardian
More Than 300 Marathons/Ultramarathons
Boston Marathon Guide Runner
World Record Holder, *Guinness Book of Records* (Multiple Events)

So, what do you wear on Marathon Monday? Well, that depends on quite a few factors (weather, pace, foot-strike preference). But let's take a closer look at your options to ensure you get it right when it counts.

Hot (greater than 75 degrees F)—Many of you who ran track sock-free in spikes back in the day would argue that no socks is the way to go, but running 26.2 miles on the roads is a bit trickier. A miler strikes the ground roughly 1,000 to 1,500 times, but an elite runner's foot will strike the road more than 25,000 times during a marathon. Slower runners often log more than 40,000 or even 55,000 steps. All of that foot trauma wreaks havoc, especially if you make some ill-conceived footwear choices on race day. Your chances of getting blisters multiply the farther you run, so training in different combinations of shoes and socks (or even trying barefoot, if that's your thing) mitigates your risk on Marathon Monday.

Plenty of barefooters have run Boston, but if you're going to give it a shot, you'd better train barefoot to sufficiently harden your feet for the asphalt concrete journey from Hopkinton to Copley Square. And if you're going to go sockless in shoes, you'll need to harden the areas of your feet (heels, toes) most inclined to rub against your shoes and blister. Whether barefoot or sockless, attempting to run Boston without training your feet properly in advance is a recipe for blood, pain, and disaster.

On average, a marathoner's foot will expand a half or full shoe size while running and foot temperature will increase (due to friction, blood flow, heat and humidity), so the temptation to run barefoot or sock-free is, theoretically, understandable. But in practice, most marathoners find socks and shoes with room in the toe box to "grow" work best.

Thin, moisture-wicking technical socks work great in extreme heat, especially for runners who like a snappy, "responsive" feel. Runners who prioritize comfort over performance may prefer socks with more cushion in the critical strike zones (heel and ball of foot). Either way, it's best to avoid cotton and socks that don't fit properly. Cotton retains moisture, heat, and friction, and socks that are too small (toe cramping, toenail loss) or too big (chafing, blisters) will come back to haunt you, likely in Newton, just when the going gets tough.

Compression socks are appealing, but it's important to have trained in heat with them prior to wearing them on race day. Some runners feel claustrophobic because the extra layer on their lower legs is too restricting in the heat. Others find the benefits (e.g., reduced leg inflammation) outweigh the drawbacks. If you're going to wear compression socks, stick to lighter technical fabrics and make sure the fit is snug so you're not feeling them sag on your weary legs late in the race.

Warm (between 51 and 75 degrees F)—Sock choices don't change a great deal when the temperatures are north of 50 degrees F. It's not cold enough to worry about heat retention, so many of the choices you make when it's 85 degrees F hold up pretty well when it's 55 degrees F.

The key is to make smart choices and, sadly, many runners don't. It's far too common to see runners spend hundreds of dollars on the latest super shoes, yet they run out of energy (and possibly money) when it comes to picking their ill-fitted socks. Toeing the line in Hopkinton in the newest, fresh-out-of-the-lab carbon-plate shoe with cruddy socks is like opening a 1787 Chateau Lafite and pouring the bottle into a pitcher of sangria.

High-end running socks have specific features designed to keep your feet happy. The amount of padding can be dialed up or down depending on your liking. Some runners are like Corvette or roadster enthusiasts and want minimal cushion to feel the road beneath them. Others prefer to absorb the shock at all costs and want thickness to protect them from the pounding.

Modern, premium socks have ventilation zones that allow your feet to breathe while running. Some have arch support that may help with your nagging plantar fasciitis, seamless toes to prevent chafing, separated toes to prevent skin-to-skin friction, multiple layers to mitigate friction, compression to improve circulation, and even anatomical feet (i.e., right and left versions to improve the fit even more).

So throw out those crusty old socks. It might be okay to train in them, but do yourself a favor on Marathon Monday and put as much thought into your socks as you do to your precious shoes.

Cool (between 36 and 50 degrees F)—It's time to start thinking about warmth, particularly if cold rain is a factor. Hypothermia is far graver than foot discomfort, but a blister or two at Mile 6 in Framingham can turn into a full-blown, bloody, excruciating disaster by the time you hit Washington Square in Brookline (Mile 23). That bunched-up sock that's soaking wet isn't going to miraculously straighten itself out.

The idea of wearing wool on your feet doesn't sound too inviting if your experience with wool is with the itchy variety (scarves, sweaters). But merino

wool has longer, softer fibers that are not only soft, they breathe, wick moisture, and help regulate your temperature.

If the temperature is cool enough, wearing snug-fitting socks with
merino wool added to technical fabrics is a great way to keep your feet
happy. Well, okay, as happy as they can be running a marathon. You are running 26.2 miles, so "happy" needs to be defined in the context of you pushing
your body to its limits masochistically by choice.

Cold (between 20 and 35 degrees F)—If you're racing in shorts in these
temperatures, compression socks will provide extra coverage and warmth
below the knee and also improve blood flow in your legs. Compression socks
come in different fabrics and thicknesses, so it's advisable to seek out the
warmer variety (perhaps with a bit of wool) when temperatures are below
freezing.

If you prefer to wear tights in this temperature range, wool-blend socks
should be considered and the length of the socks should be scrutinized,
especially if you don't like to have a gap of exposed flesh beneath your leg
wear. Another trick of the trade is to rub petroleum jelly over your toes and
heels prior to slipping on your socks. The lubricant will help prevent the friction that causes blisters. And if your feet are particularly sensitive to the cold,
doubling up with two pairs of socks is a remedy. Be sure to wear a thin, syn-
thetic moisture-wicking bottom layer with a warmer wool-blend top layer.
The friction will occur between the socks rather than between your skin and
the socks.

Also, like anything you do or wear on race day, don't forget to test this
double-sock strategy in training. It's important to know whether your shoes
have enough room in the toe box. If not, it's best to buy a pair of shoes a half-
size larger so you can wear them on the days you double up.

Wicked cold (less than 20 degrees F)—It's improbable you'll have to worry
about these temperatures on Marathon Monday, but it's not impossible. And
if you're training in Boston or similar climates, you'll be logging plenty of your
winter miles in these conditions. Feet generate quite a bit of heat while running, so it's common for your toes to feel a bit chilly at the start and then
warm up as you navigate your way through the snow, ice, and winter wickedness. Be sure to experiment with different socks and sock combinations to
ensure you make the right choice when it counts.

The heat of your feet will likely melt the snow that gathers on your shoes and socks, so your socks need to be both thermal and moisture-wicking to keep your feet their happiest. If you've ever run over the surface of what you thought was a patch of ice that turned out to be a calf-deep puddle of ice-cold water, you'll understand why sock choice is important. And if this submersion takes place at Mile 2 of a 20-mile training run, you'll be thankful for wool, sheep, and the higher power responsible for creating them.

Another polarizing foot-related topic is whether or not orthotics (i.e., insoles, prescribed or otherwise) are helpful on Marathon Monday. If a doctor has prescribed an orthotic for you and you've trained with that particular orthotic, then you should follow your doctor's orders and wear your prescribed insole on race day.

Conversely, if a medical professional hasn't prescribed an insert, you haven't trained with or fallen in love with any particular insole, and you're still testing different varieties, then you shouldn't turn your Boston Marathon experience into a continuation of your unsupervised experiment. While having a bit of cushion or support where you feel you need it seems like a good idea, the risk of getting it wrong and inadvertently sabotaging your race is far too great to take that chance.

Shoes

Despite what you may read online or in print, there is no such thing as a perfect running shoe. Sorry. Your quest is noble, but it's like sipping a 2001 Barolo that might be amazing and then discovering a Brunello di Montalcino that's even better. Plus, your palate might enjoy reds when others prefer whites.

You might think that price is an accurate criterion for quality, but, much like wine, that's not entirely true for shoes either. Some punch well above their weight. And just as certain wines pair well with particular foods, different shoes perform better at different distances, in different conditions, and on different surfaces.

The good news is there's no shortage of variety, and the more you run in different brands and styles, the more you'll learn about your feet and how your shoe choices affect your performance. You may find a neutral, spongy, high-profile shoe with significant stack height is perfect for long slow distance, but not responsive enough for workouts or racing. That's okay. You should have multiple shoes in your rotation anyway.

A smart first step in determining what shoes work best for you is to visit a running store that administers a gait analysis. Do you pronate or supinate? What heel-toe drop is preferable? Are you a heel striker? What about stack height? Are

The more shoe choices you have, the more intimidating decision-making can be.

you a minimalist, or do you favor a plusher ride? All of these questions can be answered by studying your stride.

If you've never had your gait analyzed and you're in town to race on Marathon Monday, go to Marathon Sports (adjacent to the finish line on Boylston Street), Heartbreak Hill Running Company (at Mile 20, the base of Heartbreak Hill), or Tracksmith on Newbury Street (a stone's throw from the finish line). Boston is a running mecca year-round, not just the weekend of the race, and these stores are the brightest and most passionate retailers of running paraphernalia in the city.

So, what shoes should you wear on race day? That's a highly personal question because every runner is unique. There's no magic answer. But just because it's challenging and perfection is illusory, doesn't mean you can't pursue it. You're a marathon runner. You chase unicorns. You run Yasso 800s in subzero windchills and throw up at finish lines just to carve a second off your PR. It's clearly in your DNA. Let's dig in and figure this out. Here are a few tips to get you started.

Hot (greater than 75 degrees F)—Have you ever stared at a wall of running shoes at a retail store on your quest for your race-day shoe? It's overwhelming. The shocking array of neon and electric colors alone could induce a seizure. Throw in all the competing brands and different categories of shoes (e.g., neutral, stability, motion-control, minimalist) and it's even more disorienting.

If you've taken the time to have your gait analyzed, you can eliminate roughly 80 percent of the choices and zero in on choosing from the 20 percent of shoes that are built for your specific foot type and stride. Once you know whether you pronate or supinate, strike the ground on your heel or forefoot, and prefer a minimalist or plush ride, you can turn your attention to size, heel-toe offset, and fit.

It's important to know that once you narrow down your preferences, different brands will fit differently even if the sizes are the same. If you have been prescribed orthotics or prefer to wear insoles, be sure to bring them with you when you shop for shoes. Oh, and don't forget to wear the socks you'll be training and racing in, too.

It's natural to think that hot, dry conditions don't present many shoe challenges, but there are a few things you should know prior to making your shoe selection for Marathon Monday. If you plan to run shoe-free (i.e., barefoot), you should know that the third Monday in April in Boston is a bit too early in the spring for trees to have grown back their leaves. Why is this relevant to you? Well, if the sun is blazing and temperatures are in the upper 80 degrees F range (as was the case in 2004 and 2012) or even the 90s (1976), the pavement is going to be a heck of a lot hotter. Bare trees won't provide shelter from the sun, so roads can reach temperatures in excess of 150 degrees F. That's hot enough to burn skin, so if you haven't trained barefoot in such dangerous conditions, you might want to rethink your race-day footwear, or lack thereof.

Additionally, hot and dry conditions don't guarantee your shoes won't get saturated. You'll be throwing cups of water on your head (possibly every mile), and some of that water will find its way to your shoes. In 2012 when temperatures peaked at 88 degrees, mist stations were installed along the course to encourage runners to cool down. If you've never run through a mist machine, picture running through a car wash and attempting not to get wet. Good luck.

If the aid-station water and mist don't get you, you probably won't be able to avoid streams of water from hoses held by spectators along the course. You might be able to avoid them early in the race when your legs are fresh, but at Mile 19 in Newton when your quads are trashed, you'll surrender because you won't be physically nimble enough to change direction.

Warm (between 51 and 75 degrees F)—When temperatures are in the upper end of this range, you'll still have to contend with the aforementioned saturated shoe conundrum (self-inflicted or otherwise). If you've raced or trained with waterlogged shoes before and you've figured out a good system to avoid blisters, you shouldn't have any unforeseen issues. But if you're wearing heavily cushioned cotton socks with bulky training shoes, you'll feel like you're wearing ankle weights when they're filled with water and slapping the ground like clown shoes.

If you're efficient enough of a runner to pull it off, minimalist racing flats are a fantastic choice for warm and hot days. Racing flats often feature less cushioning, lighter materials, and slimmer profiles than training shoes. It's important to have run multiple long runs on asphalt in your flats prior to race day. If your feet didn't hold up well in your training runs, don't expect any miracles on race day. Some runners need the extra cushioning to absorb the shock of more than 40,000 foot falls over the marathon distance. Just because you PR'd in a 5k in your racing flats in March doesn't mean they're the right shoe for Marathon Monday.

Cool (between 36 and 50 degrees F)—You shouldn't have to dodge hoses or pour water over your head in these temperatures, so unless rain is in the forecast, you don't have to factor in the possibility of running in soaking wet shoes. But beyond water challenges, there's plenty more to consider, including whether you have to plunk down top dollar for the latest and greatest shoes (carbon plate or otherwise) to run your fastest race.

Running shoe innovation is nothing new. Runners have been trying to figure out how to improve performance since the ancient Greeks competed naked. But significant improvements in gear, including shoes, have accelerated in the past 50 years in lockstep with modern technological advances. And prices of shoes (and gear in general) have increased egregiously as technology raises the quality of everything on your body, from head to toe.

Remember when running was an inexpensive sport? Shoes. Shorts. Shirt. Go. Well, it still is. Sort of. Relative to triathlons? Absolutely. And sports requiring access to facilities (e.g., golf, tennis, gymnastics, hockey, skiing) or costly equipment (sailing, polo, horseback riding, racecar driving)? Definitely. So, in the grand scope of costs associated with sports, running remains cheap by comparison. Those $250 to $500 carbon-plate racers you're considering don't look so stupidly out-of-reach when compared to a $40,000 polo pony, $150,000 membership fee at the country club, or a $12 million Formula 1 car.

But do you need the carbon-plate racers to PR? No, you don't. If two equally talented, healthy runners toe the line at the Boston Marathon, and one ran 120 miles per week in white bucks and the other ran 25 miles per week in carbon-plate racers, the runner in white bucks will win every day of the week and twice on Marathon Monday. A carbon-plate shoe, or any technological advancement, won't catapult you to success if your similarly healthy and talented competitor has out-trained you.

Cold (between 20 and 35 degrees F)—If you've ever trained or raced in snow, you know how important traction is, especially when roads have gathered a multitude of wintry wickedness (snow, ice, slush). Have you ever done a complete yard sale on a sidewalk or road? Sure you have. Before we discuss how to avoid it, the Runner Wipeout Checklist (page 97) is a step-by-step guide for your next fall.

There's a nonzero chance you'll see snow on Marathon Monday, but one of the "joys" of a spring marathon is you'll be training in a lot of it, so it's important to have a go-to pair of winter shoes to get you through all the fun that awaits you during your buildup. And while you're at it, embrace the cold. Seriously. If you get your gear right, including your shoes, there's (almost) no reason to be uncomfortable in these temperatures.

While warm weather calls for light, airy, breathable shoes, winter and its harsher elements beckon for waterproof shells, gusseted tongues, and aggressive traction. Many year-round Bostonians train on the Boston Marathon course, especially the Commonwealth Avenue carriage road from the firehouse (Mile 17.25) to St. Ignatius Church at Boston College (Mile 21.5). Depending on the severity of the winter, the carriage road is typically plowed and free of snow. But in 2015 (the winter of Boston's record 110.3-inch snowfall), the road felt more like a cross-country ski course, necessitating shoes more commonly seen on mountain trails. But that's okay. There are plenty of shoes to choose from to keep you warm.

If it's not too sloppy out (i.e., you actually have pavement beneath your feet) and you don't need the less than subtle traction of a winterized trail shoe, lace up shoes with weatherized toe caps that offer protection where you need it without sacrificing speed when you want it.

If the road is patchy (i.e., some pavement and some winter wickedness), you'll need more traction if you don't want winter to slow you down. Well-placed lugs on the soles make a huge difference and can allow you to enjoy some winter speedwork away from the treadmill for a change.

As conditions worsen (i.e., "you thought there used to be pavement beneath this mess, but you're not sure anymore"), you may need to enlist

Runner Wipeout Checklist

Step 1—While face down on snow, ice, pavement, or whatever lies beneath you, summon the doctor your mother wanted you to be (with no prior medical training, of course) and perform a quick diagnostic. Where does it hurt? How bad does it hurt? Is it possible you broke a bone or two? Is bone sticking through skin? Are all of your teeth still in your mouth? Are you bleeding? Where? How bad?

    i. If you feel something is broken, stay put. Don't move. And either a.) use your trusty mobile phone to call for help, or b.) curse the fact that you don't have your phone and move directly to Step #2.

    ii. If you feel you've dodged a bullet and nothing is broken, then you can survey your gear. Have you paused your smartwatch (you'll probably instinctively do this first if you aren't bleeding out)? Did you crack the display of your smartwatch? How torn up are your $125 tights? Does your vintage 2009 Adidas Boston Marathon jacket have a gaping hole in its elbow?

Step 2—Turn your attention away from yourself, lift your head, and survey the landscape. Who saw you wipe out? You're probably no stranger to eating pavement among fellow runners or in front of tables of patrons at a restaurant. Is this one of those cases?

    i. If you think you're hurt, get the attention of passersby and ask them to help and/or call for help. If they don't seem too interested in helping, show them your missing teeth, gnarly head laceration, or the bone sticking through your skin. That should get them in motion.

    ii. If you feel you're unharmed, prop yourself up into a sitting position and try out that witty comment you've been saving for such an occasion. Alternatively, feel free to borrow one of the following: "I'm falling for you . . . hard" or "Well, I guess trail running is out of the picture" or "I can't blame you. It's my own asphalt."

    iii. If you feel you're too injured to move, no one is around, and you don't have your mobile phone, now is the perfect time to put your hands together and pray. Or, better yet, if you had the forethought to purchase, own, and wear your smart safety bracelet, simply push the button and your friends and emergency contacts will instantly receive text alerts and your GPS location.

the help of more substantial lugs and water-resistant gaiters that wrap snugly around your shoes. They may be a bit weightier than your go-to summer trainers and racing flats, but with the proper winter shoes for slick and uneven terrain, you can go out and play while many of your peers are taking a snow day.

Wicked cold (less than 20 degrees F)—Can you run on ice? Absolutely. Hey, it's not easy, but it's possible. Short strides and a forefoot strike will help your efforts, as will metal ice cleats (either embedded in the soles of your shoes or purchased separately and wrapped around your shoes). An unplanned perk of running on ice is you're likely to improve your running form, too. You'll be forced to rely on a Pose-type method of running (short strides, quick turnover, forefoot strike) to stay on your feet. That rapid-fire cadence and improved balance will serve you well when you return to pavement.

Heavy snow isn't a gavel-of-judgment sentence to the dreadmill either. Okay, you're not going to PR or set any segment records on your favorite loop. But you don't have to cling to the couch or reluctantly oil up your squeaky treadmill either. There's an ever-increasing array of awesome winter shoes available, and if you can't find a pair you love, you can always build leg strength and cardiovascular endurance with some invigorating snowshoeing. If you've never tried it, you'll find that running in snowshoes, similar to running in sand on the beach, engages leg muscles you otherwise wouldn't use. You may not have the eye candy you'll find at the beach, but ogling a moose in the wild will get your heart racing, too.

TECHNOLOGY

Is there any greater feeling than running completely free, unencumbered by technology in all its forms? Just you, the road, your thoughts, nature, completely untethered from splits, social media, texts, emails, and everything else that enslaves you? Crisp autumn air on your fading tan. The crunch of leaves beneath your feet. The colors. Oh, man. Fall colors. Like a LeRoy Neiman painting on acid. Daybreak over the horizon at dawn. Or the warmth of the sun on your shoulders on an early spring afternoon. Who needs technology, right? Please.

Well, as much as we probably don't need it, we've come to really enjoy it. Bit of a paradox, but technology isn't going away. In fact, technological innovations in running are accelerating faster than Eliud Kipchoge can drop you in the last pickup on a group long run. It wasn't too long ago (2006 to be exact) that the

Boston Marathon began scoring the event by chip (net) time vs. conventional gun time. So many technological improvements (Boston Marathon app, dynamic athlete tracking, and more) have enhanced the Boston experience. My, how far we've come in such a short amount of time, and, as technology proliferates, advancements continue to gather speed.

So how can technology prepare you for Boston and help you run the race faster? For starters, a smartwatch allows you to train with greater precision, lock into a pace on race day, and monitor heart rate and other vitals that can help you control your effort more evenly. And smartwatches keep getting smarter, allowing for performance statistics (e.g., VO_2 Max) and robust form analytics (cadence, stride length, ground contact time, balance, bounce, and more). Oh, and for you music lovers, the latest watches can store hundreds of your favorite songs (no phone required). Go ahead, blast heavy metal as you grind up a hill or bliss out to some yacht rock on a recovery run.

But watches are just the beginning of a wearable technology revolution. Smart insoles gather data directly from your feet each time they hit the ground. Level of pronation, stride length, and footstrike analytics provide valuable insight into how your stride changes up hills, down hills, or when legs are fresh or fatigued.

As marathoners know (or, more accurately, learn to know [often the hard way]), figuring out a way to arrive in Hopkinton healthy is paramount to anything else you do in your marathon buildup. Thankfully, technology can help with that, too. Most marathoners are the type-A variety of humans who push themselves to the brink in training, risking injury or overuse "niggles" (a cute euphemism for pain or discomfort that won't prevent you from running). But how do you know if (and when) you're being too aggressive? How do you know you've reached the tipping point if you can't see it? How can you train smarter to mitigate the risk of injury?

Plantar fasciitis crippled my only Boston Marathon in 1998; I had been barely able to walk for a month, let alone run, but traveling to the event with Moses Tanui, who ended up winning, he said, "it's Boston, you have to try"—any other race you'd cancel, but with Boston you push adversity aside then hobble, hop, or limp to make sure you too can say you are a Boston Marathon finisher.

Toby Tanser
50+ marathons
Founder/Director, Shoe4Africa
Former Vice President, Achilles International

Rather than follow a cookie-cutter training plan, what if you could customize a plan for yourself that modified your training each day based on your body's individual needs? That would be pretty cool, right? Well, it's happening. Wearable devices for runners can help you adjust the daily time and intensity of your workouts to help you avoid the injury tipping point and absorb your training more efficiently. How? Well, modern wearables monitor the quality of your sleep, skin temperature, blood oxygen, and more. These biometric calculations are then tallied to produce a nightly sleep score that lets you know how well you slept and whether your body is ready for a workout or not. Devices will even vibrate to wake you up at the optimal time based on your sleep needs and circadian rhythms.

If a better understanding of your recuperation needs isn't enough, try slipping into recovery boots that use dynamic compression to reduce soreness and channel metabolic waste out of your limbs. They're not cheap, but, relative to human alternatives such as months and years of physical therapy or massage, the lifetime cost is comparatively undaunting. These boots are not a substitute for professional PT and massage, but they are perfect to use between visits to improve circulation and help you recover faster from your workouts.

The general idea is the compression system increases blood flow, allowing more oxygen and nutrients to get to your muscles. So the good stuff (oxygen and otherwise) heals your muscles while the bad stuff (lactate and toxins) is transported away from your muscles. You might look a little funny reclining in puffy, pulsing, inflated boots on your couch, but remember you're the one who runs in spandex in blizzards. Ya gotta do what ya gotta do. BQs don't grow on trees.

Did you know that Dick Beardsley punched his quads with his own fists over and over and over to prepare for his epic Duel in the Sun with Alberto Salazar? Yep. It worked. He may not have won that day, but he did run 2:08:53 in 1982. Not too shabby. He thought pummeling his quads would toughen them up so they could better handle Boston's undulations and Newton hills. Well, he was on to something. And he can spare his knuckles now. Percussive massagers or massage guns use vibration therapy to manipulate your body's soft tissue and, unlike boots, can target specific muscle knots and problem areas to relieve pain and accelerate healing. Boots can't reach your recalcitrant piriformis or your high/proximal-hamstring tendinopathy, but a massage gun can! Why punch yourself or pay someone to punch you when you can buy a tireless robot to do it?

When you're in the mood for something beyond being punched, try immersing yourself in subzero temperatures (cryotherapy), heating yourself without sweating (infrared therapy), rolling and vibrating simultaneously (vibrating foam roller), jump-starting your muscles electronically (EMS—electronic muscle stimulation), challenging yourself with simulated high-altitude training (elevation training mask), monitoring your holistic health (smart scale), measuring your running power (power meter), improving your safety (smart safety bracelet), upgrading your home gym (fitness mirror), or getting coached by a pro and running in exotic locales around the world without leaving your house (smart treadmill).

INJURIES

"If I waited until I was injury-free before I ran, I'd never leave the house" is not an uncommon thought among year-round runners. As healthy as running is, the cruel truth is that the very thing that is good for you is the same thing that can injure you and cause you harm. Welcome to running.

Pain management within a race is an invaluable skill for runners, and pain management (nay, injury management) in training is equally invaluable. The former allows you to lean into the unavoidable pain that greets you when you attempt to race your fastest, and the latter is necessary to manage all of the (arguably) inevitable ailments you'll encounter as you scale your winter training and attempt to arrive in Hopkinton your fittest and healthiest.

The challenge is to decipher the difference between aches, pains, and typical running discomfort and full-blown injuries. It would be easy if the lines of demarcation were distinct, but no, the lines, as you'll find the more you run, are quite blurry, making your never-ending task of discernment all the more difficult.

Should you rest your angry hamstring or get out the door for your seven-mile recovery run? Is that Achilles tendon tightness cause for concern, or are you just being soft and using it as an excuse not to run your Yasso 800s? What about your sore right foot? Is that a stress fracture, or did you just lace your shoe too tightly yesterday? Every day seems to raise new questions. And the conundrum is you're not a doctor, you're just playing one every day and you're not praying your by-the-seat-of-your-pants diagnoses are perfect, you're just praying they aren't dead wrong.

Most marathoners who have been running for multiple years traverse, give or take, many of the same injuries: shin splints, iliotibial (IT) band syndrome, plantar fasciitis, Achilles tendonitis, piriformis syndrome, high-hamstring/proximal tendinopathy, runner's knee, calf strains, and stress fractures. On any given day, you may experience symptoms related to one or more of these aforementioned conditions. Are these symptoms (and the injuries they're possibly signaling) a rite of passage? Is there anything you can do to prevent them from occurring?

Have you ever been in the middle of a training run and felt a sharp pain in your calf that stopped you in your tracks like you had been shot by a sniper with a crossbow? Well, that's an acute injury deserving of very different treatment than an overuse (chronic) injury. Acute injuries are sudden and can be violent. If you've ever witnessed someone rupture his, her, or their Achilles tendon, you likely heard a "pop!" closely followed by the injured athlete falling violently to the ground. By contrast, overuse injuries are caused by repeated forces over a prolonged period of time. These forces produce niggles that compromise your stride mechanics, speed, and volume and may well lead to the very injuries you're trying to avoid.

The best solution to the all-too-common niggle-to-injury trajectory is to prevent niggles from occurring in the first place. Sounds great in theory, but, in practice, prevention is as mythical as the unicorn on the Boston Marathon finisher's medal. That doesn't mean you can't try, of course. But even elites who run for a living and have access to all of the best medical support, training gear, and professional instruction are saddled with niggles and vulnerable to injury. If you're working a full-time job and have less time, energy, and resources to allocate toward injury prevention, you're even more susceptible to being sidelined indefinitely.

So how do you get to your corral in Hopkinton healthy? Well, prehabilitation (training specifically aimed at preventing injuries), listening to your body throughout training, and sufficient recovery are keys to your success. And know that you can't do everything alone. You'll need the help of coaches and medical professionals to not only reactively address niggles and injuries you encounter and adapt your training accordingly but also to proactively plan your training to minimize the risk of getting injured during your buildup.

Prehabilitation

In a nutshell, prehabilitation can be defined as "all the things you know you should do to improve your running but you (probably) don't do." These things include foam rolling, massage, physical therapy, gait analysis, dynamic stretching, strength training, resting adequately, anti-inflammatory treatments, and fueling properly before, during, and after your runs. Simple, right? Not really. And even if you do all of them religiously, there's no guarantee you won't get injured anyway. Thanks, running. You are a riddle wrapped in a mystery inside an enigma.

Listening to Your Body

If you run marathons year after year for multiple decades, one thing is certain: You will develop a keen awareness of your body whether you like it or not. Call them pains, niggles, injuries, or whatever you want, but you'll begin to feel like an old car with too many miles that breaks down inconveniently and requires constant care. Is that persistent throb in your third metatarsal a stress fracture, Morton's neuroma, broken plantar plate, or something else? What is that pain in your butt? Piriformis syndrome? High-hamstring/proximal tendinopathy? Sciatica? Or is it something even more egregious? Yikes. The more your body breaks down, the more you learn. When in medical school, aspiring doctors should be encouraged to train for marathons to supplement their classroom education. Never stop listening to your body whether you're training or racing. Enlist the help of medical professionals when necessary, but the front line between health and injury begins and ends with you. Happy or angry, your body is telling you something. Listen closely and you'll get better and better at understanding what it's trying to say.

Sufficient Recovery

Have you ever pulled an all-nighter and tried to be productive the next day? How did that work out for you? We humans need our sleep. Insufficient sleep can lower your body's resistance to illness and infection, negatively impact your ability to concentrate and think clearly, and increase your risk for depression and anxiety. In addition to sleep, recovery for runners includes proper hydration, adequate nutrition, thorough stretching, and active recovery (i.e., taking it sufficiently easy on your easy days, rather than running in no-man's-land).

No-Man's-Land

No-man's-land is the place PRs go to die. It's that gray area between running too fast for a recovery run and too slow for a workout. It's where plateaus are born. It's where runners tend to run when they're not training with purpose.

You're probably familiar with the 80/20 rule of running: The overwhelming majority (80 percent or more) of your training should be at a low-intensity, easy-effort pace, while the remainder (20 percent or less) of your training should be at a higher intensity. "Run slow to run fast" is the counterintuitive mantra at the heart of the 80/20 concept. That sounds great in theory, but, in practice, what often happens is the lines separating easy and hard efforts are blurred. That blurry area is no-man's-land, and once you get in the habit of going there, it's difficult to leave.

Runners' inherent competitiveness can be a blessing and a curse. Summoned on race day, this tenacity can get you on the podium. But in training, being hyper-competitive can get you in trouble, especially if you're reluctant to run paces your ego feels are too slow. For example, if you're training to run a sub-3 marathon (i.e., 6:52/mile), you may find the majority of your training mileage is in the 7:15/ mile to 8:00/mile range. That's no-man's-land. Ideally, you should be running 80 percent or more of your miles between 8:00/mile and 9:45/mile and 20 percent or less of your miles between 5:30/mile and 7:15/mile. The challenge is to train yourself to understand that running paces above 8:00/mile or 9:00/mile is not an affront to your self-esteem.

Do yourself a favor and don't run in no-man's-land!

SUPPORT TEAM

Can you be a lone wolf marathoner? Sure. Train alone. Race alone. Recover alone. Boom. You're a marathoner. One of the beauties of running is you really don't need anyone else. You can lace up your shoes, train, and race whenever you want. You may even self-navigate your way to a BQ.

But if you want to be your best, fully explore the depths of what is possible, and achieve what previously seemed impossible, you'll need some help along the way. It takes a village to unearth your true marathon potential. Friends, family, physical therapists, coaches, mentors, fellow runners, volunteers, running clubs, and medical professionals will all play important roles in your journey.

You might be the one chasing the unicorn, but your support team is why you're smiling as it dangles from your neck. Amanda Nurse

Think of all of these aforementioned people as components of your support team. Each runner's team will be unique. Runners with significant others who run marathons will benefit from their empathy and understanding (and perhaps even train in tandem on "run dates"). Runners with supportive, sympathetic significant others who don't run aren't out of luck. In fact, two marathoners in a house create laundry and schedule challenges that are minimized when it's just one of you who's sleep deprived and chronically fatigued from 5 a.m. long runs.

Every year, the Boston Marathon brings an electricity to the city I can compare only to the excitement of one of our sports teams vying for a championship—except we're not only cheering for professional athletes but our friends, family and neighbors—and I am privileged to have had the chance to be part of that as both a runner and spectator for the last 21 years.

Chrissy Horan
14 Marathons
10 Boston Marathons

But even though your support team is exclusive to you, you'll need every component to be your best. If you think you can run your fastest without physical therapy, think again. If you believe you can do your best without the help and encouragement of fellow runners, you're mistaken. If you feel you don't need a good doctor in your corner to be the best that you can be, you will learn the hard way that you do.

Surrender to the help of others. They, collectively, will lift you to higher heights and faster times than you could ever achieve on your own. Do you think Dick Beardsley and Alberto Salazar would have run sub 2:09 in 1982 without each other? Not a chance.

SOCIAL MEDIA

Camaraderie among runners isn't a modern phenomenon. Many nonrunners feel the bond runners share is unreasonable, almost cultlike. That's more true than false. Runners have enjoyed a close-knit community long before Meta's Mark Zuckerberg was born, YouTube's Chad Hurley ran his first high school cross-country race, or the internet was created. When you stand in your corral before the start of the race in Hopkinton, you feel an undeniable kinship with the runners surrounding you. The relationship you share transcends offline and online dimensions. Call it spiritual. It's okay. Because it is. And it's hard to understand, until you have that bib on your chest and you feel it yourself.

No doubt your predecessors in Hopkinton felt it, too. Can you imagine standing next to seven-time champion Clarence DeMar among a field of just 218 entrants at the start of his final victory in 1930? Goose bumps, right? But, there's a difference today. And as you shake out your muscles in your corral in Hopkinton, you'll see it all around you. Phones. Everywhere. Runners pointing them at every angle, attempting to "capture" the moment rather than living in the moment. Selfies. Group photos. Panoramas. Do they enhance the experience? Or do they cheapen it? Welcome to social media.

Much like the rest of humanity, runners have embraced social media, too. And similar to the rest of the world, the running community is both its beneficiary and its victim. In theory, the idea of connecting runners all over the world and giving them a way to share their experiences with one another is as amazing as it sounds. The running community was tight-knit in the offline days, so surely online, instant connectivity to one another would be the ultimate accentuator to something that was already hugely positive, right? Well, not so fast.

Are you inspired when you see a fit runner post a photo and workout on social media? Sounds logical, yes? Well, not everyone is. It's just human nature. Some people see poetry in a sunset. Some don't. Neither side is right or wrong. Humans are human. And social media is an amplifier of all human sides: the good, the bad, the ugly, and everything between.

Similar to money, social media is an amplifier. If you were a warm-hearted philanthropist before you won the lottery, chances are you would become an even more generous philanthropist. But if you were a penny-pinching tyrant before your windfall, odds are in your favor to become an even lousier tyrannical miser. And so it is with social media. There's plenty of bad mixed among the good. The difference is social media gives everyone a megaphone. So if you thought a person was annoying offline, just wait until he or she has more than 100,000 followers on your favorite social network. Conversely, if someone means well offline, he or she is deserving of a worldwide platform even if others are not.

But is social media a positive for runners? Well, it is and it isn't. In fairness, the positives outweigh the negatives. Just don't expect any online miracles. Can it help you BQ? Sure. There's more valuable Boston Marathon information (training plans, racing tips, course overviews) than ever before, and the volume keeps growing. Social media is a huge contributor to this deluge of positive Boston knowledge, but, much like life offline, it takes some sifting to get to the good stuff.

Social Media Personalities—
Seven Cardinal Sins

To help you separate the online wheat from the chaff and navigate your way to social media success, here are some digital personalities (whether you choose to avoid them or seek them out) you'll encounter on your journey to the Boston Marathon:

1. **Pityfisher**—Remember your grade school classmate who watched from the sidelines during the Presidential Fitness Test because he had a note from home excusing him from participating? Well, that classmate is a runner now and, more precisely, a social media–posting Pityfisher. The Pityfisher is the Eeyore of runners. You know the ones. Long posts on social media sharing (and often exaggerating) physical ailments, fishing for compliments to make themselves feel better?

   Eeyore seemed to enjoy being gloomy. It was always difficult to discern whether he was just sad or legit chronically depressed. But his mood perked up when friends remembered his birthday, much like how Pityfishers feel uplifted from the online sympathy they seek. Can you believe how cruel and vengeful the world is when the Pityfisher reveals how he might not be able to make it to Hopkinton because he tweaked his hamstring during his taper? Of course you can. Heck, you and 98 percent of the Boston Marathon field are nursing niggles and injuries. Who isn't? But let's drop everything to read the Pityfisher's 15-paragraph social media post about how life is unfair and the world might end because his hammy is tight. Oh, bother.

   After extracting every last ounce of sympathy from the internet, the Pityfisher will not only run Boston, he'll BQ and PR. And then he'll write a melodramatic race review explaining how he overcame the greatest of adversity, yet persevered. He suffered a stress fracture at the top of Heartbreak Hill and will need significant rehab prior to even thinking of running again, thereby casting his net back into the sympathetic waters of his followers and beginning the cycle once more.

2. **Speedster**—A long time ago, probably when you were seven years old, you would sprint everywhere (playground, hallways, backyard, you name it) and you may have even harbored the belief that you were one of the fastest runners alive. Illogical, but, hey, that's youth.

   Fast-forward to adulthood and turn that kid into an (arguably delusional) age-group marathoner and, voilà, you have the Speedster. You'll recognize the speedster by his social media posts because he has a marathon PR of 3:42:28 (i.e., 8:28/mile) but he never posts a run with a pace above 7:59/mile. Does he ever run over 8:00/mile? Of course. But you wouldn't know it from his social media account. Until it's race day, when the fraud would unravel if he posted a subpar time. Which he won't, of course.

The Speedster will do everything in his power to protect his dishonesty. He'll run downhill marathons (REVEL and otherwise), he'll make excuses for racing poorly (even though his training went great), and, if anyone is inclined to do it, the Speedster would resort to cheating to prove he's faster than he actually is.

Perhaps the most infamous Level-5 Speedster in marathon history, Rosie Ruiz, cheated her way to "winning" the 1980 Boston Marathon. (*Note:* Rosie's title was taken away and rightfully given to the true winner, Jacqueline Gareau, eight days after the race.) It's a shame Ruiz's stunt was pre-internet. It would have been great theater to read her social media posts.

It can be confusing on the interwebs. So here's a quick breakdown of the Speedster levels.

Level 1—refuses to post slow training times on social media

Level 2—only races on fast courses (i.e., flat or downhill) and posts PRs from the wickedly fast downhill courses without even considering an asterisk or disclaimer

Level 3—shows PRs online that are accurate, but decades old, typically from bygone high school or college track days

Level 4—lies about PRs, paces, and times in general, and selectively forgets or "misremembers" specific races (e.g., former US vice presidential candidate Paul Ryan's claim he ran a "two-hour, fifty something" marathon that was fact-checked to be a 4:01:25)

Level 5—resorts to cheating to perpetuate the fraud and never backs down from this fantastical make-believe perch (e.g., Rosie Ruiz)

Level Kip Litton—A logical question you may ask is "can a runner possibly be narcissistic enough to go beyond Level 5?" It's wildly improbable. But, yes, it's possible. Behold Kip Litton, a runner deserving of his own category. Litton cheated at dozens of marathons, primarily, in true Speedster fashion, to run sub-3. And even though he wasn't capable of running sub-3 without cheating, he attempted to manufacture false sub-3 results in all 50 states while providing online advice to other runners to help them run sub-3 marathons. And he didn't stop there. He went so far as to create an entire marathon with fictitious runners and times just so he could record yet another sub-3 marathon. Wow.

You know how you've heard stories about mothers who have lifted cars off of their toddlers to save their lives? It defies logic and is so unbelievable; yet, in the back of your head, as implausible as it may be, you're imagining a sleep-deprived mother, with a rush of adrenaline, hoisting 3,000 pounds? That's nuts, right? Well, that mother can hold Kip Litton's beer, because Level Kip Litton is everything beyond nuts.

3. **The Natural**—Unlike the Speedster, the Natural is actually fast and he or she can't help it. The Natural decides to take up running in her 40s and, within a year of running, wins age-group gold in her first 5k in sub-20. Then she starts posting about running a half marathon, hops (on a lark) in the B.A.A. Half three weeks later, and runs a sub-1:30 even though she had to stop twice for bathroom breaks. Meanwhile, you're her same age, have been running for 15 years, and have methodically whittled your half marathon PR from 2:27 to 1:53. Rawr.

You'll recognize the Natural by the posts that keep showing PRs dropping as readily and effortlessly as colored leaves in the October New England sky. To add insult to injury, the photos that accompany the posts look like Helmut Newton came back to life and collaborated with Annie Leibovitz for the sole purpose of destroying your reason to live.

Oh, and that $100 sports bra that you fell in love with when you wore it and PR'd with your 1:53 last month? Well, the Natural just became a sponsor/ambassador for the brand and posted a video where she unboxed a dozen of them that she received for free. And you know those 1,423 posts it took you to amass 702 followers? The Natural has posted 83 times and already has more than 20,000 followers. How does that knife in your abdomen feel? Thank heavens your midsection has more cushion than the Natural's fresh-out-of-bed sixpack.

4. **Monetizer**—This may (or may not) be the most comical online persona of all. Debatable only because tragedy usually precedes the comedy. The Monetizer often begins his or her social media existence as a well-meaning human (runner). You may even follow this genuinely delightful runner because of his or her fun posts and unique perspective on life. But then something weird happens. Things change.

The post that was thoughtful, punchy, and edgy months ago now is so mainstream and vapid you yawn, and it has dozens of tags and hashtags, and the photo accompanying the post shows the runner in his favorite shorts, with his favorite socks, with one hand holding his favorite electrolyte beverage and the other raised in an overly enthusiastic "thumbs-up" position. What happened?

That insipid runner who used to be astute and playful is the Monetizer. And once the smell of social media money intoxicates his bank account, your "friend" or fellow runner (or whatever you want to call him) is gone, baby, gone. You have become a number. You have become a pawn in his game. Your "relationship" as you knew it is over. Welcome to social media.

Cue the corny, exasperated action shots with products front and center (e.g., "Whew, am I tired after that tempo. Good thing I had blah, blah, blah supertastic, caffeinated energy spectacular bomb gel foam made from the collective collagen and placentae of dead Olympic marathoners to get me through that rough patch at Mile 7."). If you're not queasy already, the Monetizer will then vomit a sea of emoji your aging eyes are too elderly to see and too tired to comprehend.

While the Speedster is indisposed to posting slow paces, the Monetizer has no such problem, posting an entire rainbow of paces in his attempts to make money off anyone and everyone who will follow him. "Are your joints tired and cranky in the morning?" he'll ask beneath a sweaty photo with "5.24 mile run" and "10:14/mile" plastered in bold letters." Not any more. "Invigorate your day like I do mine with my favorite vibrating foam roller." It's followed by a rainbow of heart emoji and 27 hashtags with the exception of one he's legally bound (by consumer protection law) to provide but forgot, #ad, which it blatantly is. The hashtags are followed by a link to purchase the item which puts money in the Monetizer's pocket, but he chooses not to disclose this either.

Monetizers are product hawkers, coaches, trainers, and more. They're at their worst when they start hawking brands (particularly shoes) as if they're imparting insider knowledge when they're really getting free merchandise from the companies, building an audience they monetize, and then doing it over and over again as their posts, reels, and videos become more and more vapid. They're the same ones who shake your hand at an expo, promise to keep in touch, and disappear. Poof! But, hey, why wouldn't they? You're a number to them. As they become less human to you, you become less human to them.

Are they all bad? Absolutely not. Monetizers who are honest and upfront about their businesses or, even better, have two separate accounts (one personal account and one business account) that are separate and distinct from one another are just trying to make a living. It's the dishonesty of some misleading Monetizers (with intent to manipulate followers for personal gain) that muddies the waters for the reputable, honest entrepreneurs. Comedy and tragedy side by side.

5. **Trailer**—You know how when you see a litter of puppies they rush at you, jumping over top of one another clamoring for your attention? Their energy and enthusiasm are overwhelming. But just as you fend off their assault of cuteness, you turn your attention to their disheveled sibling whose bed head and indifference to your arrival are even more endearing. She's just vibing, doing her thing. Well, the litter is social media at large. And your new friend who's chillin' without a care in the world? She's the Trailer.

    You won't have to worry about being blindsided by ads for foam rollers from the Trailer. She's as interested in hawking products online as she is in combing her hair offline. You might see a hashtag or two, but they're the innocuous kind that aren't fishing for a thing, like "#dawnpatrol" or "#mountainsmademedoit." While Monetizers pose in laughably premeditated "action" shots, Trailers live in constant motion: running at sunrise, snowshoeing in snow squalls, and summiting mountains.

    This all sounds refreshing and good, right? Yes, too good. Just as you grow addicted to her posts, reels, and stories, she goes off the grid. Probably doing something epic in a faraway place that would be cool to see. But you can't. Poof! She's gone. And that's the sin.

6. **Bostoholic**—We're here because the Boston Marathon is special. True. But there are other races. Plenty. Thousands upon thousands, to be precise. But you wouldn't know it when you follow the Bostoholic on social media.

    The Bostoholic isn't too difficult to spot. The day he registers for Boston, he'll post the online communication from the B.A.A. confirming his acceptance with a plethora of hashtags and emoji only to be rivaled by a digitally native teenager who just got accepted to Harvard. Every post thereafter will include Boston Marathon gear. You'll ask yourself, "Is it even possible to own enough Boston Marathon gear to wear every day?" And the Bostoholic, posing in head-to-toe blue and yellow, has your answer.

    The Bostoholic runner is akin to the family that still has their Christmas tree decorated in the living room in late March. At some point you have to let the season pass and recharge for the magic of the next one.

The Bostoholic isn't doing anything wrong, per se. He's just enthusiastic. And let's face it: The world can use a little more enthusiasm. Which is awesome. Until it isn't. What does that mean? Think of The Killers's hit song "All These Things That I've Done." Can you imagine the song without the gospel choir repeating "I've got soul, but I'm not a soldier?" It wouldn't suck, but it wouldn't be as good. The bridge, when the band takes a breather before gathering itself and storming back again, transforms the song into a sing-along stadium anthem.

If the Bostoholic has a flaw, it's his unwillingness to understand the power of a bridge. Like Christmas, Boston is a yearly event that's more meaningful if you crescendo toward it and decrescendo away from it. Even Walmart knows better than to put Christmas ornaments front and center in its aisles in July. Bostoholic, it's okay. We love you. Just acknowledge that there is a bridge between Aprils, and we'll love you even more.

7. **Transformer**—You won't forget the Transformer because every third social media post will remind you. Much like the Bostoholic, the Transformer isn't doing anything wrong or nefarious, she is just really, really proud of the amazing progress made since her nonrunning days and has endless quantities of side-by-side photos to prove how transformative running can be. Again, it's okay. The Transformer isn't guilty of baby trafficking, stealing identities, or cheating in races.

But the Transformer isn't innocent either. Oh, no. She's guilty. And she's a repeat offender, a recidivist to the highest degree. When you see an inspirational quote with a side-by-side photo with multiple superfluous emoji in every sentence, you know you're following a Transformer.

Did you know the runner you follow who has a marathon PR similar to yours was once cut from her intramural Quidditch team, 37½ pounds heavier, an alcoholic, and lived in her 1978 Saab, subsisting on cocaine, Oreos, cigarettes, and Mountain Dew? Well, the Transformer will let you know.

Listen, change is good. Change is amazing. The Transformer just probably needs to read this to know we understand it; she changed her life. And she needs to know that we understood that she was a hot mess turned semi-decent hobby jogger turned BQ runner the first time she posted it. The hundreds of posts saying the exact same thing aren't necessary.

TREADMILL

Remember when you were 12 and you were sitting at the dinner table with your family and the only thing keeping you from being excused was the lump of room-temperature, untouched lima beans on your plate? The last thing on earth you wanted to do was eat them, but the alternative (heating them up for breakfast) was far more distasteful. Well, that lump of lima beans is the treadmill. It's healthy. It's feared. And the alternative (running on ice in a nor'easter with subzero wind-chills) is a nonstarter.

Did you know that treadmills were first popular in prisons and they were used as a form of punishment for inmates? Makes sense. Speaking of prisons, first-generation treadmills were similar to old-school prisons like Alcatraz, intimidating and isolating. You didn't want to get on one, and, when you did, you were on your own. Modern treadmills are like country clubs, inviting and connected. Their fancy monitors and colorful displays lure you on, and, once the belt starts moving, you discover you can run with others virtually anywhere in the world. And in true country club fashion, your smart treadmill provides you the added joy of paying membership fees and monthly dues! Now you can compete with other members and you don't even have to leave the comfort of your house.

Most runners have a love/hate relationship with the treadmill, or "dreadmill", as it's often unaffectionately known. We've all seen a sad-looking, dust-ridden treadmill with shirts and socks draped over the console and arms as if it's an expensive clothesline or closet extension. The longer it's neglected, the more likely it is to get enveloped with more clothes, boxes, and whatever else it can handle, until it's buried and put out of its misery. Because, let's face it, seeing a chronically unused treadmill is like repeatedly trying on a favorite pair of pants you've outgrown. It's far better to get the culprits out of your sight than have your lack of fitness rubbed in your nose at every turn, right?

On a more positive note, the treadmill can be a savior, especially if you overcome your fear and use it to perform key workouts that otherwise couldn't be attempted in winter. Those Yasso 800s at the MIT track aren't going to happen when there's a foot of snow atop a layer of ice. But you can fire up your treadmill and hammer out structured speed work in your favorite shorts and singlet while you watch it snow sideways through the window. Even better, there are apps that sync with smart treadmills that will allow you to run the Boston Marathon course, displaying its grandeur from start to finish while the treadmill mimics the undulations (as best it can), including Heartbreak Hill and all the fun before and after.

Budget treadmills are available for less than $500. "Smart," feature-rich treadmills exceed $3,000 and require additional monthly subscriptions to access their connected bells and whistles. If you don't have the space or upfront money to own one, you'll likely need to have a monthly membership at a gym. Either way, it's cheaper to run outside in the wide-open air.

As challenging as the Boston Marathon course is on race day, training for Boston in the heart of winter is actually more challenging. Your buildup will likely start in lateDecember and end in April, so you either a.) HTFU and run in all good, bad, and ugly conditions, or b.) pay for the comfort and climate-controlled ride of a treadmill. You'll reap benefits (albeit, very different benefits) from both.

If you prepared for the 2018 Boston Marathon by primarily running on a treadmill in windless 70-degree conditions, you would have been in for a massive shock when Mother Nature threw her best haymaker on race day. Winter running hardens you in ways a treadmill can't. However, if you hoped to PR at the 2015 Boston Marathon and prepared by running, nay trudging, outdoors in Boston's all-time-record 110.3-inch winter snowfall, you wouldn't have a prayer of opening up your stride or turning your legs over fast enough on race day after shuffling through snow and slush. The treadmill allows you to practice race pace when winter prohibits it.

Curse the treadmill. Hail the treadmill. Repeat.

PRE-RACE REPORT CARD

How do you know how fast you'll run on race day? That's a tough one. In fairness, there are dozens of factors that influence your race performance, including many surprises that are welcome (a tailwind, a random spectator's handful of ice) and unwelcome (e.g., inexplicable nausea, random cramping). You truly won't know the answer until you cross the finish line. Perhaps a better question to ask is "How fast should you attempt to run on race day?" Or, put another way, what should be your goal time (which can then be reverse engineered into a goal pace)? It'd be great to have a diagnostic of sorts to inform your goals and race-day strategy, right? Well, behold the Pre-Race Report Card, the reality check you need to perform your best on Marathon Monday.

First, a caveat: A report card is a report card, not a guarantee of success any more than a 4.0 GPA guarantees you enjoy a lifetime of wildly fulfilling professional success. That said, if you were a college administrator, you'd rather have the 4.0 student in your incoming class, and, if you were an employer, you'd prefer to have a straight-A college graduate join your team versus a middling C student, right? And if you're getting ready to run the Boston Marathon, you'll aspire to have a straight-A report card even if it's no guarantee you won't bonk in Brookline and zombie shuffle your way to Copley Square. Got it? Okay. Let's proceed.

The Boston Marathon is special to me because I wanted to test myself over the legendary Boston Marathon course, against some of the best marathon runners in the world.

Paul Sole
20 Marathons
1 Boston Marathon (2018)
Six Star Medalist

Grades will be administered by you. That's right. You're the student and the teacher. And there's no grade inflation. Nope. Instead, remember that teacher or professor you had who never graded on a curve? The one who gave you a C- on your midterm paper and handed it back to you like a remorseless robot? Be that teacher. Honesty (i.e., being brutally honest with yourself) is your best friend. Giving yourself an A when you deserve a C will hurt you, not help you. So don't be the teacher or professor who hands out an A like a heaping handful of mini-Snickers bars to everyone who knocks on the door on Halloween; be the firm, frugal one who rewards a regulation-sized bar to only the most deserving ones with the best costumes.

You will grade yourself in five areas: 1.) Fitness, 2.) Fueling, 3.) Physical Health, 4.) Mental Health, and 5.) Meteorology. You probably have some questions already, so let's dig into each topic to understand how it complements the others and contributes to your overall GPA or, more precisely, your race performance.

1. **Fitness**—How fit are you? Seriously. "Fit" isn't a one-size-fits-all, you-are-or-you-aren't type of thing. There are varying degrees. How do you stack up? Did you have a training plan and nail all of your workouts or did you wing it? Did you have a coach who dialed in a customized training block to optimize your performance? Did you hit your mileage goal? Did you blow a gasket on your long runs, or did you finish fast and feel strong? Did you run some tune-up races to help you get comfortable with discomfort? When you start asking yourself the tough questions, chances are you'll conclude you're not quite as "fit" as you thought you were.

   The more you race, the easier it is to compare and contrast training cycles, hence the better sense you'll have of what degree of fitness you're taking into your goal race. And to be fair, "fitness" for Boston is very different than fitness for Chicago, London, or any other marathon that's pancake-flat. If your long runs didn't include some hills (especially toward the end) or fast-finish efforts (i.e., running the last handful of miles at race-pace or better), then your fitness likely isn't worthy of an A and your legs may not be as prepared for Boston as you think.

So how do you know what grade your fitness earned? Well, again, it's for you to determine, but here are some general guidelines. If a Boston Marathon veteran or professional coach or runner customized a Boston-specific training plan for you *and* you executed the plan day by day from start to finish to (near) perfection, then you're in A territory. Congratulations. Alternatively, if you're an experienced runner, studied multiple marathon training plans (Higdon, Galloway, Pfitzinger, Daniels), cobbled together your own personalized plan, and nailed it step-by-step, you may well be worthy of an A, too.

If you're an inexperienced runner, you should seek the help of someone with marathon knowledge (ideally, Boston Marathon knowledge) to assist you in crafting and executing a training plan. Just because you passed the swim test in the pool at summer camp in your youth doesn't mean you're capable of swimming the English Channel as an adult. No disrespect to you or the talent you may possess, but if you have little to no running (or marathon) experience and you're building a Boston Marathon training plan on your own, the highest fitness grade you can earn is a C+ (which might be generous).

If your training is compromised for any reason (injuries, life interferences, adverse weather), you will need to adjust your score lower in lockstep with how severely it was compromised. For example, if you tested positive for COVID during the peak volume weeks of your training cycle and had to take three weeks off, then your fitness is going to take a hit. So, again, be honest, always. And grade your fitness accordingly.

2. **Fueling**—There are runners who subsist on Pop-Tarts, chewing tobacco, and grape soda, but, if you're among them, please know that you're not only frightening, but you deserve an F when grading the fueling component of your report card. There is no perfect fueling formula for success that guarantees you an A. Every athlete is different, and the fuel that works (or doesn't) is unique to each individual. Trial and error will be critical as you dial in what optimizes your training and your recovery as well as your race performance.

What works best is a puzzle that takes time to solve. For example, are you properly hydrated? We all know we should drink an adequate amount of water throughout the day, but do we even know what that amount is? And if we do know the amount, do we actually drink it? If you're chronically dehydrated, your training will suffer and your race performance will be compromised.

Speaking of drinking, do you enjoy an alcoholic beverage or two (or three, or more)? Whether you drink or not isn't the question. World-class marathoners drink. It's okay. How often do you drink? How much do you drink when you drink? And is your drinking adversely affecting your training or race performance? Again, be honest. Your "fueling" grade needs to reflect everything you put in your mouth, good and bad.

Do you have room for improvement? It's okay to give yourself a C- if you learn from your self-assessment and proactively try to improve your fueling in subsequent races. It's not okay to overinflate your grade and continue to make the same mistakes again and again.

3. **Physical Health**—You're probably wondering "Is it possible to be incredibly fit but not physically healthy?" Absolutely. Marathoners are guilty of this quite often. Fitness and physical health aren't the same. Your fitness may deserve an A or A-, but you may be so dinged up by the time you reach the starting line in Hopkinton that your physical health deserves a D.

Again, what's an honest assessment of how well your body handled your training cycle? Do you have any structural damage (stress fractures, strained muscles, or otherwise)? Is your range of motion compromised? Is your plantar fasciitis inhibiting your gait? What about your piriformis? Do you feel like an old station wagon with broken parts and six figures on your odometer? Or did your taper heal and sharpen you? Again, no grade inflation.

4. **Mental Health**—Where's your head at? You might be fit and physically healthy, but, if your mind isn't laser-focused on your mission (throughout training and during the race), your performance will be sub-optimal. Have you ever tried running when you're conflicted about a dilemma at work or concerned about a loved one? The heaviness you feel is psychosomatic. Your brain is working against your body, preventing it from operating at the performance level it's capable of achieving.

The marathon is as mentally exhausting as it is physically exhausting. If your head is muddled with doubt or stress or fear or negativity at the start in Hopkinton, you may well be in for a miserable suffer-fest on your way to Copley Square. Unlike a 100-meter dash or shorter event on the track, the demons in your head have plenty of time and opportunity to come out in a marathon. If you're not in the proper headspace to fend them off, they will exert their control. Are you mentally healthy enough to ward them off?

Again, be truthful with yourself. Are you "locked-in" and ready to battle for your new PR on Marathon Monday? Or is your brain cluttered with distractions (perhaps some that are very much out of your control)? A strong A+ or A in this category can offset lower fitness and physical health scores. Conversely, a D or low C can sabotage your straight-A fitness and physical health.

5. **Meteorology**—Okay, you're not a meteorologist. But for the sake of your Patriots' Day race performance, you will do your best to impersonate one as you train and especially as you prepare to race during the last week of your taper leading up to the Boston Marathon. And your ability to predict the weather and prepare to race in it will play a huge factor in your success.

You might be chuckling. That's fair. You probably believe your grade in this category is an easy A, similar to the ESS 247 Tropical Meteorology course you took as an elective when you were a junior at Stanford. Think again. This is far from an easy A, so far that if you choose not to study and elect to "wing it" on Marathon Monday, you will pay dearly. And the price you'll pay will be measured in precious minutes and seconds, the ones that can cost you a PR, a BQ, your pride, or all of the above.

How did Jack Fultz and Kim Merritt win the 100 degrees F "Run for the Hoses" (the 1976 Boston Marathon)? Do you think they adjusted their efforts according to the weather? The Boston Marathon list of champions is littered with the names of athletes who weren't necessarily the fastest seeds, but they were the fastest on that day in challenging conditions.

Sweltering heat. Driving rain. Vicious headwinds. Unrelenting sun. Snow squalls. Boston delivers your worst weather cocktail. Are you ready for it? Really? Then grade yourself on how ready you are. Because if you're an athlete from Orange County, California, coming from calm skies, 66 degrees F, and gently swaying palm trees, are you ready for your limbs to be frozen with ridiculous sleet pelting you in the face with a 25-mph headwind in subfreezing windchills? Are you? Okay. Grade yourself on how prepared you are.

You want to know a secret? Nobody earns a 4.0 GPA on the Boston Marathon Pre-Race Report Card. A 4.0 GPA is as fantastical as the unicorn on the Boston Marathon finisher's medal. Or, to be mathematically precise, a straight-A report card is an asymptote, a value you can approach but never reach.

Here's an example of a real-life Boston Marathon Pre-Race Report Card:

Name: Marie

Age: 51

PR: 3:21:21 (London 2018)

BQ: 3:26:59 (Berlin 2019)

Boston Marathon 2022: 3:51:34

1. Fitness = C (winter training is beastly, and aging has proven to be beastlier)
2. Fueling = B- (pandemic disrupted eating and drinking patterns)
3. Physical Health = A- (structurally sound, but untested/undertrained)
4. Mental Health = C- (life crises siphoned mental energy far away from running)
5. Meteorology = B+ (savvy, but not as weather-hardened as in years past)

The objective of the Pre-Race Report Card is not to make the Dean's List every time you toe the line. Life happens. Injuries sneak up on you. Mother Nature throws a curve. Instead, the objective is to take stock of your strengths and weaknesses so that you can more accurately adjust your goals and strategies on race day, allowing you to make wiser, data-driven decisions to perform your best on that day, in that moment.

Given her candid self-assessment, Marie knew she wasn't in PR-chasing shape. But rather than hang her head in shame and DNS or simply run Boston for fun without a goal time, she took aim at a BQ (3:55:00 for 50- to 54-year-old women) and crushed it.

You don't have to be like Marie. You don't. There's nothing wrong with running Boston for fun. The hard work is getting a BQ and getting to Hopkinton healthy. The race is your victory lap. However, if you want to push your limits and test yourself, be like Marie. Be honest. Be confident. Be purposeful. Be smart. Be realistic. Be determined.

Most importantly, don't forget to set yourself up for success by grading your Pre-Race Report Card and adjusting your goals beforehand. Being your best requires a plan. If you don't have one, the Boston course will have one for you. And chances are its plan will be significantly more painful, insensitive, and humbling (not nearly as rewarding as yours).

CHAPTER 5

The Course: A Step-by-Step Guide to Towns and Cities along the Way

HOPKINTON

We all know your journey to the Boston Marathon began years ago as a twinkle in your salt-stained eye. But don't let your origin story discourage you from posing with your arm around the "It all starts here" sign in Hopkinton Town Center. You earned this photo op. Smile wide while you have the energy. You'll be shuffling with RBF beneath the iconic Citgo sign soon enough.

Your first thought about Hopkinton will likely be on the bus from Boston, taking note of how crazy long it takes to drive to Hopkinton on race morning, more than an hour, and that's cruising 65 mph on the highway (i.e., I-90, the Massachusetts Turnpike, "Mass Pike," or, to locals, simply "the Pike"). Watching the buildings and towns whip by your window, you'll remember you have to actually run the entire way back. It's sobering to consider your fragile legs held together by athletic tape and hope will traverse the distance that has the 450-horsepower, cast-iron engine laboring in your 20-ton, galvanized-steel bus.

The B.A.A. encourages you to take the school buses from Boston Common to Hopkinton. If you do, you'll feel like a well-pampered contestant in The Hunger Games. Hundreds of volunteers will shepherd you in the proper direction and wave at you in unison as you pull away like you're Katniss Everdeen on your way to Panem.

Can you get to Hopkinton without taking the designated buses? Yes, you can. In fairness to those who try, it is a bit more challenging, but it's doable if you have a savvy driver and leave before the legion of buses starts to clog the roads. It's an unwritten Boston Marathon tradition for local runners to enlist the help of friends and family to hack the system and get to Hopkinton without hopping on one of the buses. Back in the good old days, runners would pack into cars like clowns, drive to Hopkinton on race morning, and spill out of the doors and trunk like soldiers out of a Trojan horse. But if you're prone to anxiety, the buses are your

What better way to relive your youth than to suppress the need to pee on a yellow school bus on a field trip to Hopkinton?

best bet. You'll get where you need to be before you need to be there with far less uneasiness along the way.

If it weren't for the Boston Marathon, Hopkinton is a slice of Americana you might never otherwise see. Incorporated in 1715, Hopkinton, with its white picket fences and historic homes, evokes the charm and nostalgia of America's past, as if Norman Rockwell were commissioned to paint it into existence for the sole purpose of hosting the world's most archetypically American race.

With a population just north of 18,000, the heart of Hopkinton, like the Grinch's heart on Christmas, swells to nearly three times its normal size on race day when more than 50,000 spectators, runners, volunteers, and residents flood the narrow streets. In true Patriots' Day fashion, Hopkinton takes on a party-like atmosphere that sets the tone for all the towns that will greet you on your way to Boston.

Several Boston Marathon legends have been immortalized in Hopkinton's streets. Most recently, Bobbi Gibb's *The Girl Who Ran* bronze statue was placed at the corner of Hayden Rowe and Main Streets, a stone's throw from where, in 1966, Gibbs hid in the bushes to join the race in progress before women were allowed to run. Gibb joins statues of fellow legends father-and-son team Rick and Dick Hoyt (across from Hopkinton Town Common), 1946 champion Stylianos Kyriakides (Mile 1), and 11-year Boston Marathon race manager and 33-year race starter George V. Brown (at the starting line).

Athletes' Village

Depending on Marathon Monday weather, Athletes' Village can feel like a fun neighborhood block party or a maximum security prison yard.

When Geoffrey Mutai ran the course record 2:03:02 in 2011, Athletes' Village was buzzing with excitement because conditions were perfect for racing: upper-40s and low to mid-50s, partly sunny skies and a healthy, persistent 20+mph W tailwind. The mood was even jubilant in 2004 when conditions were horrible for racing (sunny and 83 degrees), yet delightful for volunteers and spectators.

By contrast, 2018 was miserable for everyone. Andy Dufresne probably had more fun tossing a ball with Red at Shawshank than any runner had in Athletes' Village. It's no fault of the B.A.A., race officials, or volunteers who did everything in their collective powers to make the experience as comfortable and athlete-friendly as possible under such horrendous conditions.

If you've never been a Special Forces soldier on the lam living off the land like Rambo, shivering in Hopkinton in a nor'easter keen on finding shelter, warmth, and a simple banana is the closest you may ever get. Much like Rambo, you'll have stripped yourself down to the bare necessities. Everything on your person must be worn, used, or discarded due to safety and, if necessary, pandemic protocol. All that brain space that would normally be contemplating the relative merits of various race strategies will be occupied by survival instincts, such as finding a dry swath of tundra to spread the mid-2000-era Mylar blanket you folded into your clear plastic bag specifically for this purpose. Oh, and you'll hear a gunshot that will send you running out of town. Okay, okay. It's an electronic starter's pistol, but it'll get you running nonetheless.

As you leave the bus and make your way to the entrance to Athletes' Village, you'll be required to flash your race bib before officials allow you in. Unless you're already a supermodel, you'll feel like one for the first time. Not the drug-addled 80s variety, but the superfit, modern-type who's carved up from tempo runs and hill sprints, not cigarettes and heroin. Your limo is a yellow school bus, but, hey, you're cutting the line at the hottest club in town and blowing air kisses at the bouncers as they lift the velvet rope.

The party is inside and you're not only getting in, you're a VIP. And everyone knows your name, not because you're Gisele or Naomi, but because it's written with a black Sharpie above your bib in thick, block lettering in ALL-CAPS. Unlike Studio 54, where less-healthy humans waited in line to snort "Peruvian Marching Powder" in the bathroom, you'll wait in line at the porta-potty with extremely fit humans to pray to the gods of digestion and colon-health that you can fully clear your bowels before you're shepherded out of Athletes' Village to your corral.

TMI? Well, before porta-potties were popular and sufficiently plentiful, runners were known to "fertilize" lawns all over Hopkinton. Which would you prefer? A marathoner hell-bent on a PR has to do what a marathoner hell-bent on a PR has to do. It's no wonder why the Hopkinton lawns have been so majestically green each May.

All right, Hopkinton isn't a prison. And Hopkinton isn't a restroom. Hopkinton is an American oasis, and the Athletes' Village situated at Hopkinton High School is a sanctuary within its hallowed grounds. Race officials and runners can't control the weather.

If you're "running" Boston and not racing, take time to enjoy Athletes' Village, meet runners from around the world, and explore the quintessentially New England town of Hopkinton. Whoever said New Englanders are reserved and unfriendly never walked the streets of Hopkinton on Marathon Monday morning. Families open their houses to charity teams and runners, children welcome runners at lemonade stands, and volunteers and race officials treat you and your fellow runners like you're the Rolling Stones getting ready to play Wembley Stadium.

If you're racing and trying to PR Boston, you should avoid the temptation to mosey around. Rain or shine, stay off your feet as much as possible. If you really want to see more of Hopkinton, pick any day other than Marathon Monday. You'll be expending plenty of energy on your journey to Boston, so focus on conserving energy in Athletes' Village. Everyone who has a bib has a backstory about how he or she qualified and gained entry. It's natural to want to meet and greet other runners to hear their stories, but all of that milling about comes at a cost; you'll drain valuable energy that you'll need in Newton, Brookline, and Kenmore Square.

If there's a must-have item to bring with you, a plastic garbage bag (or two or three) is it. If it's raining or threatening to rain, your trusty trash bags will help keep you dry. (**Note:** Sorry, but if it's torrential rain, nothing, including your disposable bags combined with plentiful prayer, will keep you from getting absolutely saturated.) If it's cold, especially windy and cold, the trash bags will provide a bit of a buffer from the wind and can be worn to the starting corral and easily discarded. And when it's not necessary to wear the bags, you can sit on them in wet grass, mud, or whatever else looks like an inviting place to recline.

Corrals

Like other World Major Marathons, Boston's start is in waves with the elite and faster runners getting on the course first. Runners in each wave will be prompted sequentially to leave Athletes' Village when it's time to take the less-than-one-mile walk to the starting line at Hopkinton Town Common. Corrals are assigned by bib numbers, which were assigned based on qualifying times. Elites are in Wave 1, Corral 1. The next fastest runners are in Wave 1, Corral 2, then Wave 1, Corral 3, and so on until Wave 2 begins and the process starts all over again, fastest to slowest. Charity runners who have not BQ'd are assigned the highest bibs, so they are relegated to the last corrals of the final wave.

Corrals are on Main Street, so you'll see your corral in advance of the starting line and the army of porta-potties on the green lawns of Hopkinton Town Common, in close proximity to the starting line. The short walk will allow you to get some blood flowing in your legs as well as relieve some nervous energy by chatting with a fellow runner or two en route.

Once you're in your corral, it's time to stay warm and relax. You'll have ample stimuli without moving a muscle; the voice of the race announcer,

The ring entrance of a prizefighter is almost as epic as the corral entrance of a Boston Marathoner.

likely 37-time painter of the Boston Marathon starting line, Jacques "Jack" LeDuc, will boom, helicopters will whir above your head, the "Star-Spangled Banner" will echo, Air Force fighter jets will roar, and runners all around you will fidget, stretch, and buzz with anticipation. Stay calm. Stay focused. Close your eyes for a hot second and envision how the race will unfold. There will be pain. Be confident. You trained for this moment. You'll lean into the pain, race strong, and finish smiling.

Ideally, you'll make use of the porta-potties on your way from Athletes' Village to your corral. If nature calls after you're in the corral, it's okay. Don't panic. You can exit and reenter your corral. And if you take longer than expected due to lines or nature's cruelty, it's okay, too. You can start the race in the corrals behind you. (**Note:** You can start in any corral behind you, including corrals in subsequent waves, as long as it's not the first corral of a subsequent wave.)

Typically, the last runner of each wave will take less than five minutes to cross the starting line, so, even though you'll be shuffling when you hear the starter's pistol, you'll be on your way to Boston pretty quickly, especially if you're in one of the corrals near the front. But resist opening up your stride to set a 5k PR on the downhill and, arguably, fastest stretch of pavement on the entire Boston Marathon course.

Start to Mile 2

At 490 feet above sea level, the starting line in Hopkinton Town Common is the highest point on the course. By the time you reach Ashland at Mile 2, you'll have descended 170 feet. In theory, it sounds like the perfect opportunity to get out faster than goal pace and "bank" some time for when the going gets tough. First, that would be a horrible strategy, and, second, in practice you won't have that opportunity because the roads are narrow, you'll be surrounded by runners (many running your pace or slower), and you'll expend way too much precious energy bobbing and weaving around them to justify attempting to save a few seconds. If you're racing to PR, better to chill out, savor each stride, and take in the awesomeness of the Boston Marathon. You'll have plenty of time to stress out when your quads are blown out in Brookline. Your mantra should be "conserve." In this elevation drop, let gravity do the work for you. Relax. Position yourself near the middle of the street, away from the crowds. Stay light on your feet. Short strides. Slight forward lean. Find your zen. And, again, conserve energy (physical, mental, and emotional).

If you're running for enjoyment, run on the side of the road, high-five spectators on Main Street. Capture the moment with some pictures as long as you're spatially aware, respectful and mindful of runners around you, and don't disrupt

The start of the Boston Marathon is as majestic as you imagined it in your dreams. Brett Gordon and MarathonFoto

their forward progress. The first descent off the starting line is particularly memorable; where else will you witness the fastest runners in the world stretched out before you as they serpentine their way toward the most famous finish in sports?

Enjoy the gently rolling terrain. The undulations will engage all of your leg muscles and prepare them for the hard work ahead. The thick crowds will begin to thin as you leave Hopkinton, but don't worry; rowdy crowds in the village of Ashland are waiting for you.

ASHLAND

Each town you pass through on the road to Boston has its unique personality. You'll feel something different. It's hard to explain, until you run the race, and then you'll fully understand. The Ashland vibe is very different from Hopkinton. To paint an overly generalized picture, it's like the black sheep of the families inside the historic homes with the white picket fences in Hopkinton grew up, left the nest, and relocated down the road in Ashland.

That's not a slight. You'll hear quite a bit of polite "golf-clapping" in Hopkinton. In Ashland, AC/DC's "Thunderstruck" will blare at full-volume out of houses' open windows and the clapping from parties spilled across the lawn will be generous and equally deafening.

The Patriots' Day party starts early at TJ's Food & Spirits.

The children's lemonade stands in Hopkinton are replaced with adult tail-gates in Ashland. You get the sense as you pass through town that whatever is in the Solo cups that are raised in your direction must be darn good. And whatever parties you're witnessing got started long before you arrived, particularly impressive given the increasingly earlier start times that began in 2007.

Prior to the starting line being moved to Hopkinton in 1924, Ashland hosted the start at the site of Metcalf's Mill from the Boston Marathon's inception on April 19, 1897. Thomas E. Burke, who won gold medals in the 100- and 440-yard races at the Athens Olympics in 1896, drew a line in the dirt that day for the 15 runners who started the race. We've come a long way. And Ashland has been at the heart of the Boston Marathon from the start. Literally.

Biker Bar

If you didn't know Ashland and Hopkinton aren't twins, you'll begin to get the picture when you pass TJ's Food and Spirits at Mile 2. You'll hear Bruce Springsteen's "Born to Run" a quarter-mile before you see the speakers blaring it, and you'll see dozens of Harley-Davidson motorcycles and pickup trucks you couldn't have found in Hopkinton even if you were looking. Welcome to Ashland.

Being the first restaurant on the route of the Boston Marathon, TJ's Food & Spirits naturally draws in crowds for those who want first glances of runners passing by, but we like to think that the energy, loud positive cheering and music filtering from spectators at TJ's sets the tone for runners, and gives them that jolt of energy needed to propel them to the finish line in Boston.

Jill DellOrco
Owner/Operator, TJ's Food & Spirits (Mile 2—Ashland, MA)

What's nice about TJ's is that things get quieter and decrescendo as you leave the hoopla of Hopkinton, and then BAM!, TJ's gives you this much-needed adrenaline rush that reminds you you're running the Boston &%$#ing Marathon. It's like hearing music as you meander peacefully through a cornfield and then realizing you're in the middle of Woodstock and Jimi Hendrix is on stage.

Clock Tower

You may not know that Ashland is known as "The Clock Town" and its sports teams are known as "The Clockers." You probably do know that when lightning struck Hill Valley's clock tower, it provided the 1.21 gigawatts of power necessary to transport Marty McFly back to 1985. That fictitious clock tower sits on a backlot at Universal Studios.

Ashland has the real McCoy, a genuine, made-for-real-life clock tower built in 1927, more than 20 years before Universal Studios got around to it. You'll run right past it at Mile 4 of the Boston Marathon. Rumor has it, if you're running 8.8 mph and lightning strikes, you'll be transported straight to the finish in Copley Square. Well, maybe not. But you wouldn't want that anyway. The real fun is just getting started.

Miles 3 to 5

You'll drop another 110 feet or so during your three miles in Ashland. Mile 5 is actually slightly uphill (about 25 feet) prior to things beginning to flatten out in Framingham. PR chasers should again focus on the "conserve" mantra. If you heel strike when running downhill, you're actually braking repeatedly. Instead, take short strides, keep your turnover quick, and land on your forefoot or midfoot. A good rule when running downhill is to stand tall but look toward the pavement at a 45-degree angle to the horizon, giving you a slight forward lean that will eliminate braking and take advantage of gravity as you navigate Ashland's downhill section from Miles 2–4.

Those less concerned about finish times might consider grabbing an out-stretched Solo cup at TJ's, jumping up onto the bed of a pickup truck (there will be plenty to choose from), making a poetic toast to the town of Ashland (bonus points if you're Irish or can nail an Irish accent), shotgunning the contents (beer, straight whiskey, or something indefinable), and releasing a primal scream. The already raucous crowd will go full-send ballistic. If you stage dive off the pickup into the arms of the outstretched mob, someone will likely snap your photo. You'll be immortalized on the bar's wall, elevated to legend status, and have your beverages comped at TJ's for life. Okay, maybe not the last one, but, hey, it's worth a shot.

Before leaving Ashland, all the amazing women who run the Boston Marathon each year can pay homage to Kathrine Switzer, who in 1967, before women were permitted to run the race, was shoved unceremoniously by race official Jock Semple when he attempted to remove her now famous and historically significant bib #261 at Mile 4. After the assault in Ashland, Switzer contemplated quitting the race. Thank heavens she persevered. Every female runner at Boston owes Switzer a debt of gratitude.

Take a look to your left and right at Mile 4 and admire the strong, determined women around you. Switzer and Bobbi Gibb (the other woman in the race that day, albeit without a bib) got it all started. Switzer's refusal to leave the race on the pavement beneath your feet in Ashland helped jump-start improvements in gender equality.

Being able to run the iconic course in the footsteps of the women who proved, as females, we are capable of running 26.2 miles and thus giving me the opportunity to follow my own big dreams and travel the world racing marathons make the Boston Marathon special to me.

Amy Sole
20 Marathons
1 Boston Marathon (2018)
Six Star Medalist

The ancient Greeks had two words for time: *chronos* (i.e., sequential, quantitative time) and *kairos* (i.e., infinite, qualitative time). It's fitting that Ashland, "The Clock Town," is home to Switzer's timeless moment. Switzer's heroism in Ashland is a reminder to Boston Marathoners that the clocks that measure chronological time don't tell the whole story. Beyond the clock, our races have significance that is timeless. It's hard to understand it when you're racing against the clock, but, much like Switzer's ordeal, your race-day trials and tribulations will take on greater meaning as the years pass. You'll come to appreciate the spiritual, *kairos*-like significance of your Boston Marathon experience even more.

FRAMINGHAM

In addition to the five towns you'll traverse during the Boston Marathon, you'll pass through three cities, Framingham being the first. The course continues to roll ever so gently downhill as you enter Framingham, but it begins to flatten out for the remainder of your time in the city, allowing you to settle into a nice rhythm (if you haven't found one already).

Unlike the "conserve" mantra that guided you in Hopkinton and Ashland, you can begin switching gears to "cruise" mode as you focus on locking into race pace and perhaps even finding a few runners with similar time goals so you can work as a group and share the fun as you move along.

If you're racing for a PR, it's time to "cruise" in Framingham. Amanda Nurse

The crowds get a bit larger the closer you are to the Framingham MBTA train station, just beyond the 10k mark. If you're running Boston for enjoyment, this is your chance to hug the rails and high-five spectators. Food trucks, live music, face painting, and family-friendly celebration seem to grow in this section year by year. Keep your eyes and ears open and soak in the energy that surrounds you.

PR chasers should remain in the middle of the road away from the hullabaloo and focus on clipping off these Framingham miles as close to goal pace as is possible. If all is going according to plan, these miles should feel like you're on autopilot, allowing your body and mind to continue to expend as little effort as possible.

If goal pace doesn't feel relatively effortless here, then you could either be a.) experiencing a temporary bad spell (it happens, so don't panic), or b.) beginning to second-guess your training. Don't listen to either voice. A cardinal rule of marathoning is "never make decisions when you're feeling bad." You may continue to slide off the rails or you may rally and have the PR of a lifetime. Either way, you won't be able to tell in Framingham. So, best to bury those seeds of doubt, stay true to your mission, trust your training, and HTFU.

Train Station

In 1907, runners had to wait on the course as a train switched tracks in front of Framingham's most recognizable landmark, its MBTA train station. Designed by the renowned architect Henry Hobson Richardson who, along with Louis Sullivan and Frank Lloyd Wright, is known to be one of "the recognized trinity of American architecture," the Boston & Albany Railroad Station (as it was originally called in 1883) will be a welcome sight for you.

Big crowds gather to cheer you on, so you'll get a nice boost of energy before things quiet down on the approach to Natick. Remember to watch your step as you run beside and over the railroad tracks. You no longer have to worry about trains interrupting your run, but the tracks themselves can be a hazard.

Miles 6 to 8

Despite the enthusiastic support from spectators and slices of Revolutionary and Civil War history that surround you throughout Framingham, PR chasers should have little to no recollection of these miles. Ideally, you want to be completely immersed in finding a steady rhythm that you can ride through Natick and Wellesley on your way to the Newton hills, where the real work starts. It's okay to have your head on a swivel if you're running for fun, but PR chasers need to stay laser-focused, especially in these flat miles before the hills.

Boston is special because it's not only about unifying amazing runners to run a prestigious race, but it also unifies all the communities along the course as we all come together on one day to celebrate the unwavering spirit of what it means to be Boston strong!

Heather Schulz
45 Marathons
14 Boston Marathons

The "cruise" mantra is appropriate because when someone asks you "How was Framingham?" after the race, you want to look at them with a blank stare and say, "I have no idea. I was 'in the zone' and don't remember a thing." That's not to disrespect Framingham. It's just the mindset you should have if you want to finish strong in Brookline and Boston.

As you pass the train station, you'll notice the crowds begin to thin, so it's even more important to stay on task when the adrenaline rush from the fans begins to wane. Stand tall. Keep the cadence steady. And if you've found a like-minded group of PR chasers, help one another by alternating in the front of the pack, particularly if there's a persistent east or northeast headwind.

As you approach the train station, for the first time on the course, you'll have what seems like unlimited line of sight. You won't just see a few dozen runners in front of you, you'll see thousands of runners ahead of you. This can be unexpectedly demoralizing and get your spirits spiraling downward.

Don't get stressed if runners zip by. Let them go. You have your agenda. They have theirs. The finish line is in Boston, not Framingham. One important thing to remember about marathoning is that the overwhelming majority bonks and positive splits (i.e., runs the second half of the course slower [often egregiously slower] than the first half of the course). By virtue of negative splitting or even splitting (just not slowing down), you will pass hundreds, if not thousands, of runners in the final four miles. Remember that now. Remember that always.

On your immediate left, train tracks run parallel to this straight-as-an-arrow stretch of course, reminding you that there are far faster ways to get to Boston than by foot. Do not let these negative thoughts and PR-sabotaging demons get comfortable in your brain. Much like your limited glycogen stores, you have only so much mental energy to expend during the race. Save as much as you can for the Newton hills and beyond. Chase out the demons. Get back to your zen. And cruise. Mentally and physically. Cruise.

Enjoy the calm of Natick before the storm of Wellesley College. Heather Schulz

NATICK

It's not out of line to consider the name Natick to be a misnomer. "Natick" comes from the language of the Massachusetts Native American tribe and is commonly thought to mean "Place of Hills." You will enter Natick at nearly the same elevation you exit Natick (180 feet above sea level). You will have subtle ups and downs, but should be able to stay locked into the "cruise" goal pace established in Framingham, holding steady throughout your four miles in Natick.

If your legs are feeling wonky in Natick, channel the heroics of its famous native son, Doug Flutie. Flutie has run the Boston Marathon multiple times (2014, 2015, 2017, and 2023). But his greatest athletic accomplishments were achieved on a football gridiron, none more memorable than his Hail Mary pass in the "Hail Flutie" game (aka the "Miracle in Miami") when he led Boston College to a last-second win over Miami, catapulting himself into a Heisman-winning New England sports legend.

The diminutive Flutie did the unthinkable when it looked impossible, so, if you're hurting in Natick, summon your inner Doug Flutie and remember miracles only occur if you believe in them.

Lake Cochituate

Water is said to be the foundation of everything. Without it, life wouldn't exist. There's something comforting about water, but you won't find a lot of it on the Boston Marathon course (other than the cups you drink and spill over your head). Lake Cochituate at Mile 9 is your Boston Marathon feng shui moment that can help you re-establish harmony between you and the universe.

Two-time winner (1936 and 1939) and Boston Marathon celebrity Ellison Myers "Tarzan" Brown found his version of harmony in 1938. Leading the race on an unseasonably hot day, the oft-whimsical Brown veered off the course, waved to the Natick crowd, and proceeded to jump in Lake Cochituate for a refreshing swim. After exiting the water, Brown jumped back into the race, and dripped dry all the way to a 51st place finish in Boston. Legen . . . wait for it . . . dary. Legendary.

You'll be surrounded by glorious H_2O (Lake Cochituate to your immediate left and Fisk Pond to your immediate right) as you approach the 15k checkpoint. Savor the views and smile wide because, even if you don't stop for a respite like Tarzan Brown, there's a photo bridge at the 15k checkpoint and you'll want to look wicked fast and happy in your race photos, right?

Town Center

Now that the waters have calmed you and renewed your focus, you can settle back into that metronome-like rhythm you've been rocking since Framingham. You'll be in the midst of Natick's Henry Wilson Historic District as you approach Mile 10 at the intersection of Routes 135 and 27. As if entering double-digit miles isn't exhilarating enough, you'll have thick crowds of families emerging from time-honored homes in and around Natick Common to boost your spirits as you carve your way through the center of town.

Former B.A.A. president and CEO and current luminary Tom Grilk has a uniquely powerful way of describing why he feels the Boston Marathon is special: "In Boston, everyone owns the marathon," he says. "We see it everywhere," he explains, "numerous acts of personal kindness" that demonstrate how all stakeholders (spectators, volunteers, town officials) take ownership of and protect the Boston Marathon.

This relationship between stakeholders and participants is unlike any other marathon in the world, and it's on full display in Natick. The B.A.A. and the town of Natick have a partnership: The B.A.A. provides invitational Boston Marathon bibs to local nonprofit 501(c)(3) organizations to field teams of runners who will raise money specifically for programs and services that benefit Natick residents. This reciprocity is woven into the fabric of the Boston Marathon, and you'll feel it here in Natick Town Center as readily as you'll feel it when a volunteer places your hard-earned finisher's medal around your neck in Copley Square.

Miles 9 to 12

Much like the elevation, your pace shouldn't fluctuate too dramatically during this stretch and your energy should exit Natick at the exact same level it entered Natick. Have you ever seen world-class runners in the second lap of a mile? They're stoic, almost robotic. They know the pain and the real fight lies ahead, but their training has prepared them to remain remarkably calm as they ratchet up their effort. They're in "cruise control" at sub-4-minute/mile pace, just like you should be at your goal marathon pace throughout Natick.

Even if you're running for fun, refrain from getting too giddy in Natick. You may not be redlining, but a marathon is still a long way and the parts of the course that truly test you are still in front of you.

From the history and legends of the past, to the dreams it inspires in present-day runners, the Boston Marathon offers so much to celebrate in our sport; just as Pheidippides journeyed from Marathon to Athens, we journey from Hopkinton to Boston, following in legendary footsteps while weaving ourselves into the race's history.

Deena Kastor
Bronze Medalist, Olympic Marathon (2004)
Winner, Chicago Marathon (2005) and London Marathon (2006)
Ranked #1 in the World, Marathon (2006)

One of the beautiful things about the Boston Marathon course is the almost poetic ebb and flow of the energy it exudes along the way from Hopkinton to Boston. It's like Queen's "Bohemian Rhapsody" shapeshifted into the form of a road race. Both are considered to be the greatest, and both tell epic stories. Part comedy. Part tragedy. Completely captivating.

Like Freddie Mercury's voice rising, falling, and traversing four full octaves, the Boston Marathon takes you on an epic journey of ups and downs. And, because Boston is a point-to-point course, you feel transported and transformed by the experience.

Natick is the tail end of the operatic interlude ("for me . . . for me . . . for meeeeeeeeee"), right before the heavy guitars and Wayne and Garth's headbanging begin. In Boston, you're on your way to a cacophony of sound that's, arguably, even more inspiring, the legendary Wellesley Scream Tunnel.

WELLESLEY

As you leave Natick, you'll enjoy a relatively quiet mile or so that is wooded and peaceful and the perfect time to perform a self-diagnostic. Things will get a bit more frantic from here on out, so take this time to ask yourself the important questions that will shape the remainder of your race. And be honest with your answers. How's your stomach? Are you behind on fuel? Have you hydrated according to plan? Any nausea yet? How's your chronically tight upper hammy doing? Has it affected your stride? Are you overheating? Should you shed a layer? How's the GI doing? Cramps? Tightness? How does goal pace feel right now?

You don't have to rush to any conclusions yet. But the answers from your candid assessment will help you make some data-driven decisions when the going gets tougher. Rather than lament the lack of noise as you enter Wellesley, you should instead bliss out to the tranquility while you can. You'll roll up and down some gentle hills as you approach Wellesley College, so focus on maintaining an even effort more so than an even pace.

Then, just as you embrace the serenity and comforting sounds of competitors' footfalls, your rhythmic breathing, and birds chirping, you'll hear a murmur. And the murmur will grow with every stride until it swallows everything, including your own breath. It's an inimitable chorus of high-pitched screams that will soon test the upper limits of the decibel scale. It's possible you've heard your name screamed a time or two before. But nothing can prepare you for the adrenaline rush that's about to catapult you into Wellesley Square.

Scream Tunnel

Have you ever wondered what it feels like to be Taylor Swift being adored by an entire stadium filled with fans? Well, here's your chance. Your very own swooning Swifties await you at Wellesley College (Mile 12.2), an entire campus of college women shrieking in unison.

If you want the experience to be even more intimate, write your name in large letters on your singlet. Hearing hundreds of women scream your name with enthusiasm is a rush. You may never experience such a jolt of energy again in your life, so take it all in while your name is echoing in the open air. Oh, and if you're wondering, their revelry isn't just for men anymore. The women of Wellesley embrace women, nonbinary runners, wheelchair racers, and all athletes. Their cheers are thunderous and their kisses are wondrous for everyone.

And it gets better. Unlike Taylor, who is shielded from fans by layers of bodyguards and police, you have ready access to your Wellesley College fans, many of whom are holding signs such as "Kiss me, I'm a freshman!" or "Smile if you're not wearing underwear" or "Love your stamina. Call me!" or "Kiss me, I talk dirty in 4 languages!" or "I won't tell your wife!" or the all-girls college favorite, "FINALLY . . . Some men around here!"

What happens in Scream Tunnel stays in Scream Tunnel. Joe Findaro

Is the Scream Tunnel as awesome as advertised? Perhaps this sign answers your question. Joe Findaro

If you're chasing a PR, it's advisable, no matter how enticing it may be, to refrain from stopping to kiss a girl or multiple girls. In fact, it's best to stay toward the middle or the left side of the road, away from the mayhem that lines the campus to your immediate right. Runners will cut across you or stop in their tracks in front of you to high-five or kiss the girls who lean over the metal barricades lining the roadside.

If you do it correctly, you can be in eyesight of the girls so they can cheer your name (written in Sharpie above your bib) while avoiding the traffic jam created by the screaming girls and weaving runners who covet them. The only drawback is you'll have to save your kisses for your significant other. But, hey, that's no different than every other day of your life, so suck it up, and, for the first and only time in the race, focus on keeping your cadence slow. All the excitement tends to get your legs turning over too fast for your own good. Relax. Keep cool. Bottle up the energy you're feeling. You'll need it in an hour when it feels like you're carrying a refrigerator up the Newton hills.

Regardless of your gender, if you're running for fun, Wellesley College, rivaled only by Boston College, is as fun as it gets. And you can enjoy it far more at Mile 12 than you will when you're feeling janky at Mile 21. For starters, be courteous. Be respectful to the legions of Wellesley College girls and be considerate of fellow runners. It's easy to get swept up in the moment and lose all sense of propriety. Don't be that runner, ever. And don't be that runner now.

Instead, indulge in the spectacle with reverence. Begun in the inaugural 1897 Boston Marathon when some Wellesley College students cheered on a friend from Harvard, the Scream Tunnel tradition is one of a kind in sports. Even better, it has grown year by year, yet has remained remarkably unchanged. Unlike many modern college fraternities and sororities, which have become watered-down versions of their former glory, the Scream Tunnel is as raucous and bold as ever. Let's keep it that way.

Yes, you can kiss the girls who request to be kissed. Yes, you can high-five the girls with outstretched palms. Yes, you can stop and take a selfie. Just maintain decorum on your end, even if the daring and bawdy signs encourage you not to. It's woven into the heritage. They're just being playful, which is part of the fun.

Wellesley Square

Just beyond the Scream Tunnel is the center of Wellesley, Wellesley Square, home of the halfway point (Mile 13.1) of your journey. Well, it's the physical halfway point. We runners know the true halfway mark is Mile 20, at the base of Heartbreak

Hill. The energy you'll expend to get to Heartbreak Hill is equal to the energy you'll need to get to the finish line.

Wellesley draws huge crowds outside its quaint shops and idyllic New England streets, but happening upon Wellesley Square after the Scream Tunnel is like listening to Barbra Streisand in the car on the way home from a German underground techno club. Both are enjoyable in their own separate way, but it's a tough transition from one to the other.

You'll still be riding the high from the Scream Tunnel as you pass the chip-pad and 13.1 sign, but be prepared for your energy to drop precipitously as you move through Wellesley Square. It's no fault of the townsfolk; it's just your heart rate that spiked out of the atmosphere a half-mile ago is now coming back to earth. This is very much a good thing, because you can't sustain that level of revelry for 13 more miles.

But it's also a critical juncture for your psyche; don't let your spirits sink too low after the Scream Tunnel lifted them so high. That angry calf that hurt at Mile 12 (and you forgot about as you were high-fiving and kissing Wellesley students who were shouting your name) is now angrier than your remember it, and no one's going to run across the front lawn of their stately suburban mansion to kiss you and take your mind off of it anymore. C'est la vie.

Upon leaving Wellesley Square, you'll veer off Route 135 for the first time, merging onto Washington Street (Route 16) and providing you with a scenic tour of Wellesley's charm and suburban opulence on your way to Newton. If you've ever yearned to jump into a New England postcard, work at a tony venture capital firm, and run along the white picket fence and sprawling lawn of your $5.8 million estate, this is your chance to play out that fantasy. You might even high-five your fictitious kids as you pass by. But, on second thought, don't bother. They're at boarding school or on Nantucket with the nanny.

Miles 13 to 16

To run the Boston Marathon successfully, you need to think of the race course as a rollercoaster. But Boston isn't a traditional rollercoaster. If it were, you'd never make it past the Newton hills.

Traditional rollercoasters rely on a simple formula: A motor pulls the rollecoaster to its steepest point, amassing a sizable chunk of potential energy which is released when the cars plummet. This potential energy turns into kinetic energy, a combination of gravity and inertia, along with g-forces and centripetal acceleration, propelling you around the track until you reach the end of your ride.

You may notice that each successive peak on your journey is shorter than its preceding peak because friction slows a rollercoaster down as it moves. If a peak were higher than the previous peak, the rollercoaster wouldn't have the energy to make it up the hill. That said, if Boston were a traditional rollercoaster, your ride would end at the right turn onto Commonwealth Avenue at the fire station in Newton.

But, no. Boston isn't a traditional coaster. You need to think of Boston as a new-age, modern, multi-launch coaster, one whose motor re-engages on the Newton hills, pulling you toward the precipice of Heartbreak Hill and hurtling you once more to the finish in Copley Square.

Alas, you can't go (relatively) straight downhill forever, unless you're running a REVEL marathon, of course. So enjoy the undulations in Wellesley like you would the end of a rollercoaster ride. And know you'll take pleasure in the steepest descent on the course, a 100-foot drop on Grossman's Hill (a stone's throw from Maugus Hill, the highest point in Wellesley Hills), to the Charles River just before you transition to Newton.

This Grossman's Hill downhill stretch beginning at Warren Park at Mile 15.4 is a shocker for two reasons: 1.) Up to this point you've been rolling up and down gradually, and you're not used to going downhill so violently, and 2.) once you hit the bottom, similar to a rollercoaster, your gravitational potential energy will need to sustain you until you get to the firehouse, when the real work begins and your motor needs to re-engage to "click" your way up the Newton hills.

Much like your initial descent off the starting line in Hopkinton, you'll want to keep your stride light and short. Overstriding causes you to brake and put additional stress on your quads. If your stride is short enough, you can land on the balls of your feet or, at the least, midfoot, which might be more realistic since your legs are likely starting to feel some heaviness at this point.

NEWTON

The second of three cities (in addition to Framingham and Boston) that you'll traverse on Patriots' Day, Newton is actually a patchwork of 13 villages without a true city center. Like the neighboring town of Brookline, Newton is also one of the most densely populated Jewish locations in the United States (roughly 30 percent of the Boston suburb's population), giving rise to the notion that "The Garden City" is known as such not just because of its tree-lined streets and gardens, but because there's a Rosenblum on every corner.

Tradition is strong within the Jewish culture, so it's no surprise that Newton families are hard-core, veteran Patriots' Day spectators. They've been doing this for generations. You'll see lawn parties up and down picturesque Commonwealth Avenue on both sides of the street, and they've got serious Marathon Monday "game." This is prime marathon viewing territory, and families who live on the street host huge soirees for extended family, friends, marathon enthusiasts, and what appear to be tailgating professionals. No joke. Rain, shine, or epic nor'easter, these events are the envy of mint julep–sipping dandies in seersucker at the Kentucky Derby, well-hydrated alumni at Ole Miss football games, and preppies quaffing Bloodies at the Head of the Charles.

Oh, and treats for runners abound: Orange slices, bananas, pretzels, licorice, Swedish fish, jelly beans, ice, Vaseline, and paper towels are an arm's length away somewhere in the Newton hills. It's uncanny how much is available. It would be like running through your favorite drugstore and grocery store simultaneously, only everything you're looking for is conveniently located in the same aisle and handed to you on demand. During the "Perfect Chaos" of 2018, Newton fans weren't only out in droves, they tied shoelaces of runners whose frozen hands were incapable and offered dry clothes off their backs to runners who were hypothermic. Epic, indeed.

Hell's Alley

You've probably heard of the legendary right turn at the firehouse that serves as a gateway to the Newton hills. And you're likely (to some degree) aware of the challenges you're about to face. But what you may not know is the first hill you'll tackle in Newton is situated more than a mile before the firehouse, and it has far less fanfare. Welcome to the I-95 overpass and Hell's Alley.

Immediately upon reaching the bottom of the hill that transitions you from Wellesley to Newton, you'll begin a sneaky climb toward the concrete I-95 overpass that deserves your attention, lest it surprise you and sap your legs and spirit before they've even had a chance to flex on the marquee, tree-lined hills ahead. This devious ascent isn't steep, but it's protracted (which is unexpected), exposed to the elements (which is unpleasant), and understandably devoid of fans (which is a bummer). In one word? Devilish.

Hell's Alley has earned its name. It isn't spectator-friendly. Who wants to stand in the sun (or rain) and wind on a highway overpass? And it isn't runner-friendly. The good news about this incline is it truly is preparing your legs for the greater ascents ahead. Everything was (mostly) downhill until this point, so the gradual uphill serves as a nice transition, even if the lull in fan support is a temporary downer.

Newton-Wellesley Hospital is mercifully positioned just beyond the overpass. Thick crowds gather in this area, especially enthusiastic charity team supporters. So if things get bad (nay, really bad), take solace in knowing you have cheers of encouragement and a safe haven of medical professionals awaiting you.

Firehouse

Once I-95 is in your rearview, you'll enjoy a flattish stretch of pavement that leads you past Woodland Golf Club (on your left) and the Woodland MBTA train station (on your right). It's easy not to enjoy this stretch because your quads are probably on fire more than you imagined at this point and you're likely stressed about how they'll hold up on the hills.

> *Though Boston qualifiers arrive with commitment and experience, they are filled with fear because the course demands constant focus and creativity; its roller-coaster hills are discussed in hushed tones, like approaching a labyrinth, leaving racers exhausted, baffled, and ever-eager to return for more.*
>
> **Peter Bromka**
> 20 Marathons
> 8 Boston Marathons
> 10th Place, Masters Division, Boston Marathon (2023)

Instead, use this time to gather yourself. Remember that self-diagnostic you performed early in Wellesley? Now's the time to make a few decisions that will shape the remainder of your race. Commonwealth Avenue mania is close at hand. And the firehouse (Mile 17.3) at the corner of Washington Street (Route 16) and Commonwealth Avenue is where it begins. You'll want to assemble a game plan for the hills before the hoopla distracts you.

If you haven't experienced any goose-bump-worthy moments yet, there's something about the turn at the firehouse that feels unforgettable. Have you ever wondered what it felt like to be Boston's beloved Carlton Fisk in Game 6 of the 1975 World Series when he lifted a flyball toward the left field foul pole, jumped to his right waving his arms above his head as the crowd rose, and coaxed the ball into fair territory and over the Green Monster? Well, this magic turn is as close as you'll get.

The generous enthusiasm that greets you at the firehouse sets the tone for the entire duration of the five miles you'll enjoy on Commonwealth Avenue. The crowd is at this critical turn for a reason; spectators know what difficulties you'll face and they genuinely want to encourage you. It's almost like you're going off to war, your boat is leaving shore, and your loved ones are lined up at the water's edge. The cheers are real. The cheers are loud. But the cheers come from Solo-cup wielding civilians in street clothes. You and the soldiers around you with the bibs on your chests are the ones going off to battle.

Young at Heart

If your spirits are flagging, there's a beacon of hope just beyond Mile 19. After you pass Newton City Hall, at the corner of Commonwealth Avenue and Walnut Street, stands a tribute to two-time winner and 58-time finisher Johnny "The Elder" Kelley. The bronze statue, *Young at Heart*, depicts a 27-year-old Kelley when he won in 1935 holding the raised hand of an 84-year-old Kelley when he ran his last Boston in 1992.

Thick crowds at the intersection may block your view of the statue, but it's comforting and inspirational to know it's there, particularly when two more hills and seven more miles remain. Local runners often drape medals around the necks of the Kelleys and decorate the statue in celebratory garb befitting the season or holiday. Another tradition is to make a wish while tapping (or placing something in) the hat held in the 84-year-old Kelley's left hand.

If you're chasing a PR, don't bother to stop, but feel free to pay tribute by making a wish or saying a prayer on your way by. If you're running for fun and you want to take a timeless selfie, carve your way through the crowd to the statue and snap a picture or two. Regardless of whether you're racing or merely running, channel Kelley's grit as you move up the hills. If he could do it 58 times, you can summon the strength to do it once.

Heartbreak Hill

If there's solace to be found in the Newton hills, it's because they're a series of hills with rests between them, much like steps ascending multiple floors. And there's only one thing nicer than getting to the top floor: making it to the final step and rejoicing in knowing there's just one more to go. That's the vibe at Mile 20 at the base of Heartbreak Hill.

Even better, nobody ever applauds or offers you free food as you make your way up steps, but you'll have thousands of fans cheering for you by name, ringing cowbells, and offering complimentary snacks to you as you tackle Heartbreak Hill. Hankering for an Otter Pop? You'll find one. How about some gourmet jelly beans? Pretzels? Yep, those, too.

As you cross Centre Street, you'll see Heartbreak Hill Running Company on the corner, the Mile 20 sign, and the MassGeneral "Fighting Kids Cancer . . . One Step

The GOAT, Eliud Kipchoge, attacks Heartbreak Hill during his Boston Marathon debut (2023). Kevin Gunawan

at a Time" Marathon Team party that occupies multiple blocks on your right. These crowds are substantial, and this isn't their first rodeo. Also, it's tough to pinpoint year by year where they'll be situated, but a unique hand-drumming group of more than 50 West African *djembe* drums provides a rhythmic boost to your ascent at the base of Heartbreak, give or take a quarter-mile or so. Regardless of their exact coordinates, there's nothing quite like more than 100 hands thumping rawhide in unison to remind you that your cadence needs to be picked up a notch to PR.

Interestingly, Heartbreak Hill, on the other 364 days of the year, is a rather normal looking hill with delightful suburban homes on either side. It's as menacing as a miniature Shetland pony at a rodeo. And you couldn't pick it out of a lineup if your life depended on it.

Yet, on Marathon Monday, Heartbreak Hill is like Sasquatch in the wild, feared and revered, the stuff of legends. In all fairness, whether intimidating to you on race day or not, it deserves its laurels. It's broken hearts, Johnny Kelley's included. It's connected hearts. (Did you know Heartbreak Hill proposals are almost as popular as finish line proposals?) And it's overwhelmed hearts with joy. (Have you ever seen an eight-year-old pediatric cancer patient greet the Mass General Hospital charity runner who has raised more than $25,000 on his or her behalf?)

It's hard to know in advance how, but Heartbreak Hill will leave its impression on you. Its sacred turf, more than any other part of the course, is where the wheat separates from the chaff, just as it did in 2021 when winner Benson Kipruto, like so many Boston Marathon champions before him, made his decisive move. It's Heartbreak #$%*ing Hill. Love it or hate it, you will come face-to-face with it. And, for better or worse, you will be woven into its history, as it will be woven into yours.

Boston College

It seems fitting that after you "summit" Heartbreak Hill the universe would offer up some type of reward. Sure, you get to run down the back side of the hill, which, in theory seems rewarding, but, in practice, after 21 miles of challenging terrain, your blown-out quads equate to pain, not pleasure. Thankfully, just when you're ready to curse the universe, it delivers the reward you deserve. Behold, on the horizon, it's Boston College.

Similar to Wellesley, you'll probably hear Boston College before you see it. But this wall of sound has a more baritone, fraternity tone than the high-pitched soprano, sorority-like shriek you heard at Mile 12.

And speaking of fraternities, Boston College is a Catholic Jesuit university without a Greek system, so it feels like the campus has a lot of pent-up party energy that is unleashed on Marathon Monday. You may not find a kiss as readily as you did in Wellesley, but there's no shortage of beer if you're looking to wash down your fifth vanilla gel with a Narragansett or PBR.

Legend has it that some Boston College students have a "marathon" of their own, one that's remarkably less healthy than running a marathon, a "marathon of beers" requiring quaffing 26 beers within Marathon Monday's 24 hours. That's no small task, but neither is running from Hopkinton to Boston. Since most runners will be making their way past Boston College around noon (give or take), that means participants are at the halfway point of their liquid marathon, much like you are in your foot version (in effort-based theory). Thankfully, you'll be done within an hour or so, but they'll still have a dozen beers to go, at which point you'd probably be ready to take one off their hand, if you haven't already.

What's comforting about Boston College spectators, unlike the well-dressed Wellesley girls, is they look as disheveled and haggard in their revelry as you do in your glycogen-depleted wonkiness. Gray sweatpants, yellow "SuperFan" T-shirts, and bedheads are the norm here. The downhill stretch leading to St. Ignatius Church looks like a hoard of Solo cup–wielding zombies. That's what happens when you start at midnight. But you should take note: Just like you, these zombies have stamina.

Haunted Mile

Beyond Boston College, you'll follow the train tracks of the MBTA Green Line's B train toward Cleveland Circle. Because the throngs of college students are behind you, the tracks are situated to your left, and a burial ground is to your right, the crowds in this area are noticeably lighter.

Described by *Boston Globe* writer John Powers as "the spooky place where contenders go to die," the Haunted Mile is where whatever adrenaline got you over Heartbreak Hill and past Boston College is now gone. Runners considering throwing in the towel have all the excuses they need to surrender. To add insult to injury, it's quiet, and Evergreen Cemetery looms like an ominous reminder that pushing your body to its limits like you're doing is equally healthy and unhealthy.

Legendary Boston Marathon coach Bill Squires called Evergreen the "Cemetery of Lost Hope," an appropriate moniker because the struggle you face to get to the finish is as much mental, spiritual, and emotional as it is physical. Staying mentally strong as you're physically breaking down is easier said than done. But it's imperative if you want to fulfill your potential at the marathon distance, particularly at Boston throughout the Haunted Mile.

Cleveland Circle

Remember how at the train station in Framingham you had line of sight for what seemed like miles on end? Well, assuming it's not like 2018 and you can see more than 50 feet in front of you, once you make the left turn onto Beacon Street, you'll have déjà vu all over again. A sea of runners as far as the eye can see will be laid out in front of you, making you painfully aware you still have a long way to go and that thousands of runners are faster than you. Once again, don't get down on yourself. If you've run the course properly and you have the heart to pull it off, you can pass plenty of them in the last four miles. Prior to your right on Hereford and left on Boylston, this turn will be the last you make.

The MBTA Green Line's C train tracks are situated to your immediate left as you approach Cleveland Circle, but you'll cross over them when you make the turn, so be careful not to trip. The raised tracks present a challenge for wheelchair and handcyclists, too. The obstacles wouldn't seem too intimidating in the early miles, but tired athletes at Mile 22 aren't as nimble as they were in Hopkinton. Be careful not to trip, turn an ankle, or completely wipe out.

Miles 17 to 22

There's a lot to love about the six miles you'll spend in Newton. These are known to be the most famous miles. But these aren't the easy miles. These are the miles you trained for and the reason you did hill repeats until your lungs burned when you could have picked up a more relaxing sport like golf or a less-stressful hobby like needlepoint or Frisbee.

But these are the rewarding miles. Once you crest Heartbreak Hill, it's more or less downhill to the finish, and that's pretty darn comforting even if your quads are on fire, your calves are cramping, and you're beginning to understand why Rosie Ruiz took the T.

Bostonians run the Newton hills (specifically the carriage road running parallel to Commonwealth Avenue) year-round, creating friendships and camaraderie among local runners, especially those who run the Boston Marathon. It's not uncommon to see hundreds of runners on the Newton hills on any given weekend between January and early April.

If you run the course often enough, you'll see a lot of the same faces. You'd think that all those miles logged on the course would give Bostonians an edge on Marathon Monday, but the reality is the course is as perplexing to locals on race day as it is to everyone else.

On the last Saturday of March, thousands of marathoners gather in Hopkinton to run the course from the starting line in Hopkinton to the top of Heartbreak Hill (Mile 21). It's a ceremonial final long run before the taper, complete with anxiety-ridden rides to Hopkinton, runners of all ages and paces, aid stations, and support from local charities.

The irony is that this dress-rehearsal run often goes far better than the main event (despite tired, untapered legs and the absence of the more than a million cheering spectators you'll see on race day). Go figure. Again, don't feel bad if you bonk on Patriots' Day. Boston is a riddle, even to the locals. Or, as a true Bostonian would confess, "My PR (pronounced 'pee-ahh') was in the hoppah on Hahtbreak, khed. All a yiz bettah know Bahstin's wikkid hahd."

BROOKLINE

Remember you're running gently downhill. It's easy to forget this when you're physically and emotionally exhausted, probably in some degree of pain, and likely questioning why you run. But it's critically important to play Whac-A-Mole with all of the seeds of doubt that try to see the light of day in your brain. Crush those evil thoughts and lean into the pain.

These Brookline miles can be fast. If you were to race them on fresh legs, you would be in heaven; there are no unwelcome twists and turns, no steep inclines or declines, and no distractions (vistas, propositioning college students, or otherwise) to sway you from your mission. And, even with more than 20 miles in the rearview, you can attack these miles. Everybody's legs are hurting at this point. The question is "Are you mentally tough enough to finish strong?"

Another cool element of the Boston Marathon is how the communities you traverse on your point-to-point passage from Hopkinton to Copley Square get more and more urban the closer you are to the finish line. The pastoral woods and rural homes are long gone now. Brookline's brownstone-lined streets provide the first real city vibes of your journey. If you have the strength to turn your head to see them, you'll notice spec-

You know you're having a good day if you have the energy to smile and high-five spectators in Brookline. Amanda Nurse

tators hanging out of the windows of their fifth-floor condos are holding martini and wine glasses (not Solo cups) as they cheer for you. That's right. Real glass. These fans are adulting.

Washington Square

After you've made the left turn onto Beacon Street at Cleveland Circle, you will follow the MBTA Green Line C branch train tracks (to your immediate left) in nearly a straight line to Boston.

As you move deeper into Brookline, it's like you're watching a time-lapsed movie of spectators aging before your eyes. The college students who were offering you beer and hard seltzer in Chestnut Hill morph into young professionals working on PowerPoint presentations over video conference calls as they watch you out of their windows on Beacon Street. By the time you approach Washington Square, they've fast-forwarded to parenting and pushing strollers filled with children. And when you happen upon the shops and restaurants of Washington Square, spectators have transmuted once more; retirees dine al fresco and trade photos of puppies and grandchildren while you shuffle by as if you were on set with George Romero. Witnessing the entire life cycle of humanity in such short order is a testament to the multigenerational family-friendliness of Brookline in general, and Washington Square in particular. What's interesting about what you just experienced is you'll do the exact same thing in reverse as you work your way to Boston through Coolidge Corner (families), Audubon Circle (yuppies), and Kenmore Square (Boston University students).

Coolidge Corner

Have you seen the 1982 footage of Dick Beardsley leading Alberto Salazar through Coolidge Corner? If you're going to race Boston and chase a PR, drop everything and watch it before Marathon Monday. Seeing two warriors completely depleted, refusing to give up, throwing caution to the wind, and racing each other full-throttle all the way to the finish is exhilarating. "Mind over matter" is just a clever phrase until you see the Duel in the Sun and understand it's real.

You'll recognize the heart of Coolidge Corner (Mile 24) when you see the clock tower of the Tudor-style S.S. Pierce building to your left as you cross Harvard Street. Thick crowds will surround you at the intersection as you continue to move downhill for 400m until the course begins to flatten out when it intersects St. Paul Street.

Boston has been a heartbreaker in many ways, but at the same time, it has made me feel alive, challenging me and continuing to inspire me to come back and give my all.

Fernando Cabada
3 Boston Marathons
Masters 50k American Record Holder (2022)
US National Marathon Champion (2008)

Again, everyone is hurting, even the elites. Unlike you, they're used to it. The very best find comfort in it, like an old friend. Whether you're racing or running for fun, do your best to welcome it. You're just 2.2 miles from glory. If you didn't think this would hurt, you fell in love with the wrong sport.

Miles 23 to 24

These Brookline miles are critical miles. You feel like you're in the city, but the reality is you're a 5k away and the Citgo sign is only faintly visible to inspire you until you approach Coolidge Corner. These are the miles where, if your negative thoughts set up camp during the Haunted Mile, your demons are holding hands and singing songs by the campfire in Brookline. Conversely, if you've fended them off to this point, you'll need to double-down your efforts to keep those PR-sabotaging thoughts at bay.

The crowds are strong, but not in a substance-fueled, all-day party kind of way like Boston College. Brookline's aura is "I'll cheer for you because I'm thankful for the day off, but I'm still: a.) working on a side-hustle project, b.) taking care of the kids who are off from school, or c.) running late for my lunch date with Eleanor and Doris."

Now is the perfect time to hit "play" and have your mantra on infinite loop in your groggy head. Many runners write their mantras on their arms or hands with a Sharpie as a reminder. This is a good practice because you want your mantra to be short, and you want it to be easily recalled, especially when your brain is mushy. A good mantra is any word or simple phrase that keeps you in positive spirits during this difficult stretch. "Compete" is a good one, but you do you.

Whether you're running or racing, you'll need to dig deep. Do whatever it takes to stay strong, because that massive Citgo sign on the horizon is farther away than it looks.

BOSTON

When you were in your corral in the woods of Hopkinton practicing your best positive visualization, contemplating how your race would unfold, you probably envisioned how euphoric it would feel when you finally saw the Boston skyline. Well, here you are. And, yes, euphoria is a valid emotion. But, chances are, what you're feeling is far more complicated, like a mother whose baby is crowning in the latter stages of labor.

It's a long, strange trip from pregnancy to birth, and it's Mr. Toad's Wild Ride from a BQ to Boston. Both involve significant preparation, none of which truly gets you emotionally ready for the raging tempest of feelings that overwhelms you in the moment.

And, much like childbirth, you'll be utterly exhausted at the exact moment you should be most overjoyed. In the moment, this feels cruel. But in retrospect, you'll appreciate everything more because the journey to get there was so darn challenging. You probably cursed the Lamaze class that made everything look so easy, and now you're ripshit with online marathon gurus who failed to mention the severity of the Mass Pike (I-90) overpass (Mile 25), which feels as gnarly as you envision summiting Mount Everest would be.

The left on Boylston will take your breath away no matter how many unicorns you've earned. Becca Pizzi

What I love most about the Boston Marathon are the Citgo sign, the deafening crowd support, and the excitement of running the most iconic marathon, but most of all, crossing the finish line on Boylston Street!

Becca Pizzi
99 Marathons
19 Consecutive Boston Marathons
1st American Woman to Complete World Marathon Challenge
(7 Marathons/7 Continents/7 Days)

Struggles aside, savor every step here. You may not ever feel as alive and dead at the same time ever again in your lifetime. This is as memorable as it gets. The hallowed ground beneath your feet is paved with the hopes, dreams, and grit of three centuries of warriors just like you. Kelley. Switzer. Rodgers. Nderba. Van Dyk. Driscoll. Keflezghi. Linden. Keep moving forward. It's your turn now.

Citgo Sign

You've likely never been lost at sea, but, if you had, you would be awfully excited to look into the darkness to find a beacon of light from a distant lighthouse. That's a fair metaphor for what it feels like to be in a sea of runners on Beacon Street and see the Citgo sign for the first time.

Built in 1940, the iconic Citgo sign in Kenmore Square guides you home. Much like a lighthouse, this legendary beacon of hope, primarily due to its enormity (60-feet square), gives you the impression that you're closer to it than you actually are. This is disconcerting as you approach it, but it makes the act of finally running beneath its shadow (Mile 25.2) all the more fulfilling.

Fenway Park

If you forgot Patriots' Day was a statewide holiday, you might remember as you approach Fenway Park (Mile 25). Depending on how fast you are, you'll either run past the "cathedral of baseball" during the late innings of the Red Sox game or after it is over. Either way, you'll smell beer and hot dogs, which envelop the park like a biodome of sorts. Fans in full Sox regalia will spill out of the park into Kenmore Square, adding multiple concentric layers to an already well-established marathon party.

And if you've been on a quest to hear an actual Bostonian utter the term *wicked* in the wild, this is as good of a chance as you'll get. Sox fans converge on Fenway Park from all directions and neighboring towns (Lynn, Revere,

Swampscott, Cohasset, Milton, and more), and Kenmore Square turns into a melting pot of various Boston accents (yes, there are many).

Kenmore Square

If you're in the shadow of the Citgo sign, you're in Kenmore Square, a mile away from the finish line. It's time to exit zombie shuffle mode. This is your last chance to HTFU, find another gear, and pick up your cadence for the homestretch. If you need encouragement, you'll have plenty of rowdy spectators shouting at you regardless of whether you're running, walking, or writhing in pain in attempts to calm down cramping quads, hammys, and calves. Kenmore fans are well aware that you're one mile from the finish, but what they don't know is that all of their cheers of support sound like they're being yelled through a McDonald's drive-thru.

No matter your pace, you'll be deep in the pain cave in Kenmore Square. Heather Schulz

Participants in ultramarathons like the (roughly) 100-mile Barkley Marathons describe sleep-deprived hallucinations and the inability to recognize faces, including friends, family, and running partners by their side. But you're not running in the woods in silence at Boston. Instead, just as you're feeling your wonkiest, you'll approach the city and have thousands of people screaming at you. It's a rush, for sure, but it also takes on a dreamlike quality because your glycogen-starved senses are overloaded with stimuli, rendering a psychedelic peculiarity to the experience.

Reality starts to blur. Sounds are muffled. Colors are muted. Thankfully, you won't be able to drift aimlessly off course at Boston and wander around in circles like at Barkleys. Follow the "Boston Strong" sign on the bridge above your head. And if you're too wrecked to see it (not just possible, but probable), there are thousands of runners ahead of you, thousands behind you, and thousands of fans alongside you to help you reach your destination.

Tommy Leonard Bridge

You'd think an innocuous underpass beneath a road wouldn't present much of a challenge for a tough marathoner like you, but you'll be cursing this little dip and ascent when it's upon you. Why couldn't the B.A.A. just keep the course flat for a few more meters?

Legendary coach John Wooden said, "the true test of a man's character is what he does when no one is watching." Do you have the mettle to fight beneath the spectator-less underpass? Andrew Kastor/ Nico Montanez

Traversing this quick roll down and up (the underpass named after Boston Marathon legend Tommy Leonard) seems unnecessary and cruel. You'll be surprised at how many defeated runners will be walking here, but don't give up and become one of them. You're only a few strides away from two of the most famous turns in road racing.

You know how you think back on races and lament all of the precious seconds you lost in stupid ways? Well, don't make this one of them. HTFU and power through this dip. All of the good stuff is, literally, around the corner.

Right on Hereford

You've come a long way to get here (past prestigious colleges, historic train stations, quaint New England towns, exclusive country clubs, colonial burial grounds, and even Fenway Park), but you know you're in Boston proper when you're surrounded by the Commonwealth Avenue Mall, confusing one-way streets, and Victorian-era brownstones.

You know you're fast when your bib is three digits and you're all alone for your "left on Boylston." Sumner Jones

No matter how stoic you are, the most celebrated street corner in road racing will stir up your emotions.

It may (if this really isn't your day) or may not (if adrenaline is carrying you) be important to tell you that Hereford Street is ever so slightly uphill, the type of incline you wouldn't even notice if it weren't Mile 25.8 of a marathon.

Left on Boylston

There are plenty of cool twists and turns in marathons all over the world, but only one can be the most famous turn of all, the Boston Marathon's "left on Boylston." If you've been running for decades and you've questioned whether a moment could simultaneously take your breath away and supercharge you with adrenaline unlike you've ever felt before, your left on Boylston will provide the answer.

A few important things you should know: 1.) Smile, there's a photographer situated on the corner. 2.) If you haven't been moved to tears yet, this epic turn and seeing the finish line in the distance might do the trick. 3.) The tears you shed could be overwhelming joyful, or they could be because the finish is farther away than you may have suspected (600 meters, give or take, but it looks like a mile). 4.) Crescendo your effort as you move toward the finish. You don't want to pull a hamstring or cramp up with a quarter-mile left, so step on the gas (if you have any left) gradually, in sync with the growing cheers surrounding you. 5.) Other than Wellesley, if there's ever a time to swivel your head and take it all in (the crowds, the buildings, the aura, everything), and savor every step, it's now.

It's time to celebrate! You've reached your destination, the heart of Boston's Back Bay. Brett Gordon / MarathonFoto

That finish line ahead isn't a mirage. You're in the homestretch of the Boston #@$%ing Marathon!!! Pump your fists. Raise your hands. Let out a primal scream. You do you. It's possible you'll never feel what you're feeling in this moment ever again.

Copley Square (Boston Public Library)

If you ever wanted to find a single location where you could witness the breadth of the transcendence of the human spirit, all you need to do is position yourself at the finish line of the Boston Marathon. Where else will you see smiling, weeping, laughing, writhing, vomiting, praying, collapsing, leaping, hugging, grimacing, and everything good, bad, and ugly in between?

In the shadow of the Boston Public Library, the Boston Marathon finish line delivers it all. Much like the books inside the library itself, the finish line provides something for everyone. As an athlete nearing the finish, it's hard to anticipate what emotion(s) will bubble to the surface until you're there and whatever it is involuntarily overwhelms you. Take a mental note of the moment. You'll want to treasure what you're feeling and tuck it away in your mental vault so you can recall it again and again.

The first step over the sacred Boston Marathon finish line, across the timing mat, beneath the press box suspended above you, is pure bliss. As you're shepherded down Boylston Street to receive your Mylar blanket, finisher's medal, more photos, and water and treats, you'll be pampered and congratulated by hundreds of volunteers. Soak it up. Their praise is genuine. You earned it. But don't get too carried away with yourself and forget to thank them. No matter how amazingly awesome or tragically terrible your race went, thank them. They earned it, too.

Miles 25 to 26.2

The only thing better than seeing the Citgo sign get bigger and bigger as you approach it is no longer seeing it because you passed it. You'll finally get that opportunity when you're in the heart of Kenmore Square and have just one mile left. Unlike the typical Brookline fan who happened to see you running whilst en route to finishing a sales deck for a local blockchain startup or taking grandchildren to Amory Playground, fans in Kenmore Square and Boston are laser-focused on their top priority: losing their voices screaming your name and finishing whatever is in their Solo cups, flasks, or "water" bottles.

When you have the day off work (or school), a Red Sox game at 11 a.m., and an all-day marathon, Bloody Marys and pancakes segue seamlessly into several Sam Adams Summers and Fenway Franks before you fill your Hydro Flask with a

The paradox of the homestretch on Boylston Street is that you'll wish you had run faster (to improve your finish time) and slower (to preserve this moment in time). Yudelman

dirty martini. That's the vibe in Kenmore Square and Boston. You'll feel like you've run 25 miles to join a very cool party. The velvet rope is lifted for you in Kenmore Square, like you're entering Studio 54 to meet with Andy Warhol in a secret room you never knew existed. Attendees have been waiting for your arrival so they can really let loose. Everyone is super excited to see you. You may feel like an imposter, but you're not. Spectators are screaming your name in unison. And it's wild.

Back in the old days (i.e., prior to 1990, when the field had yet to ever exceed 8,000 runners), spectators created a narrow chute barely large enough for runners to pass through single file, an impossibility if they were side by side. The relationship between spectators and runners was intimate, more so than at any other race in the world. You would think the metal barricades lining the streets and increased security measures instituted after the 2013 bombing would have compromised that relationship, but the rapport is stronger than ever.

You'll feel the close connection as you navigate the course's final two renowned turns. Just before you, in true Boston fashion, "bang a right" on Hereford, you'll dip beneath the Tommy Leonard Bridge adjacent to the home of the Boston Marathon's onetime "unofficial finish line," the Eliot Lounge. The bar at the Eliot was commandeered by distance-running fanatic, Falmouth Road Race founder, and Boston legend Tommy Leonard.

The Eliot became the social club for local runners, and soon word spread and runners from around the world would gather at the Eliot after finishing the marathon, elevating it to its mythical status of "center of the Marathon universe" until it was unjustly shuttered in 1996. If thousands of living, breathing, shouting fans don't hype you up enough, the added bonus of being in the midst of spirits of Boston Marathon legends past should propel you the last half-mile to the finish.

Speaking of inspiration, as you approach the finish line, you'll pass the memorials to the victims of the 2013 Boston Marathon bombings. The hallowed pavement beneath your feet was desecrated where

The Boston Marathon Bombing Memorial stands less than 50 meters from the finish line.

spectators, runners, and volunteers were harmed. But the city of Boston and the running community returned in force, packing both sides of the street with fearless enthusiasm.

The thick crowds lining Boylston Street and cheering for you are reclaiming sacred turf. You and the athletes surrounding you are reclaiming sacred turf. Suffering can and does lead to joy. Together, runners and spectators strengthen their bond, renewing it year after year.

If you have yet to allow the history and significance of the Boston Marathon to gain entrance to your soul, perhaps this final stretch of pavement past the memorial and across the finish line will open that door.

CHAPTER 6

Pre-Race

The Boston Marathon experience isn't confined to the streets between Hopkinton and Copley Square. The Monday race provides you with extra weekend time to sightsee, carbo-load, and enjoy a city that's in full-send party mode.

TAPER

A steady decrease in training volume in the final weeks leading up to your goal race, a taper is not a one-size-fits-all garment you buy off a rack. A proper taper is the bespoke suit that begins with exact measurements and ends in tailored perfection that fits like a glove.

A taper is uniquely yours. It's personal. A two-week taper that works for one runner might be far too short for another, rendering legs too fatigued to race their best on Marathon Monday. Conversely, a four-week taper can be too long for some runners, resulting in runners "losing their edge" due to a slight loss of fitness (or mental toughness) that peaked before race day. So, how do you dial-in the proper taper?

You need to find the taper duration and intensity that work best for you, and the only way to arrive at your answer is through trial and error. Practice is necessary with tapers, too. To be clear, the goal of a taper is to improve your performance, accomplished three ways: 1.) absorbing your training, 2.) healing, and 3.) getting you to the start in Hopkinton physically and mentally refreshed. That's it. Sounds easy, right? In theory, yes. In practice, no.

If there are two adjectives to describe how you'd like to emerge from your taper, they would be *healthy* and *confident*. An off-the-rack taper would begin immediately after finishing your last long run three weeks before race day (or in Boston terms, the last week of March). The most important thing to remember throughout your taper is "the hay is in the barn." No workout from this point forward will improve your fitness beyond where it's at. You will do more damage than good if you continue to train as intensely in April as you did in March.

Equally as important as caring for your physical health is enhancing your mental health. You'll need both to be in top form to be your best on Marathon Monday. Chances are you feel pretty darn invincible after finishing your last long run in a snowstorm in March, but it's natural for phantom pains and real doubts to surface in April. You're not alone.

Top 10 Taper Do's

1. Cut back on volume progressively (e.g.,70–80 percent of peak weekly volume three weeks out, cut to 50–65 percent during week two, and 50 percent or less in the final week).

2. Rest. Sleep more. Take naps. You earned it.

3. Trust your training.

4. Maintain intensity (to keep that "snap" in your stride).

5. Fine-tune nutrition and hydration and make final decisions for race day.

6. Chill. A proper taper takes confidence. You know how poker players can %#$& up if they are not chill? You, too. Chill. Taper with confidence.

7. Detach from analytics. You've probably been super-excited to see your step count and VO$_2$Max rise in March like Episcopalians after Communion. But if you want to PR at Boston, you better not meet that goal. If you do, as they say in Boston, "yah pee-ah's goin' to Chelsea." (Translation: You might as well drink your face off at L Street on Sunday night, because your PR is long gone.)

8. Consider a short race (10k is ideal), preferably two weeks before Marathon Monday. A solid 10k effort two weeks before race day accomplishes many positives: allows you to have a dress rehearsal for your Boston Marathon gear and fuel, gives you an opportunity to turn your legs over and compete, provides a good indication of your level of fitness, and makes your goal marathon pace feel a bit more comfortable.

9. Develop your race plan.

10. Stay healthy (i.e., don't put yourself at risk of catching a cold, virus, or anything else you'd prefer not to have in Hopkinton). Take any and all precautions you can (wash your hands, don't jump in a McDonald's ball pit, don't elect to chaperone your child's or grandchild's elementary school field trip).

Top 10 Taper Don'ts

1. Freak the &$%# out, especially during the weekend of the marathon. In case you didn't get the "chill" memo from the "Taper Do's" list, you need to take your penchant for worrying down several notches or you're going to be a hot mess by the time Monday rolls around. Everyone struggles with the taper. Everyone. Get in line.

2. Second-guess your training. Yes, "the hay is in the barn," but, to keep the clichés rolling, "you've made your bed, now lie in it" is fitting, too. You'll have plenty of time post-race to assess what went right or wrong during your training block, so don't waste valuable time and mental energy ruminating about all of the things you could have done differently during your taper. You don't even know whether or not they worked yet, so, again, chill. You got this.

3. Pick up a brand-new cross-training discipline (skiing, mountain biking, kite surfing). If you've been itching to try something new, take time during your marathon taper to read about it, strategize, and plan. You'll have an entire lifetime after Marathon Monday to do whatever your heart desires. But, please, do not pour your pent-up energy into anything new. You'll be pouring out your PR or BQ.

4. Spend too much time on your feet. There's plenty to do in Boston. Don't do it on Sunday.

5. Be a hypochondriac. Many of the out-of-nowhere aches and pains you're feeling are "phantom pains." Your body is healing from months of training. Let it heal. Don't assume your fifth metatarsal is fractured because you spent six hours looking at websites that hint that it could be.

6. Weigh yourself. Unless you have a medical condition that your doctor ordered you to monitor with daily weigh-ins, do not even think of getting on a scale during the tail end of your taper. You'll be running less and eating more to maximize your glycogen stores before Patriots' Day. If you don't weigh yourself regularly, don't start now. If you do weigh yourself regularly, take a break. Your body is a temple. Worship it, not the scale.

7. Forget the awesomeness of your support team. Tapers can make runners irritable. For many (possibly you, too), mileage is therapy. With less mileage (hence, less "therapy"), you'll have more time on your hands for other things. One of those other things should be to thank anyone and everyone who helped you prepare for your Boston Marathon (family, friends, teammates, fellow runners). Remember how your significant other met you at your favorite brunch spots with warm clothes and your smiling children after your long runs? Now's a perfect opportunity to find a creative way to return the favor(s).

8. Lose your focus. You know how you're keeping your legs and body sharp for race day? Keep your mind sharp and confident, too. Rehearse the race. Visualize executing your "Conserve, Cruise, Control, Compete" mantra on each section of the course. Plant the seeds of your success and water them throughout your taper.

9. Go overboard with your taper. "Taper" doesn't mean sit on your couch. Too much "taper" can dull your competitive edge and leave you sluggish. In fact, many runners feel "tapering" is a misleading descriptor that should be replaced by a term that articulates what your mindset should be as your race approaches (e.g., *polishing*, *fine-tuning*, or *peaking*). Whatever you call it, remember that the reason you're doing it is to improve your performance on race day.

10. Be too serious. Have fun. Boston Translation: "Enjoy yah taypah. Yah earned it. Yah runnin' Boston, khed. Remembah?"

Remaining positive as your goal race approaches is an unforeseen, yet unavoidable, challenge you'll face throughout your taper, especially in the final days. Take the opportunity to craft the mantra you'll use on race day and practice some positive visualization on your runs. Picture yourself passing runners on Heartbreak Hill, high-fiving spectators in Kenmore Square without breaking stride, and finishing with your goal time above your head in Copley Square.

GOAL SETTING

What's your race strategy? Do you have one? What are your goals? Do you have more than one? You've probably heard the expression "If you don't have a plan, someone has one for you." Well, at the Boston Marathon, if you don't have a plan, the course has one for you; it will chew you up and spit you out. And even if you do have an "A" plan, you should have contingency plans "B" and "C."

Even when you believe you're perfectly prepared and ready to run, Boston's deceptively easy start, ill-timed hills and variable weather can crush your soul; but when you get it right, and the stars align, it can soar you to new heights.

Susan M. Simmons
12 Marathons
5 Boston Marathons
Top American, 45–49 Age Group, London Marathon (2018)

So, how can you "win" at Boston? Easy. Have a race strategy. Have a mantra. Have three goals. Boom. Bonus points if your mantra dovetails nicely with your strategy. Don't let the course win. Don't let the weather win. Don't let the negative gremlins in your head win. The seeds of your success are planted before the race. Here's an example:

Mantra—"Conserve, Cruise, Control, Compete"

"A" Goal = 3:15:00 (BQ-5)
"B" Goal = 3:20:00 (BQ)
"C" Goal = sub-3:34:12 (CR)

Strategy

- Conserve—Run as effortlessly as possible through Mile 6. Don't panic if behind schedule.

- Cruise—Dial in 7:27/mile goal pace through Mile 15. Be on "autopilot."

- Control—Run the hills with controlled confidence.

- Compete—It's "game on" at Boston College. Start to step on the accelerator and reel in competitors. Increase effort gradually, relentlessly, and mercilessly. HTFU.

If you're not chasing a PR and you're running Boston for fun, then you can be more playful with your strategy and goals, but that doesn't mean you shouldn't strategize and plan prior to race day, too. How many spectators can you high-five before you get to Ashland? Can you be a "Sherpa" for a friend or help a fellow runner PR? What if you ran for fun until Wellesley and then picked up the pace to see how fast you can run the back half? Or, how about you create your own Boston Marathon trifecta: Kiss a student at the Wellesley Scream Tunnel, donate a $100 check to the Mass General Marathon Team at Mile 20, and shotgun a beer you grab from the outstretched arm of a Boston College SuperFan? Make your own fun. The possibilities are endless.

DEFERRALS

Historically, Boston is not a "deferral-friendly" race. The official B.A.A. statement on the matter is "deferment of entry into the next year's race will not be accepted for any reason."

So, if you get sick, injured, or move across the globe during your marathon buildup, you will not be able to defer your entry to a subsequent year. Check with the B.A.A. if you feel you have reason for an exemption, but it's clear that your hopes shouldn't be high, lest you be disappointed.

The one current exemption is participants at the Boston Marathon and all B.A.A. events (as of January 24, 2023) may defer if they become pregnant prior to race day or "have recently welcomed a child into their families" and elect not to compete as a result. According to the B.A.A., "athletes seeking a pregnancy or post-partum deferral may submit a request in writing to registration@baa.org any time between receiving confirmation of acceptance into the event and up to 14 days before race day."

As efforts move forward to refine accommodation enhancements for mothers, the B.A.A. is "consulting a group of mother runners to help facilitate best practices" at its events. The race once known for its reluctance to change is listening to participants and stakeholders, balancing its intention to improve the race experience with its understanding that traditions help differentiate the Boston Marathon from its peers.

GETTING AROUND BOSTON

Walking

Boston is a very walkable city. If you're not familiar with the area, it's natural to assume the North End is far away from Beacon Hill which is distant from the Back Bay which just might be farther than you thought from the South End, but in reality they're all very close. So before you hail a cab, take a bus, summon an Uber, or consider the "T" (slang for Boston's MBTA, Massachusetts Bay Transportation Authority), pull up a map and see how far your destination is from your location. Chances are, it's closer than you think.

The T

Okay, one caveat. If it's Sunday and you feel like you're spending too much time on your feet when you should be resting, then your first choice should be the pride of Boston, the T, the oldest subway system in the United States. You can purchase a CharlieCard at self-service kiosks at T stations. Your best bets are to either purchase a day pass (good for unlimited rides for 24 hours) or pay trip-by-trip by loading your CharlieCard with a dollar amount you feel you'll need during your stay. Check out www.mbta.com to determine up-to-date adult fares per one-way trip (as well as reduced fares for seniors, students, military). Children under the age of 11 ride for free if accompanied by an adult.

Boston is the birthplace of public transit in America, including the T, the first subway in the United States.

No matter where you are in Boston city proper, the T is nearby, ready to shepherd you away to your destination. For example, if your hotel is in the Battery Wharf/Waterfront area, you can hop on the Blue Line (inbound) at the Aquarium, take it to Government Center, change to the Green Line (outbound) and take it four stops to Copley (right on top of the finish line) or one more stop to Hynes Convention Center (home of the Expo). Easy peasy.

Duck Boats

Speaking of riding things, Boston is the home of many sightseeing tours and fun modes of perusing famous landmarks around the city. Boston Duck Tours, amphibious boats that take you around Boston (60 minutes) and into the Charles River (20 minutes) and back are hugely popular, so you'd better book well in advance if you want to experience this Boston classic. No matter your age, there's something about driving down a ramp straight into the water that never gets old.

Swan Boats

Hoping to find your zen before race day? Head to Boston's Public Garden and take a ride on Boston's famous Swan Boats, a relaxing, warm-weather tradition since 1877. Tickets are purchased at the Swan Boat dock prior to boarding, you guessed it, swan-shaped boats that propel you around the Public Garden lagoon for 15 minutes (give or take). The Swan Boats often open for the season during the weekend of the Boston Marathon and reservations are not required, so, again, expect a line when you get there, but the peaceful sojourn that awaits you is well worth the wait.

Trolley

If you're aquaphobic or just prefer to stick to land, you'll be happy to know you can explore Boston's rich history via trolley. Like the duck boats, you'll have a conductor who will drop historical knowledge on you as you traverse Boston neighborhoods, landmarks, and key attractions. Unlike the duck boats (where you remain in your seat for the duration of your trip), you can hop on and off the trolley at various locations to explore by foot throughout the day. Billed as "transportainment," a combination of transportation and entertainment, trolley tours can be purchased in various day or multiday passes to suit your curiosity and length of stay.

Taxi, Ride App, or Car

Are you the "I'd rather be in a car" type? Well, your best bet is to find a taxi or hail a car via a ride app outside your hotel. Taxis aren't as plentiful as you might think in Boston, but they do tend to congregate outside hotels. Apps such as Uber and Lyft are quite popular in town, so if that's your go-to method of avoiding your feet and you're T-averse (for whatever reason), then hail away via your ride-sharing app of choice.

If you're anywhere near downtown Boston, do yourself a huge favor and don't rent a car. A car is way more of a hassle than a convenience. Finding parking on the street is as easy as getting into Harvard via its restrictive early-action program. And if you think you'll just park in a garage, good luck. You may find one, but you'll carve deep into your Boston Marathon merch budget to make it happen. A few nights in a garage and you can say goodbye to the money you earmarked for the official Adidas Boston Marathon jacket you've been coveting.

Bus, Commuter Rail, and More

The MBTA bus network is another option available to you. You'll find it a bit more complex to navigate compared to the T, but there are some great shortcuts if you study the map before you head out the door. For example, if you're in Cambridge near Harvard University, you'd have to take the Red Line to the Green Line on the T to get to the Expo. But the MBTA #1 bus from Harvard takes you straight down Massachusetts Avenue directly to within a block of the Hynes Convention Center in half the time. Also, the CharlieCard you purchased for the T can be swiped to ride MBTA buses. Not too shabby. But, again, it'll take some homework to figure it all out.

If you find the T and bus don't quite get you to and from your destinations, give the MBTA's Commuter Rail, ferry, and paratransit services a look. The Commuter Rail extends geographically beyond the T and reaches places the T doesn't, including numerous popular spectator spots on the Boston Marathon course (e.g., Framingham and Wellesley). Boston Harbor cruises are also popular, as are ferries to and from Provincetown on Cape Cod.

If you have a disability that prevents you from using the T, bus, or trolley, under the ADA you can use MBTA paratransit services (aka "The RIDE") for up to 21 days in a 12-month period. You will need to contact The Ride Eligibility Center (TREC) and provide your eligibility information (including documentation of your disability [ADA Certificate or otherwise] and a letter from your health care provider) roughly a month before Marathon Monday. Be sure to contact TREC for all pertinent details to ensure you're all set in advance of your arrival.

Bike

Popular in and around Boston, "Bluebikes" are Boston's public transportation bike alternative (with more than 400 stations and 4,000 bikes available to you). Riding around the busy streets can be a bit nerve-wracking if you're not used to pedaling around a city, but, if you can get yourself to the Charles River Esplanade, the views are spectacular and the bike- and runner-friendly path along the river is free of cars. Single-ride purchases are available, as are various pass and membership options. Whatever you do and wherever you go, have fun, be careful, and remember this isn't the Tour de France. You're in Boston to run a (pretty cool) road race. Take it easy and save your quads for Monday.

SITES TO SEE

You're going to want to put your feet up in your hotel room as often as you can (especially on Sunday night), but you're doing yourself a disservice if you don't explore Boston and enjoy all of its rich history (e.g., Freedom Trail, Bunker Hill

Monument, Boston Tea Party), world-revered learning institutions (Harvard, MIT, and more), beautiful parks (e.g., Charles River Esplanade, Public Garden, Greenway), cultural attractions (Museum of Fine Arts, Boston Symphony Orchestra, Isabella Stewart Gardner Museum, New England Aquarium), and charming neighborhoods (Beacon Hill, South End, Back Bay, and North End, among others).

Your greatest challenge in Boston won't be finding something to do; it will be refraining from doing too much for your own PR-chasing good. Do you remember in grade school when you read about "Old Ironsides" (the naval hero of the War of 1812)? Well, you can visit Old Ironsides (aka the USS *Constitution*) floating in Boston Harbor at the Charlestown Navy Yard. What about Paul Revere's famous ride? You can visit the colonial home (c. 1680) of American patriot Paul Revere in Boston's North End. And remember how zany the Boston Tea Party and Boston Massacre sounded? Well, you can go to Griffin's Wharf in Boston and see where the tea was destroyed and visit the Old State House at the corner of State and Congress Streets to see where the riot ensued that turned colonial sentiment against King George III.

If American history isn't your cup of tea, then how about gleaning a little inspiration from some big (and small) screen magic? Be like Norm and grab a beer at *Cheers* (84 Beacon Street) to see the namesake bar that inspired the hit television show. Or consider taking a stroll in Boston's Public Garden to sit on the same bench that Robin Williams and Matt Damon sat on when Robin delivered the monologue that was greatly responsible for his Academy Award for his role as Dr. Sean Maguire in *Good Will Hunting*.

Or go to Harvard and take a picture in front of Kirkland House, the dorm where Mark Zuckerberg and his cofounders birthed Facebook, as immortalized in *The Social Network*. Or walk the streets of Charlestown where Ben Affleck and Jeremy Renner plotted their brazen heist at Fenway Park in *The Town*. Boston's landmarks and charming streets have provided the perfect backdrop for many well-known films and television series. Perhaps Hollywood's obsession with Boston can motivate your legs to reach their own *Fever Pitch* on Monday.

Now that I'm at the halfway point of my life's journey, I can distill why the Boston Marathon is special into one word, hope: I hope I didn't go out too fast, hope I have my legs to make it through the challenging hills, hope the hard work through the winter pays off, and hope as the finish line approaches on Boylston, I can say "I gave it my all."

Shane O'Hara
Former Store Manager, Marathon Sports, Boylston Street (2001–2019)

If history, art, TV, and film aren't motivating, you have plenty of running attractions to get you in the marathon mood. Multiple pop-up stores (Asics, Brooks, Rabbit, Bandit) and retail stores (Tracksmith, Marathon Sports, Nike, New Balance) are scattered about the Back Bay. These stores host events that allow you to meet and greet elite athletes (Des Linden, Meb Keflezighi, Sara Hall, Ben True, Kara Goucher) and check out the latest and greatest gear (super shoes, electronics).

If you'd like to see other athletes dig deep into the pain cave before it's your turn on Monday, enjoy the B.A.A. 5k (8 a.m. start on Saturday) or cheer on the elites racing the B.A.A. Invitational Mile and talented school kids racing various distances immediately after the 5k. Races start and finish at the Boston Marathon finish line, so you'll get a taste of the thrill of victory and the agony of defeat, the perfect appetizer before Monday's main course.

EXPO

Hosting more than 200 exhibitors, the Boston Marathon Expo is a running love-fest of the highest magnitude. The Expo is free, open to the public, a mere 600 meters from the finish line, and is the perfect way, if you're not amped up already, to get wicked stoked for Marathon Monday. Typically located at the Hynes Convention Center at 900 Boylston Street (on the corner of Hereford Street) in Boston's Back Bay, the Expo is a perfect opportunity to take a glimpse of the finish line and perhaps even pose for a picture near it.

You'll meet runners all over Boston, but the epicenter of prerace activity is the Expo. Norman Lang

The Expo is open pretty much all day Friday, Saturday, and Sunday and is jam-packed with the latest running gear, fuel, gadgets, and more. If you arrive in town early enough, you might want to avoid Sunday because it's easy to get caught up in the excitement and spend way too much time on your feet than is recommended the day before your race. The Expo has a way of getting you emotionally and mentally ready to race, but it also has a sneaky way of sapping you physically. Better to attend on Friday or Saturday (or both), relax and enjoy yourself and the friends and family that accompany you, and not be hyper-concerned that you're leaving your PR on the convention center floor.

Don't forget to grab your bib (yah numbah), race packet, and T-shirt at the designated pickup section at the Expo before you leave. Bring a photo ID and the official runner passport you received digitally from the B.A.A. You'll need them to claim what's rightfully yours. The Expo is extremely well organized, but, even so, you may have to stand in queue for a bit, the perfect opportunity to strike up conversations and create some friendships with marathoners from around the world. Everyone has a unique journey to Boston, and, as you know, runners love to talk about running.

Make certain you retain the clear bag (and the sticker with your bib number you'll affix to it) when you get your swag. The clear bag is your gear-check bag that must be used on race day. Oh, and don't be shy with photo opportunities at the Expo. You're capturing a significant life moment. Even if you're a streaker, it's fun to look back at the memories and how young you looked when it all started. So put your stress about the race, weather, GI, and everything else on the back burner for a hot second and enjoy your Expo and Newbury Street experiences.

SHAKEOUT RUN

In addition to the B.A.A. 5k on Saturday, Boston has a plethora of choices for your shakeout pleasure. A flat, go-to place to calm your nerves or jump-start your GI is the Charles River Esplanade. If your hotel is situated within walking distance of the finish line (in Boston's Back Bay neighborhood), simply run north until you hit water (the Charles River). The footpath along the Charles is considered one of the best places to run in the world. You can run on both the Boston and Cambridge sides of the river, so create a loop or just go out and back and enjoy the tranquility. There are many shakeouts orchestrated by brands and influencers, so hook up with a group if a solo shakeout isn't your thing.

My incredible experience running the B.A.A. 5k and traditional experience spectating the Boston Marathon have been true celebrations of the human spirit, where thousands of individuals from all walks of life come together to achieve their goals and inspire one another.

Mary Darling
11 Marathons (3 Chicago, 3 London, and 5 NYC)
BQ'd and Preparing to Run Her First Boston

Another strong idea for a shakeout is to run the Boston Marathon course in reverse. Just start at the finish line and head as far out as you'd like and then turn around. You'll have to run on the sidewalks to avoid cars (the streets will only be blocked off from traffic during the marathon), but that's no different than the other 364 days of the year. This shakeout route is especially helpful for any athletes who haven't navigated the course before. It'll look quite different with thousands of screaming fans on Marathon Monday, but it's still nice to know what you're getting yourself into late in the race.

Other shakeout routes worth considering include the Freedom Trail (a 2.5-mile route from Boston Common to the Bunker Hill Monument in Charlestown), the Emerald Necklace (one of Bill Rodgers's favorite routes, particularly The Fens in the Fenway-Kenmore area), the waterfront in Southie (especially near Castle Island), and Fresh Pond (a 2.5-mile reservoir loop in Cambridge).

Your running experience in Boston isn't complete without a run along the Charles River. The Charles River Esplanade is a flat running oasis, affording all types of loops and distances to please Boston's vibrant running community. But as popular as the Esplanade is, it's nearly impossible to find rules of decorum of any sort. Until now.

Contrary to what may seem to naïve newcomers as "make up your own rules" Wild West lawlessness, the scenic pathway for pedestrians, dog walkers, runners, bikers, skateboarders, and anyone else intent on enjoying it has unwritten and unspoken rules of engagement that will henceforth be readily accessible to Bostonians and visitors alike. Behold . . . (see The 20 Golden Rules of Running Along the Charles River).

You never know who you'll run into along the Charles. Aurelien Scagnolari

The 20 Golden Rules of Running Along the Charles River

1. **Stay to the right**—There are parts of the path that have a solid line separating the path, there are parts that have a dotted line, and there are parts that have no line whatsoever. Regardless what the path looks like, you must behave as if traffic is two-way (because it is) and you are relegated to the right half of the road (because you are). And, just like a highway with a double yellow line, if you veer across into oncoming traffic, you risk instigating a head-on collision.

2. **The slower you are, the farther to the right you should be**—The slowest walkers should be on the far right; faster walkers should be on the far right before passing slower walkers on the left (i.e., on the left of the slower walkers, but on the right of the path, *not* on the left side of the path). Runners and slow bikers will do the same, staying right before passing. Faster bikers are best situated in the middle of the right side of the path prior to passing slower bikers, runners, and walkers to their left. Again, envision a double yellow line in the middle of the road, so cross it at your own risk (and thereby risking the health and life of anyone in oncoming traffic, too).

3. **No littering**—You'd think this would be a commonsense no-brainer, but one glance at the not-so-occasional bottles and debris along the water's edge of the Charles and it's clear this Golden Rule still needs to be included in writing. So, for those of you (i.e., ungrateful miscreants) who need to be reminded, please, don't litter. For the love of the fish, the geese, the squirrels, the swans, and all of humanity, let's keep this running paradise clean.

4. **Never come to a complete stop on the path**—Do you notice how there's not a caveat like "without checking behind you" or "when you're on a bike"? That's because there's no need for a proviso. Would you ever hit the brakes in your car and come to a complete stop smack dab in the middle of a highway? Of course not. If you did, you would be correct to expect to be rear-ended, just as you will be on the Esplanade pathway (ruining your day and the day of the person behind you who crashes into you).

   If you must stop, get off the pathway completely. Then you can fix whatever caused you to stop and hop back on the path when you're ready to move again. It's that simple. It's not your path. You're sharing it. Don't behave like no one else is using it.

5. **People not on foot (e.g., bikers or skateboarders) yield to people on foot (walkers, runners)**—This really shouldn't need to be explained, but (disrespectful) bikers who weave in and out of runners and walkers at high speeds need to be reminded that pedestrians have the right-of-way (100 percent of the time, all the time, every time). Got it? Good.

6. **Pass to the left**—Whether you're walking, running, skateboarding, or biking, you pass to the left, always. And as you approach the person or persons you're passing, you announce yourself by exclaiming confidently "ON YOUR LEFT!" The phrase has become the preferred warning cry to signal your intent to pass people ahead of you.

    Never pass on the right. Never. Also, it's best to wait to pass until you're sure people are not coming toward you, especially if there's not enough room to pass without veering into their lane and putting them and you at risk of a head-on collision.

7. **Leash and clean up after your pet**—Owners must be responsible and leash their pets and dispose of any waste created by their pets. Pets should be at their owner's side (i.e., no leashes that extend across the path diagonally or perpendicularly that trip runners or catapult cyclists over their handlebars). If you want your pet to live (not be run over by a bike or inadvertently kicked into Rainbow Bridge by a runner), then either a.) carry your pet, or b.) keep your pet within a six-inch radius of your feet while on the path. Ideally, you should walk on the far right of the path and your pet should walk beside you (to your right) off the path. And if you want your pet to be unleashed and wander away from you, the Esplanade pathway is not for you.

8. **Educate and clean up after your children**—It is incumbent upon parents to teach their children the do's and don'ts of walking, running, biking, or skateboarding on the Esplanade pathway. A child on a bike meandering into oncoming traffic on the Esplanade pathway is not cute, in the same way a wide-eyed toddler walking onto an interstate highway isn't cute. And, please, do not leave bikes, toys, food, or anything on the pathway. Don't be that parent. Again, the pathway isn't just for you and your children; it's shared by everyone.

9. **No "human chains"**—You know how frustrating it is to run around a group of slower runners that are side by side, right? Especially when you're in Brookline at Mile 23 and your legs don't change direction too well. Well, imagine running (or biking) on the Esplanade when a family of four has decided to form

a "human chain" across a pathway that is, give or take, one-eighth the width of Beacon Street. It's a recipe for anger, at best, and an accident, at worst. If you're walking, running, or biking with family or friends, do not form a perpendicular or diagonal chain across the pathway. Be courteous. Two abreast tops, and even that is troublesome in narrower sections. Single file is best, always.

10. **It's called a "pedestrian footbridge" for a reason**—Chances are you'll cross a pedestrian footbridge (e.g., the Arthur Fiedler Footbridge in front of the iconic Hatch Shell used for Boston's July 4th concerts) to get to the Esplanade. Whether you're biking, skateboarding, or running, it is proper to walk across the footbridge. Get off your bike or skateboard and walk. Period. Runners may "lightly jog" if they must, but walking is best for the safety of you and everyone around you.

11. **Be respectful of wildlife**—As much as we humans like to believe that the Charles River Esplanade is a gift from the running gods for our enjoyment, the reality is we share the paradise with all the fish, animals, birds, and critters that inhabit it. You'll see swans, herons, ducks, geese, bald eagles, hawks, squirrels, rats, bass, perch, carp, turtles, and more. Steer clear of them, including their nests, and refrain from feeding them no matter how cute or hungry you perceive them to be. They will survive and thrive without your Gummi bears, Sour Patch Kids, bread, potato chips, M&Ms, or whatever else you errantly believe will enhance their day.

12. **Go early to go fast**—The Esplanade park "opens at dawn and closes at dusk," so you probably won't be surprised to learn that foot traffic on the pathway surrounding the Charles River is lightest in the early morning. Hence, experienced cyclists and runners, especially those training for upcoming races, are best able to crank up the velocity and volume at sunrise, when most civilians are prepping for work, nursing hangovers, or asleep. If you think later in the day is another good option, you'd be wrong. The park attracts strong after-work crowds, many of whom like to linger until sundown, making biking and running fast far more challenging and dangerous.

13. **Daylight is your "frenemy"**—Depending on what you're looking to accomplish on your run, daylight can be your best friend or your worst enemy. If safety is your prime concern, daylight is your best friend. Ample sunlight, better visibility, and more people add up to greater safety. If you'd like to crank out your last speed session before Marathon Monday, daylight isn't so friendly.

You'll be dodging recreational bikers, strolling families, and the unpredictable movements of pets and small children. Choose the time of your run according to the purpose of your run.

14. **West is best**—As a rule, the farther west you run along the Charles, the less congested the pathway will be. Most of the foot traffic on both the Boston and Cambridge sides of the Charles is between the BU (Boston University) Bridge and the Charles River Dam Bridge (Museum of Science), a picturesque 5.63-mile loop. Once you get west of the BU Bridge, you won't be announcing "on your left!" quite as frequently and you can open up your stride a bit. So if you're interested in an up-tempo effort without much interference, go early and go west.

15. **Report any accidents or suspicious activity**—Call the Massachusetts State Police (617-727-6780) to report any theft, injury, or behavior worthy of police intervention. The paradise that is the Charles River Esplanade isn't policed heavily because, for the most part, parkgoers are law-abiding and respectful. However, like any public place allowing access to all, the potential for unfortunate incidents occurring is nonzero. If and when an event arises, please call the police to ensure they're aware of it and can dedicate proper resources toward resolving it in a timely fashion.

16. **Acknowledge other runners (or not)**—Boston is an incredibly runner-friendly city, filled with runners of all shapes, sizes, ages, ethnicities, and genders. You'll discover that there is no right or wrong answer regarding whether or not you should make an effort to acknowledge runners you cross paths with along the Charles.

    If you're accustomed to nodding, smiling, or gesturing (politely) to runners in your hometown, don't be shy about doing the same on the Esplanade. Just don't take offense if your kindness isn't returned. It's not that these runners are being blatantly rude (well, okay, some might be), but runners are a focused bunch, and sometimes that concentration is so strong that it overrides common courtesy. Again, don't be offended. And don't give up. Keep making other runners' days better. Keep spreading your love. Eventually someone will reciprocate your good manners. So keep nodding, smiling, and gesturing if that's your thing. It just might boomerang back to you and make your day, too.

17. **Beware of ice**—This isn't a grave concern in April, but in the heart of the winter, the Charles River will be covered with ice. The hardy among you

might be inspired to run, snowshoe, or ski across the river from Boston to Cambridge (or vice versa). Don't do that. The chances of you making it all the way across are horribly low. A more likely scenario is the ice breaks and you fall through. So, yeah, don't do that.

Speaking of ice, beware of black ice! When it snows in Boston, the pathway along the Charles will typically be plowed (some sections far better than others, but not too shabby overall). On warm days when the snow melts, it will gravitate toward the pathway and freeze overnight, forming a runner's nightmare, black ice (a clear glaze of ice on the pavement that you can't see). Many a runner has fallen prey to the Esplanade's black ice. Don't be another victim.

Oh, and the fair-weather corollary to "beware of ice" is "beware of raised pavement." Sure, ice is dangerous, but have you ever been picking up the pace in a tempo run when all of a sudden the toe of your extended carbon-plate super shoe jams into a dastardly ridge in the pavement that sends you, face-first, violently to the pavement?

Those patches of raised pavement are often attributed to tree roots that cause the pavement to rise and fracture. Sometimes it's just shoddy workmanship or expanding and contracting water and ice that are to blame. Regardless of the culprit, the Esplanade has an abundance of pavement that isn't level or smooth, so beware of these imperfections and be careful year-round.

18. **Know thy wind**—Bostonians who run year-round know how the speed and direction of the wind can influence a run (good, bad, or ugly). The majority of the Charles River flows east and west, but there is a section from the BU Bridge to Weeks Footbridge that runs north and south.

That said, if you're running from Boston west toward Newton, prevailing westerlies will typically be in your face on your way out and will be at your back on your return. The wind along the Charles is more intense as it whips (unimpeded) over the water. In the winter, a 20 degrees F day with a 25 mph west-northwest wind will make it feel like it's closer to 0 degrees F or subzero on your way out to Newton and more like the advertised 20 degrees F on the way back to Boston.

However, if the winds shift and are from the east or northeast as they are during a "nah'eastah," you'll want to rethink your strategy because running back to Boston in a subzero windchill after you've sweat beneath the surface of your layers of clothing could be a recipe for hypothermia.

19. **Jump in the water (at your own risk)**—If the sun is blazing, humidity is through the roof, it's 92 degrees F, and you just finished a 12-mile run, it's so darn tempting to jump in the Charles, right? But you should know a few things before you run off a nearby dock and take the plunge.

Have you ever approached an alluring building surrounded by a fence, barbed wire, and police tape, and you strangely feel compelled to go inside, but, just as you approach, a security guard stops you and says the building is "condemned" and you can't enter? Well, in liquid terms, the Charles River was condemned for more than 50 years. Due to years of oversight and abuse (primarily industrial contamination), resulting poor water quality, and necessary safety precautions, swimming in the Charles was prohibited for a half-century. Efforts to clean up the river began in earnest in the 1990s.

Does that mean it's okay to take the plunge now? Well, technically, swimming in the Charles is still prohibited without a permit issued by the Massachusetts Department of Conservation and Recreation (MassDCR). For example, City Splash, an annual community event (typically in June), allows the public the opportunity to swim in the Charles off the Fiedler Dock for the day (including a sanctioned one-mile swim).

Outside of such permitted events, will you be arrested if you jump off a dock into the Charles and splash around for a second? It's possible, but improbable. Whether the rewards (quick cooldown, body temperature reset) are worth the risks (bacteria, oncoming boats, and more) is up to you to decide.

20. **Make use of the public facilities**—Thanks to ample open space and a plethora of public facilities, there's no shortage of things to do along the Charles River if you'd like to stray from the comfort of the Esplanade pathway. You can relax with friends on a dock overlooking the water, picnic or play catch in a field, chill out while your children enjoy a playground, rent a boat and go sailing, work out on exercise stations, row a skull, windsurf, skipper a kayak, and more.

The Charles River Esplanade can be enjoyed year-round, and, during the warm months when the park is most crowded (late spring through early fall), public restrooms are open and water fountains (aka "bubblahs") are turned on, too. So if your GI is janky and you like to keep hydrated in the heat, you don't have to be shy about spending afternoons along the Charles.

BLESSING OF THE ATHLETES

One of the cooler traditions for Boston Marathon participants is the "Blessing of the Athletes" at Old South Church, the Gothic-style home to a religious community established in 1669 and known for its platform of equality, social justice, and peace.

On the Sunday preceding Marathon Monday, Old South Church welcomes all Boston Marathon participants by inviting them to worship and receive a traditional blessing asking that the athletes "be kept safe from harm or injury, exercise respect for each another, and persevere to endure the competition."

The Boston Marathon is a gift from God, embodying the human spirit—the world's fastest runners and handicapped racers, dedicated charity participants, toughest weather conditions and terrain, alumni teams (I'm talking to you, Tufts), athletic associations (including my own B.A.A.), runners of all ages (including two 81-year-olds I met in 2023), unrelenting energy from the most vocal sports fans in the world, and unlimited support from family, friends, and fans—reinvigorating my life goals of consistency, durability, longevity, and socialization in one blissful weekend celebration.

Joe Findaro
40 Marathons
15 Consecutive Boston Marathons

If you believe in divine intervention or you just want to cover all of your bases in your never-ending attempts to be your best on Marathon Monday, you should make a trip to Old South Church at 645 Boylston Street, a mere few feet from the Boston Marathon finish line. The service includes an inspiring rendition of "Highland Cathedral" for bagpipes, organ, and drum. And, hey, is your trip to Boston truly complete without bagpipes?

PRE-RACE "SUPPAH"

One of the cool things about running any of the World Major Marathons is all of the incredible restaurants available for your pre- and post-race enjoyment. Whether you're in New York, Chicago, London, Tokyo, or Berlin, there's no shortage of amazing food of all varieties close at hand. Boston is no exception, particularly when it comes to what many of you will be choosing for your pre-race meal, pasta. Boston's North End neighborhood is the city's official "Little Italy," home to its largest Italian-American population as well as dozens of Italian restaurants, bakeries, and shops. The North End is a popular Sunday night carbo-loading destination, so get your reservations early. Oh, and bring some dead presidents, too. Some of the most popular places, including Mike's Pastry (home of legendary cannoli), are cash-only.

Beyond the North End, Boston offers plenty of carb-friendly choices, including the Boston Marathon's own pre-race Pasta Dinner at City Hall (the Government Center stop on the Blue and Green Lines of the T). The city's best Italian (sorry, North End, and no offense to the group feast at City Hall) is a hidden gem called Rino's Place in Boston's original Italian neighborhood, East Boston ("Eastie" to locals). Rino's is particularly convenient if you're situated in a hotel near Logan Airport (also in Eastie). But if you thought it was difficult to get a table in the North End, Rino's seats about 35, so either a.) you know someone, b.) you know someone who knows someone, or c.) you're out of luck.

If Italian isn't your go-to pre-race meal, then, fear not; Boston has you covered, offering a cornucopia of choices from Thai (an excellent pre-race choice according to Boston luminaries Amanda and Ian Nurse) to Chinese (go to Chinatown near the Theatre District) to Irish pub fare (literally all over Boston) to, well, just about anything you can imagine (Indian, French, Greek, sushi, seafood [yes, chowdah and lobstah], and much more). If treats are your thing, you already know about the cannoli at Mike's Pastry (and its across-the-street archnemesis Modern Pastry) in the North End, but Boston also has top-shelf carrot cake and Boston cream pie (Flour Bakery, multiple locations), chocolate chip cookies (Levain on Newbury Street via NYC), and maple bacon donuts (Union Square Donuts, multiple locations) that will emerge from the octagon victorious if pitted against any you'll find in your travels around the globe.

For those of you in the habit of having a carb-rich beer to help calm your nerves and sleep more soundly before a big race, you'll be pleased to know that Boston and beer have been synonymous since the Puritans began crafting creative brews in the 1600s. The Greater Boston area is home to more than 130 craft breweries, including several brewers of world renown (Sam Adams, Harpoon) and many innovative young upstarts (Trillium, Jack's Abby, Cambridge Brewing Company). So wash those carbs down with more carbs, if that's your thing.

If wine and cocktails are more your speed, you won't have to venture far from the Boston Marathon finish line to find the perfect Perfect Manhattan or Boulevardier at Boston's iconic Oak Long Bar at the Fairmont Copley Plaza. Alternatively, you can head up Boylston Street to the ever-popular bar at Abe & Louie's steak house for a tasty glass of Brunello di Montalcino, or just stay at the Hynes Convention Center after the Expo for a dirty martini at the Capital Grille. Pick your poison, and then get home and get to bed so you can be wide-eyed for your 4:25 a.m. wake-up call.

PRE-RACE CHECKLIST

Whether it's your first Boston or your 27th, you'll want to make sure you remember everything you need to be your best on Marathon Monday. Sunday should be a day of rest, so it's best to have all items on your checklist prepared on Saturday. Heah's yah Boston checklist, khed.

Shoes

"Lightly tested" (10 to 30 miles). Never brand-new. Bring a gnarly old pair to wear until it's time to get in your corral. Then donate those workhorse shoes (i.e., place them in the clear donation bags hanging from the railings of your corral) and switch into your racing shoes. You'll avoid mud, wet grass, and anything else devious, and you'll feel like a boss when you slip on your shiny, dry super shoes.

Socks

You do you on this, but stay away from cotton and bulky, heavily cushioned socks if it's raining.

Bottoms

There are dozens of options here, but whatever you wear should be battle-tested (preferably trained and raced in before). Wear some threadbare pajama pants or crusty old sweatpants that you can throw out or donate before the start.

Tops

Layers are key. You can always shed as necessary. Bringing a throwaway layer or two is encouraged if it's cool. Like your bottoms, the top (or tops) you're wearing for the entirety of the race should be seasoned and combat-ready.

Gloves

If you know you'll be taking them off, consider slipping old, threadbare socks on your hands that you can just throw away.

Compression sleeves

Your arms and calves deserve love, too. If you're in the habit of wearing compression gear, or if you have "tween" weather that may (or may not) require limb coverage, throw your compression sleeves in your Start Area bag. If you think you might not need your arm sleeves all race and the thought of tossing your precious (and expensive) sleeves out is too heart-wrenching to fathom, consider wearing an old pair of tube socks or dress socks (simply cut a hole in the toe area, and, boom, you have arm sleeves). Then you can just throw them out without remorse.

Hat

Wool if it's raining. Brimmed if it's sunny. Technical, breathable if it's hot. And don't forget hair ties to tame your locks further, if needed.

Sunglasses

You may or may not be a fan of sunglasses in general, but, when you're running, sunglasses reduce glare; protect you from damaging UV rays, wind, and debris; and provide stress relief for your eyes. Oh, and sunglasses hide your RBF and look cool. So there's that.

Bib

Yah numbah. Don't leave for Hopkinton without it. If it's not already pinned to your singlet, make certain it has four safety pins affixed to the corners. Oh, and fill in the identification and medical information on the back of the bib. If something goes horribly wrong on the course, medical professionals will be able to act quicker knowing your vitals (name, allergies, emergency contact). It takes one minute. And that one minute could save your life.

Garbage bags

Large (33-gallon or larger). Bring several. Share with fellow athletes. Permanent marker—Sharpie or otherwise, bring a marker with you so you (or a fellow athlete, who just so happens to be a calligrapher) can write all over your body. Most importantly, inscribe large letters on your chest with whatever you want the crowd to shout at you for the next two, three, four, five, or six hours (depending on your degree of fitness). Oh, and there are some people who think you shouldn't write your name on your chest. They're the same people who are the first to tell children there isn't a Santa Claus.

Sunscreen

There aren't a lot of leaves on trees in April in Massachusetts. That said, sunscreen is a highly personal thing. If you're a bronze Adonis from Miami, you may be sickened at the thought of sunscreen blocking your pores and dripping into and stinging your eyes. But if you're from Buffalo, you might be a "lobstah" by the time you hit Copley Square. Your call.

Lubricant

Whether it's Body Glide, Vaseline, or otherwise, you're going to want to lubricate yourself in Hopkinton like you're the Tin Man who needs his oilcan in the Land of Oz. Don't be shy. Slather all the usual places and the not-so-usual places (like your undercarriage, feet, and between your toes).

Gear check bag

You'll part with your gear bag (provided at the Expo) before you board your bus, and then you'll take a separate clear plastic bag, your Start Area bag (also provided at the Expo) with you to Hopkinton. The bag you take to Hopkinton will contain items you either make use of before you start the race, or you'll have to discard them. The bag you leave behind in Copley Square will contain all the items you'll want when you finish (dry clothes, hat, sandals, towel, keys, a few dollars). Volunteers closely guard the bags, but the B.A.A. makes it clear that they are not responsible for lost items. If possible, refrain from placing valuables in your bag. If you need to bring something of value, hide it from plain view.

Start Area bag

Provided at the Expo, this clear plastic bag is the only bag you're allowed to take with you on the bus to Hopkinton. All other bags are prohibited (with an exception or two listed on the "Allowable and Prohibited Items" page of the B.A.A. website). Whatever you place in this one-gallon bag (food, drink, garbage bags, or otherwise) must be used or discarded in Hopkinton.

Sponge

For the love of all that is holy, if the temperature is above 60 degrees F, bring a sponge to Hopkinton. Your relationship with sponges will never be the same again.

Smartwatch

There will be digital clocks positioned at every 5k mark as well as key mile locations (e.g., the half-marathon mark in Wellesley). These clocks will begin running when the runners with the lowest bib numbers cross the starting line. So the times displayed will be pretty meaningless to you if the bib number on your chest is 8242 and you crossed the starting line 4:32 after the gun. You might be able to do the quick math in Ashland, but if John Nash were running Boston, even he would be hard-pressed to calculate his split when he's glycogen depleted in Brookline.

Don't forget your watch. And don't forget to fully charge it the night before. Oh, and even if you wear a smartwatch, please know the GPS will not (okay, this deserves to be capitalized . . . WILL NOT) register perfectly with each mile marker. This isn't Fantasyland. You're running a marathon with tangents into a city, so expect your GPS to be off (e.g., registering your 10-mile split a good 178 meters in advance of actually crossing the 10-mile sign in Natick). Don't panic. Everybody's watch is doing the same thing.

Pace band or tattoo

Do you have any clue what your split should be at 20k or Mile 22? Well, if it's written on (or affixed to) your arm, you'll know the exact time. Channel Guy Pearce in *Memento*. Write it down.

Lip balm

Sometimes when you run a marathon, it's the little things that make the biggest difference. If you're one of those people who has lip balm at the ready on the daily, tuck one in your pocket on race day. Your lips will be happy even if the time above your head in Copley makes you unhappy.

Pain reliever

Consult with your doctor regarding over-the-counter pain reliever use before, during, and after your marathon. Non-steroidal anti-inflammatory medications (e.g., Advil, Motrin, and Aleve), acetaminophen (aka Tylenol), and aspirin all have pros and cons. Many runners nursing overuse injuries and niggles rely on pain relievers, but they aren't familiar with the negative side effects, particularly when running at high-intensity for two to six hours. That said, if the doctor gives you a thumbs-up, don't forget to tuck some tablets in a baggie in your shorts (they'll dissolve if moisture, including your sweat, finds them).

Paper products

Toilet paper, tissues, paper towels. Pick your poison. It's disheartening when you're in a porta-potty and discover (albeit too late) that TP is MIA.

Adhesive bandages

If you're prone to chafing (nipples, ankles, toes, or otherwise) and you've trained with bandages before, then don't forget to throw a few of your fave bandages in your Start Area bag.

Athletic or kinesiology tape

Similar to bandages, if you've trained with and relied on tape during your marathon buildup, don't abandon it on race day. However, if you've been nursing a niggle or injury and your bright idea is to tape it on race day for the first time, then you should think again. Taping a part of your body improperly when you haven't tested it beforehand is a recipe for disaster.

Fuel

To be your best on your journey from Hopkinton to Boston, you'll need three types of fuel: fluids, carbohydrates, and electrolytes. The B.A.A. provides water and Gatorade stations at every mile marker (beginning at Mile 2) and energy gel stations at 11.8 miles (just before the Wellesley Scream Tunnel), 17 miles (in advance of the right turn at the firehouse), and 21.5 miles (immediately after Boston College). If your fueling strategy calls for more (sodium tablets, jelly beans, energy bars) or you have an aversion to what's offered on the course, you'll need to carry fuel with you or rely on your support crew to deliver it to you at strategic points along the way.

Money

Throw a few dollars or a credit card in your shorts in case of an emergency.

Cellphone

If you're used to running with a cellphone or you're running Boston for fun (and not a PR or BQ), bring it. If you typically don't run with a cellphone and you're chasing a PR or BQ at Boston, do yourself a favor and don't take it to Hopkinton. Does Eliud Kipchoge carry a cellphone? Please. Will you miss out on a photo opportunity or two? Sure. But you'll feel free and untethered and much less encumbered (physically and mentally) and you'll be hyper-focused on what matters: staying in the moment, listening to your body, and optimizing your performance.

Camera

The B.A.A. "discourages" the use of "action cameras" such as GoPros, and insists that footage is for personal, noncommercial use only. Some runners post videos of the race on YouTube and various social media, and the B.A.A. turns a blind eye. Others post videos and the B.A.A. insists the footage of the race violates their deals with partners. So if you intend to bring a camera, capture your race experience, and share the footage, you may (or may not) be contacted by the B.A.A., who could ban you from participating in future B.A.A. events. If (potentially) being on the wrong side of the B.A.A. concerns you, either a.) contact the B.A.A. in advance of sharing content, b.) refrain from filming in the first place, or c.) post across social media and lawyer up.

GETTING TO HOPKINTON

The best way to get to Hopkinton on Marathon Monday is to take the official B.A.A. buses from Charles Street, between Boston Common and the Public Garden. Check the B.A.A. website for exact timing; but, as a rule, the buses begin around 6:30 a.m.-ish and are boarded in waves corresponding to your bib number and color-coated wave on your race bib, beginning with the lowest bibs (i.e., fastest runners) in Wave 1, who start first, of course.

Transportation to the start is for official participants only, and volunteers will be checking your bib numbers to ensure no bandits or stowaways of any kind occupy a seat reserved for you and your bibbed brethren. Remember to check your clear plastic Finish Area gear bag at the designated area (on Boylston Street and Berkeley Street east of the finish line) before you board the B.A.A. bus. Once your glossy yellow chariot is on its way to Hopkinton, it's too late.

Also, don't forget to take care of all of your GI needs as best you can prior to boarding the bus. These are yellow school buses (the same ones that took you to elementary school), so there aren't any toilets. You and more than 40 of your fully hydrated and carb-loaded adult competitors who are all trying to clear their GIs before the start are tempting fate by opting to board a bus together.

If you thought having to run 30 seconds faster than goal pace on Boylston Street to barely BQ was stressful, try listening to the life story of your overly sharing seatmate from Sylacauga, Alabama, while fighting the urge to "evacuate" all of your pancakes and coffee on a crowded bus that's idling in traffic.

Can you get to Hopkinton without taking an official B.A.A. bus? Yes, you can. But it's important to know that, even with the aforementioned potential GI challenges, you're making your morning incredibly more stressful if you do. Many charity teams have vans or private buses that transport their runners to Hopkinton. They've been doing this for years, so they know the drill. They get to Hopkinton early (typically before 7 a.m.), and many of the teams have arrangements with local Hopkinton homeowners, setting up de facto headquarters for the entirety of Marathon Monday morning. If you're on a charity team, follow the lead of "The Cruise Director" (i.e., your teammate responsible for all items of logistical importance).

Every year on the third Monday of April, Boston becomes a focal point with a world-class event; it is a special feeling being a part of it.

Rich "Shifter" Horgan
25 Boston Marathons
Dana-Farber Marathon Challenge Team

If you're a bibbed runner who is not on a charity team and you're determined (for whatever twisted reason) to make your life more difficult and not take an official B.A.A. bus to Hopkinton, then you'll need to enlist the help of a friend who's willing to wake up before sunrise to pick you up and take you to Hopkinton in his or her car. The earlier, the better, because roads begin to get clogged with buses after 7 a.m. (give or take, depending on traffic). That's a pretty big ask of a friend, so, if you find a very generous soul who's willing to help you, you'd better return the kind favor after the race. Oh, and plan to walk a good mile or more once you get to Hopkinton. Even if you beat the rush, you'll likely be stopped by security well short of the starting line, necessitating a longer walk than your bus-riding competitors will be taking.

If you have a bib, you can chill out in the Athletes' Village. Nineteen times out of 20, it's an absolute blessing to have access to this runners' sanctuary, home to some much-appreciated complimentary amenities (e.g., water, Gatorade, bananas, bagels, energy bars, porta-potties, tents). The Achilles' heel of Athletes' Village is foul weather. If it's anything like 2018, the only place you'll want to be is indoors. A tent won't comfort you much from 30-mph winds, sideways rain, and freezing windchills. If the forecast is calling for horrible weather, do everything in your power to befriend a charity group or Hopkinton resident who can provide you with shelter.

Lastly, if you're a bandit, you're going to have to be wily. This shouldn't come as a shocker to you. After all, you're a bandit, so you'd better be innately cunning or you wouldn't consider sneaking into the greatest race in the world for free, right? That said, you're going to want to dial up your guile to "11" if the weather looks bleak. There's only one thing worse than being pummeled by Mother Nature with all of your bibbed friends in Athletes' Village, and that's roaming the streets of Hopkinton alone as you shiver and look for shelter.

CHAPTER 7

The Race

If you're running a "typical" marathon (i.e., a marathon with less challenging undulations), your race mantra should have three basic Cs:

1. Conserve—Miles 1–10: Conserve as much energy as possible.
2. Cruise—Miles 11–20: Lock into your goal pace and cruise as if you're on autopilot.
3. Compete—Miles 21–26.2: If you executed the first two Cs, now's when you'll be passing all of the runners who didn't.

Given Boston is unique, it may come as no surprise to learn that the typical race mantra needs to be adjusted. What might that look like? Look no further. Herein is your (nearly) foolproof Boston Marathon Race Mantra.

Write your mantra on your body with permanent marker so your increasingly woozy brain can't forget it. Sienna Berg

THE FOUR Cs

1. **Conserve**—Miles 1–6: Conserve as much energy as humanly possible. No weaving. No miles faster than goal pace. No "banking" time. Roads are congested and you're going downhill, so your well-tapered, carbo-loaded, finely tuned machine of a marathon body should feel like it's jogging. Jog and enjoy.

2. **Cruise**—Miles 7–15: This is where the course "flattens out" (code for "rolling hills," but nothing too egregious), so this is your golden opportunity to dial in your goal marathon pace and hit the "cruise control" button that you press in your dreams. Framingham, Natick, and Wellesley are beautiful. Go visit them before or after the race. On Marathon Monday, you cruise past them like a pilot preparing a cappuccino at 30,000 feet.

3. **Control**—Miles 16–21: Control your effort. You're on the Newton hills now, so it's important to run by "feel," not pace. Is your breathing labored? Dial it back a notch. Or are your legs enjoying using muscles you hadn't engaged before? Okay, then increase your tempo a skosh. Listen to your body, not your watch. There's no prize money for the "fastest up Heartbreak Hill," but there is a price to pay in Brookline if you fail to control your effort on your way to the summit.

4. **Compete**—Miles 22–26.2: Same drill as a typical marathon, but exponentially better or worse depending on how you executed the first three Cs. The final 5+ miles of the course are downhill and (potentially) fast. If you're not completely wrecked, you can finish the race far quicker than you imagined. Conversely, if negative voices are swirling in your head, the Citgo sign in the distance will seem like a cruel mirage.

SMILE FOR THE CAMERA(S)

Like most big-city marathons, Boston has race photographers situated pretty much everywhere on the course, waiting to immortalize you at your absolute best or worst (probably the latter). Your race pictures will look like your middle school photos in the 1970s, the ones where you have braces and blemishes and the photographer made you crane your neck until you looked like an alien.

The difference is, in your race photos you'll be in motion, caught in awkward poses, and wearing next to nothing. Awesome. Suffice it to say, you'll be shocked and appalled as you peruse your photos after the race, just like you were when you had to find the lesser of all evils from the proofs of your class photos.

I used to watch the Boston Marathon and wonder why runners put themselves through so much pain, then I became one of those runners and I now understand; the Boston Marathon is special because I thought I would be a "one and done" marathoner, but I was overcome by such a sense of exhilaration when I crossed the finish line that I haven't stopped chasing the physical and mental challenge/accomplishment, and in fact just completed my 29th marathon (in Boston).

Kate Kennedy
29 Marathons
14 Consecutive Boston Marathons

If you're chasing a PR, you'll likely be locked in to the task at hand (i.e., maintaining your goal marathon pace mile by mile); hence, you'll be oblivious to how many photographers there are and where they're situated. That's perfect. Whether you look fast or slow in a race photo won't help you PR. Your arbiter is the clock, not the camera.

But if you're running Boston for fun, you can be far more playful with the cameras. For starters, you'll need to make sure your bib is plainly visible on your chest. Not your shorts. Not your leg. Not (please say it's true you don't do this) your back. Your chest. The only way for race photographers and their AI-robot colleagues to sort through hundreds of thousands of photos and know which ones belong to you is by assembling all photos that match your bib number.

Next, you'll want to understand where the cameras are. This can vary year by year, but there are some areas where the odds are heavily in your favor. There are typically photographers' bridges at the 15k mark (adjacent to Lake Cochituate in Natick) and 30k mark (a half-mile before the Johnny Kelley statue in the Newton hills), so look up and smile at the photographers perched above you when you cross those checkpoints.

Two other camera spots that are unlikely to change are the right on Hereford Street and the left on Boylston Street. If you swing wide (away from the masses) and ham it up a bit (smile and perhaps flex your weary arms), you'll get the photographers' attention and have plenty of gems to choose from when you're sipping a celebratory beverage (or two, or more) and sifting through your photos.

There's no doubt you'll be in a rush to cross the finish line, but, before you do, take a moment to celebrate in your own unique way. Cameras will be drawn to you if you show a little enthusiasm. Whatever you do, do not have your head down and fiddle with your watch as you're crossing the finish line. That's like having your eyes closed for your high school senior picture. You'll have to look at those photos for the rest of your life.

Your chip will register your official net time. If you're that hyper-concerned about your Garmin or Strava data that you can't even celebrate your finish at, as said by a true Bostonian, the Boston friggin' Marathon, then you might have some issues you need to work out.

The "one mile to go" mark in Kenmore Square has become a camera hot spot, too. You're physically and mentally struggling, likely nauseous (to some degree), angry at the universe (because, why not?), and angry at yourself (because you actually chose to do this), but smile. You're almost at Hereford Street. Almost.

Back in the old days, runners could dress in elaborate costumes that attracted attention from a lot of cameras. You would be ambling through Welles-ley Square and be simultaneously passed by a lobster, Elvis, and Superman, click-ing off sub-seven-minute miles, side by side. In the wake of 2013's tragic events, Boston's tolerance of costumes has waned considerably, particularly bulky cos-tumes that cover the head and disguise the identity of the wearer. If you plan to don a costume of any sort, make sure you take a look at the latest version of the "B.A.A. Boston Marathon Rules and Policies" to ensure what you are wearing is allowable.

THE 10 COMMANDMENTS OF BOSTON MARATHON ETIQUETTE

Just because you've been running for a long time doesn't mean you're doing it right. So how do you know if you're doing it right at Boston? For starters, read the most recently updated version of the "B.A.A. Boston Marathon Rules and Policies." Yes, there are rules, policies, procedures, and guidelines that the B.A.A. states all Boston Marathon participants must "be knowledgeable of and abide by," so do yourself a favor and learn them, lest you do something egregious before, during, or after Marathon Monday.

The Boston Marathon holds a special place in my heart because it unites individ-uals from all corners of Boston and beyond, transcending differences and cele-brating a day steeped in rich history, lively energy, and deafening cheers.

Sumner Jones
10 Marathons
2 Ultramarathons
2 Boston Marathons

But, as is the case in any sport, rules and regulations in long-distance running are merely the skeleton of an elaborately complex organism. For example, in baseball, if you're up to bat with a 30 count and your team leading 13–1, you take ball four just off the outside corner, and you walk to first base, you might think you did your team a favor, right? Incorrect.

You'll understand why when your teammate batting behind you gets a 97-mph fastball thrown at his head. There are unwritten, unspoken rules, one of which is "If your team leads by 10 runs or more, you swing away on a 3–0 count if the ball is anywhere close to home plate." If you don't, your teammate behind you will get thrown at, and you likely will, too. That's not in the rule book. That's just how the game is played.

So it is with running, especially on running's brightest stage, the Boston Marathon. Unwritten rules. Oral code. Tradition. Convention. Etiquette. Call it whatever you want, but it's real. And you will learn it (or not), to your own benefit (or detriment).

So if it's not in the rules and regulations, how will you know? Behold, as established by historical precedent atop Heartbreak Hill and delivered to you in print to guide you in perpetuity:

#1—Thou Shalt Not Have Other Races Before Boston

Yes, there are other races and other marathons. And, yes, they occur before and after (and perhaps even during) the Boston Marathon. And, yes, there's no doubt that they are awesome and memorable in their own fantastic ways. But, Boston is well . . . umm . . . Boston.

Is there joy to be found on the Champs-Elysées at the Paris Marathon? Absolutely. Does running over the Verrazzano-Narrows Bridge with the Statue of Liberty to your left and the skyline of Manhattan in the distance at the New York City Marathon send chills up your spine? You bet. And passing through Brandenburg Gate in the homestretch at the Berlin Marathon is an adrenaline rush, too, right? Yep.

You can have a soft spot in your heart for one of them, some of them, or all of them. Just understand that they're part of a separate group. A really cool group. A group that includes some of the greatest road races and marathons in the world (Tokyo, London, Chicago, and more).

But your relationship with them will be very different than the one you share with Boston. That's okay. You're not doing anything wrong, nor are they. It's like when you greet a litter of puppies, and one runs toward you wagging its tail, and there's a special connection you share that you don't have with the others, no matter how amazing they are. That puppy with the happy tail and warm tongue is Boston.

#2—Thou Shalt Not Defile Thy Bib

When Bill Rodgers won the first of his four Boston Marathon titles in 2:09:55 in 1975, he looked like he was running a local 5k. And you could probably tell he wasn't if his race bib hadn't been folded into a tiny square on his chest, revealing nothing but the number "14." You couldn't tell if Rodgers was running the Boston Marathon or Michael Scott's Dunder Mifflin Scranton Meredith Palmer Memorial Celebrity Rabies Awareness Pro-Am Fun Run Race for the Cure.

Elites like Rodgers during the early running boom era will tell you that it was the "cool" thing to do to fold race bibs into the size of a cocktail napkin, partly for fashion purposes, but also because the tiny bibs didn't flop around on their tiny chests, and, perhaps most importantly, there weren't many rules governing what you could or couldn't do with your bib anyway. Modern bibs aren't just pieces of paper anymore. And bib defilement has escalated far beyond origami. Plenty of rules, guidelines, and general common sense govern "yah numbah;" hence the Second Commandment.

First, as it says in the rules, don't "cover, bend, fold, or cut" your official B.A.A. bib. It's no longer a cool thing to do (i.e., it's decidedly uncool and is grounds for disqualification). The B.A.A., Adidas, and lead sponsor (formerly John Hancock, now Bank of America) all occupy precious real estate on the bib and will not be pleased if their logos are compromised. Also, your contact and medical information reside on the back of the bib, so if it's illegible or gone, your life might be in jeopardy. If the possibility of unnecessary death isn't incentive enough, your timing chip is attached to the back of your bib, and it would be unfortunate to run the entire race and PR only to find your chip didn't register over any of the timing mats, including the finish.

Beyond wearing your bib improperly, there are several other ways to defile it that must be avoided. For example, never take a photo of your bib and place it on the internet (social media or otherwise). Thieves will photocopy your bib and wear it, resulting in a very awkward collection of race photos, namely half of the images being of some random criminal wearing an exact replica of your bib. Only the person assigned a bib is authorized to run with it.

Do not switch bibs with another runner, allow someone else to run with your bib, sell your bib to the highest bidder, or act as a "bib mule" for other runners. You will be disqualified from the race, and it's possible you'll be banned for life from all B.A.A. events going forward.

Take your selfies and group photos in front of, behind, or anywhere around the finish line, but don't tempt fate by mugging the camera atop the line. Heather Schulz

Wear your bib front and center on your chest. Do not dishonor the bib by wearing it on your back, displaying it on your shorts, folding it up in your pocket, or holding it in your hand. That number on your chest isn't random; that number is your hard-earned seed in the race. Oh, and your color-coded wave and corral information on the front of the bib needs to be readily accessed by race officials and volunteers throughout the day (boarding buses, entering Athletes' Village, slipping inside your proper corral, receiving your finisher's medal).

#3—Thou Shalt Not Cross Thy Finish Line Before Marathon Monday

It's so tantalizing. The Boston Marathon finish line, that sacred swath of pavement in front of the Boston Public Library, is like a magnet to runners, and its attraction is even stronger when it's freshly painted, surrounded by grandstands and press booths, and converged upon by runners across the globe on Patriots' Day weekend. But don't do it. Don't stand on it. Don't cross it. Save it for when it counts. Save it for Marathon Monday.

Can you take pictures alongside it? Sure. Can you pose in front of it? Yep. How about taking a majestic wide-angle photo from a distance on Boylston Street? Have at it. Just don't set foot on it. Or, more aptly put, set foot on it at your own risk.

When you're at the zoo, do you reach in the lion's den to pet the mane of the king of the pride? No, you don't. That's insane. You're way too concerned about losing a limb to even think about touching that luscious mane. And that's exactly how you should feel about the Boston Marathon's shiny finish line.

"What if you're a streaker and this is your 23rd straight Boston?" you ask? Can you take a picture on the finish line then? No. You can't. And it's really a moot question. Streakers with 22 Bostons under their belts aren't anywhere near the finish line. They're in their hotel rooms popping anti-inflammatories and stalking the weather.

If you want to tempt fate and any other karmic forces that exist in the world (juju, voodoo, sorcery, alchemy, whatever), then hop on that finish line, run over it, across it, and then stand smack dab on it and take a smiley picture on Friday, Saturday, Sunday, or, heck, all three (why not?). Just know you're breaking Commandment #3 when you do it. So whatever happens on race day, well, as they say in Boston, "that's on you, khed."

Vintage merch is the real flex on the streets of Boston. Sienna Berg

#4—Thou Shalt Not Wear Thy Swag or Merch Before Crossing the Finish Line

You know all of those athletes wearing their just-purchased official Adidas Boston Marathon jackets at the Expo? Similar to crossing the finish line before the race, wearing "year-of" merch is inviting all of the karmic evils that exist to &%$# up your Marathon Monday. Do you want that? No, you don't want that.

If you want to make a statement at the Expo, wear your tattered, salt-stained 1997 jacket (you know, the crusty orange one whose lining has disintegrated). That's a power move. Bonus points if you still have a T token (highly improbable, but very cool) or some unrecognizable food item (highly probable, but disgusting) in your pockets.

And what about those athletes wearing the swag shirt (the one you get for free in your participant bag at the Expo) at the starting line in Hopkinton? No. Please, no. Wearing your swag shirt on race day is like a baseball player mentioning to his pitcher in the dugout that he has a no-hitter before taking the field in the ninth inning. If you're going to ignore one of the greatest superstitions in all of road racing, you might as well just go out to Hopkinton on Sunday night and run the entire course at race pace as a "dress rehearsal." Either way, your PR dreams are "in the hoppah."

#5—Thou Shalt Not Commit Banditry

To bandit or not to bandit? That is the question. And the answer is no. Always no. You shouldn't bandit. "Boston bandits are legendary," you say. Yes, they are. "Boston was bandit-friendly for more than a century," you argue. Yes, also true. "Boston needs bandits. It isn't the same without them," you might implore. Yes, you're not wrong.

In a way, bandits built the Boston Marathon. Without bandits (many of whom were local college students, executives, or crossover athletes), the Greater Boston community wouldn't be woven into the fabric of the Boston Marathon as it is. Here's an example of The Circle of Boston Marathon Life:

- Age 7: Your legendary uncle Tommy runs as a bandit (1969).
- Age 20: You're a Boston College sophomore and run as a bandit on a dare (1982).
- Age 22: You stay in town to work after graduation (1984).
- Age 29: You become a Dana-Farber charity runner (1991).
- Ages 29–38: You raise more than $100,000 to eradicate cancer (1991–2000).

- Age 39: You get so fast you finally BQ (2001).
- Age 51: You have hip surgery and transition to pickleball (2013).
- Age 52: You pass the baton to your oldest daughter, who runs for Dana-Farber (2014).
- Age 61: You place your Boston Marathon medals in your granddaughter's nursery (2023).

And it all starts again.

Before charity running became a thing, banditing was the thing. Banditing was the seed from which grew concentric layers of the mighty Boston Marathon oak.

So that makes banditing okay, right? No, it doesn't. As many (necessary) cultural transformations have proven (including the addition of para-athlete and nonbinary divisions at Boston), just because something is a tradition doesn't make it morally or ethically right. And so it is with banditing. Hence, the Fifth Commandment has made it so.

#6—Thou Shalt Not Covet Thy Fellow Runner's Wave, Bib Number, PR, BQ, Gear, Mileage, Medals, Calves, or Anything Else

Unlike other marathons where you might greet a fellow numbered runner before the race and not know whether he or she is faster than you, the number on your chest at Boston doesn't lie. Your number is your seed in the race, but that doesn't mean you should envy the lower-numbered runners in the corrals and waves in front of you. Your number is unique to you just like your journey to Boston is unique to you.

One of the Boston Marathon's greatest treasures is the incredible camaraderie shared by its participants. Sure, you're an individual on a journey, but you're not running 26.2 miles alone. All of the athletes surrounding you have their own journeys, complete with their own challenges, injuries, doubts, niggles, insecurities, vices, and everything else that makes them human just like you. But the beauty is you're all in it together, especially at Boston, where you've all earned your right (via BQ or fundraising) to be there. Shared struggle builds unbreakable bonds. And whatever jealousy or resentment you may have had in your heads begins to melt away as you dig into your hearts and perform something epic in unison.

So stop ogling the things that aren't yours. A mind and heart filled with charity for others doesn't have room for anything else.

#7—Thou Shalt Honor Thy Race Officials, Spectators, and Volunteers

The intimate relationship you share with spectators at the Boston Marathon is unlike any other race on this earth. As former B.A.A. CEO Tom Grilk said best, "In Boston, everyone owns the marathon." Boston Marathon officials, spectators, and volunteers are models for races around the world and they pour their hearts and souls into the race, taking ownership of their respective roles in making the Boston Marathon special. Runners speak with reverence about the Boston Marathon, and their admiration is largely due to the people responsible for transforming an otherwise unassuming 26.2-mile stretch of pavement into the Super Bowl of road racing.

Running Boston without acknowledging the hard work of officials and volunteers or the unending enthusiasm of its spectators would be like sleepwalking through college and never thanking the professor responsible for changing the trajectory of your life.

You know the woman who was been standing in the rain on Boston Common for five hours to ensure you got on your bus to Hopkinton? She woke up before you did just to make your life easier. Or how about the gentleman who handed your bib to you at the Expo? He's been on his feet for 10 straight hours and still cracks a smile, takes your picture, and answers your questions to make your Boston Marathon experience special.

Remember in 2018 when the woman tied your shoe in Cleveland Circle because your hands were like two frozen bricks attached to your arms? Her hands were numb, too. Or what about 2012 when you were overheating in Natick and the handful of ice and Otter Pop given to you by a local middle-school student rejuvenated you? That interaction may inspire her to run Boston when she gets older.

Volunteers, like you, just want to participate in this awesome event. You might be in town for a PR. Volunteers are there for you.

Like athletes and volunteers, race officials share a deep respect for the race, its traditions, and the athletes who descend on Boston each spring. Impassioned race director Dave McGillivray is the most dedicated of all, setting the tone for officials before, during, and after the race. You may be amazed by Dave's (and his team's) enthusiasm and attention to detail for a few days over an extended weekend, but managing the Boston Marathon is a year-round labor of love.

So how do you honor all of these amazing people? Well, it's easier than you think. Throughout your extended Boston Marathon weekend, you'll have opportunities galore to honor race officials, spectators, and volunteers. It's okay to be hyper-focused on your PR. But you can be in full-on PR-chasing mode and still be respectful and gracious.

The Boston running community embraced Meb Keflezighi and Des Linden not just because they won Boston Marathon titles (2014 and 2018, respectively), but because they honor and adore the city as generously as it admires them. Carry yourself around the Expo and city streets like Meb and Des. Boston will open its arms to you, too.

#8—Thou Shalt Not Cheat

Committing this sin didn't work out too well for Rosie Ruiz in 1980, but sadly, cutting the course by hopping on the T is child's play compared to the numerous, innovative ways athletes can cheat to gain entries into Boston and improve their performances on Marathon Monday. Thankfully, timing mats and race photos make it more difficult for course cutters today, but criminal minds continue to push the envelope, necessitating the vigilance of the B.A.A. and honest athletes like you.

The lengths to which runners will go to qualify for Boston are beginning to look like they have no bounds. Since non-elites who aren't competing for money aren't blood-tested, one nefarious way to improve performance is do what disgraced cyclist Lance Armstrong did before he was caught and stripped of his Tour de France titles: repeated blood doping (i.e., removing blood, storing it, and then transfusing it back into the body) and using performance-enhancing drugs or PEDs (e.g., testosterone to improve recovery).

Injecting and transfusing substances into your body may seem ridiculous for non-elites, but the athletic world has gone a bit crazy, so crazy that your tuna-fish-at-his-desk-eating co-worker who just missed a BQ at CIM (the California International Marathon) in December might just be storing his red blood platelets next to his Lactaid in his refrigerator to BQ at Chicago next October. That's the level of absolute insanity we're at.

Even if the cheater isn't injecting himself or herself with God knows what, he or she still has myriad ways to stand next to you in Hopkinton. Another way to underhandedly get into your corral is to enlist the help of a "bib mule" who runs a qualifying race with the cheater's bib tucked (undetectable by photos) beneath a layer of clothing. A real-world equivalent of such chicanery would be if you nearly flunked out of law school before graduating and then enlisted the help of an attorney to pass the bar for you.

How many more ways are there to cheat? Infamous cheat Kip Litton invented an entire fictitious race just so he could "run" a sub-3 marathon. Some marathons have caught twins relaying a race to BQ. That's right, one twin would run a stretch, duck into a porta-potty, the other twin would emerge and eventually do the same, and, well, you know how a relay works.

Some USATF-certified courses (hence, BQ-able courses) have fewer timing mats than the Boston Marathon, and, unlike Boston, the courses are loop courses or meandering courses that traverse less territory, allowing cheaters to exit and enter the courses at will. These courses are perfect for cheaters. It's a solvable problem, but the onus must be shared by race officials and runners to protect the sanctity of road racing.

More subtle cheating occurs at Boston each year, too. For example, runners who are injured share bibs with runners who can finish the race on their behalf. It's tougher to pull off with race photos, but these cheaters dodge that bullet by instructing their co-conspirators to simply hide their bibs beneath a layer of clothing, hence no photos to call attention to their deceit.

It's frightening how simple course-cutting in the early years of the running boom has escalated to such villainous levels. And because the Boston Marathon requires a (very difficult to obtain) qualifying time or (also difficult to attain) fund-raising bogey, cheaters are particularly attracted to it, cutting corners to gain entry without doing the hard work.

It's hard to even fathom what might be next. Cheating is an affront to the integrity of the race, and it's up to the honest, commandment-abiding non-sinners to continue to identify cheaters who disrespect the sport in general and violate the sanctity of the Boston Marathon in particular. As they say on the T in Boston when you encounter something suspicious, "If you see something, say something." Justice takes a village. And everyone in the village, including you, has responsibility for maintaining law and order within it.

#9—Remember Patriots' Day, to Keep It Holy

Whether you're making the journey from Hopkinton to Copley Square, volunteering at Mile 15, or spectating in Cleveland Circle, one thing is true: The third Monday in April, Patriots' Day, will take on greater meaning for you.

There will be a day, alas, when Boston will keep going without you. That's life. It happened to Meb. It happened to Shalane Flanagan. It will happen to you. But that doesn't mean the third Monday in April will be any less special. The bond you share with the city and the event will stay with you, providing a lifetime of replayable good vibes. Mondays get a bad rap, but you'll find a way to set your beloved weekend-extending Marathon Monday apart from the far less memorable weekend-ending Mondays.

Remember Patriots' Day. Hold the memories and the feelings close to your heart. Reliving Boston is like listening to the one saved voicemail you have from your mother who passed away. It chokes you up, but you can't stop rewinding it to hear it again. Set it apart and keep it special.

#10—Thou Shalt Curse the Weather

It's what runners do. It's what Boston Marathoners do. The weather is so front and center at Boston that runners identify different years by the weather that plagued the event on race day. For example, if a runner says she ran in 2007 and 2012, you can sympathize instantly without her saying another word. The race was nearly canceled in 2007 due to a "wikkid nah'eastah," and temperatures reached a beastly 87 degrees F in 2012. That's hot.

The irony is that most Bostonians are stoically nonchalant about the wicked weather that defines their hometown. They deal with it year-round, so what seems "epic" to someone visiting from LA is just "Monday" to a New Englander. That might explain why neither snow nor rain nor heat nor gloom of any sort keeps locals away from lining the Boston Marathon course with enthusiasm every year.

The funny thing is weather, particularly bad weather, is so intertwined with Boston that even the relatively good weather years get criticized. After the "Perfect Chaos" of 2018, the 2019 race started in rain and ended in relative sunshine with temperatures in the upper 50s F to lower 60s F for the better part of the day. Is that perfect? Probably not. But looking at social media posts from some runners would lead you to believe they ran through a catastrophic tempest of biblical proportions. Clearly, the complainers hadn't participated the previous year, or they would be grateful for Mother Nature's mercy.

It's like the athletes who run in good-weather years are strangely jealous of the athletes who participate in the bad-weather Boston years. One very convenient reason for this envy is because bad weather is the perfect excuse for poor performance. Of course your massive positive split and complete collapse had nothing to do with you being undertrained or Boston's challenging course chewing you up and spitting you out. It was the weather's fault that you BQ'd with a 3:24-low on a REVEL ski slope course and ran 3:58:07 at Boston, right?

Boston's average high temperature in mid-April is 55 degrees F, and its average low temperature is 42 degrees F, a pretty dreamy range for marathoners. So why is it so popular to curse Boston's weather? Well, one reason is because the course stretches 26.2 miles from Hopkinton (inland) to Boston (on the water). Bostonians know that it can snow two feet near I-495 in Hopkinton while it's raining politely in Boston. The weather patterns are significantly different, which creates a little havoc, especially if storms are coming and going on- and offshore on race day.

Can Boston weather ever be perfect? Yes. Yes, it can. Runners in 1975 and 2011 will tell you that not only were temperatures nearly ideal (mid-50s F), but tailwinds (25mph west) were persistent all day. So, as a rule, bank on ideal conditions twice in roughly 50 years. The odds (4 percent chance) aren't in your favor to have Mother Nature completely on your side. But, hey, that's Boston.

So go ahead. Curse the weather. You have a number on your chest. You've earned the right.

CHAPTER 8

Post-Race

Congratulations! You've finished the Boston Marathon. You are one of less than 1/1000 of 1 percent of people in the history of the world who can claim they've finished the race since its beginning in 1897. Whoa.

Bliss is a reclusive emotion, but you'll find it at the finish on Boylston Street.
Rachel Anderson

CROSSING THE FINISH LINE

So, now that you're essentially a superhero among mortals, what do you do after you've crossed the finish line? Unlike Chicago, where you can kick back and sprawl your limbs in every direction over the inviting manicured lawns of Grant Park, Boston more or less shepherds you away from Copley Square. It seems a little abrupt in the moment, but it's actually partly out of necessity (there's not enough space for everyone in Copley Square) and partly a blessing in disguise (you really should shower and move on with your day).

When you cross the finish line, the medical tent is to your immediate right, directly in front of Trinity Church in the reflection of the glass of 200 Clarendon, the former John Hancock Tower. You really can't miss it, but you'll likely be full-on wonky at this point, so enlist the help of the legion of volunteers if you need them. Inside the medical tent, you'll have unlimited access to medical professionals, physical therapists, and sports massage therapists who are there to nurse you back to health, including getting you to one of Boston's nearby world-class hospitals if you need one.

If you think you can manage without immediate medical attention, follow the lead of volunteers and proceed forward on Boylston Street, where you'll be greeted by offers of more water, Gatorade, and the usual post-race fare of bananas, energy bars, and potato chips. It's important that you don't linger too close to the finish, because more and more athletes are finishing behind you. Besides, continuing to move (shuffling, walking, whatever you can muster) is important for your recovery. One of the best things you can do after finishing a marathon is to continue walking to allow your heart rate to come down gradually as it returns to its resting rate. So keep moving forward.

But don't make too much haste. This is your moment to take it all in for a hot second and savor the fruits of your labor. Revel in the majesty of the place that opened its arms to Johnny Kelley 58 times, christened "Boston Billy" and "Catherine the Great," rejoiced in the freezing rain with Des, and celebrated with Meb and Dick and Rick Hoyt.

Congratulate fellow runners. Thank officials and volunteers. Pose for the photographers. Drape your complimentary Mylar blanket around your shoulders. Your body temperature will plummet pretty precipitously now that you're no longer running. Don't worry. Volunteers will swaddle you and tape your blanket together to keep it secure.

Show your bib to the volunteers and they will place your well-earned finisher's medal around your salt-stained neck. Unless you feel your physical well-being is in danger (in which case you shouldn't have bypassed the medical tent), take

Don't cry because it's over. Smile because it happened.

advantage of every photo opportunity you can. Some will have official B.A.A. Boston Marathon backdrops; others will just be candid photos with random runners and the splendor of Boston's Back Bay over your shoulder.

The photos where you're finished and smiling will likely look far better than your RBFs at Miles 18, 20, and, well, pretty much anything during and after Newton, and those smiles will be priceless (and may even inspire your children, grandchildren, and great-grandchildren to run) in years to come.

As you continue to make your way down Boylston Street, you'll eventually have to make a right turn toward the bag-drop pickup area, where you'll be reunited with all the wonderful items you packed. It's perfectly acceptable to grab your bag and move along or just have at it and start changing into your delightfully soft, loose-fitting clothes straightaway. Discretion isn't high on the priority list when you're borderline hypothermic and your chafed skin is bleeding through your sports bra. What happens in bag-drop pickup stays in bag-drop pickup.

Now that you have your medal and your personal effects, you can focus your efforts on making your way back to wherever you came from (home, hotel, friend's house, or otherwise), preferably while avoiding stairs and anything else daunting (e.g., curbs). Volunteers encourage you (albeit politely) to exit the area. So it's best to take their hints, get yourself to a hot shower, and commence part two of your day, the celebration.

CELEBRATING

Much like the diverse choices you had when you were considering where to carbo-load, your selection of post-race ways to celebrate can go a wide variety of directions. What does victory taste like to you? Do you want a white-tablecloth, high-end experience? How about an awesome burger at a local watering hole? Or, if celebratory beverages are top-of-mind, how about a tour of a local brewery? Are you getting together with friends, kicking back with family, or going out on the prowl like Alberto Tomba in the Olympic Village? Regardless of how you define "celebration," Boston has you covered.

The Boston Marathon is a mirror reflection of your entire running journey, with a destination you get to celebrate in real time.

Nick Renfro
10 Marathons
2 Boston Marathons

For starters, let's address the elephant in the room and answer the question "Is it appropriate to wear your finisher's medal after you shower?" The answer is "yes." Naysayers would argue it's tacky and you're clamoring for attention. Those are solid opinions, but here's the bottom line on this matter: This is your one chance to wear it.

Most runners lose 2–3 percent of their body weight during a marathon. That means if you weighed 185 pounds in Hopkinton, it's likely you'll arrive in Copley Square beneath 180 pounds. Counterintuitively, the faster you finish, the more weight you lose on a percentage basis. But whether you finish in slightly more than two hours (Kelvin Kiptum's world record is 2:00:35 and the Boston course

Boston Marathon Medal Etiquette

There's an unwritten "day-of rule" with medal wearing: Upon the stroke of midnight (unless you're still celebrating), your medal will go to its rightful home (shining in a display case, hanging from a hook on a wall with its siblings, never seeing the light of day again in a drawer, gathering dust in your garage), anywhere but around your neck.

Can you break the rule? Yes, under one condition; if a bare-chested Mark Spitz rings your doorbell and offers to re-create his iconic poster with you, put on your medals and snap the picture together. Then, you and Mark will take off your medals, put on your shirts, shake hands, and move on with your lives.

So go ahead, wear your medal (or don't), get out the door, and explore Boston. Move quickly. Seriously. Chances are, if you get too comfortable indoors, you'll be too tired to rally and celebrate. You'll find yourself curled up in your comforter on your bed, surrounded by completely empty room service dishes, a half-empty beer, ibuprofen, and the remote control (or, as said correctly in Boston, "the clickah"). That sounds pretty cozy, but it's hardly the best way to celebrate your epic fabulousness, right?

record is Geoffrey Mutai's 2:03:02 in 2011) or just shy of six hours (the official Boston Marathon cutoff is 6:00:00, or six hours after the last athlete crossed the start), eating a hearty, nutritious meal after the race should be atop your list of priorities.

If you have your heart set on celebratory cocktails, delay that part of your celebration until you've fortified yourself. You're going to crash hard if you don't have a solid base of carbs and wholesome food.

Are you craving iron, red meat, white tablecloths, and your water glass refilled in a timely fashion? Excellent. Replenish your exhausted muscles with an incredible steak and some decadent sides at the following top-shelf Boston steakhouses: Grill 23 (161 Berkeley Street), Abe & Louie's (793 Boylston Street), Capital Grille (900 Boylston Street), Ruth's Chris (45 School Street), Boston Chops (1375 Washington Street), Ocean Prime (140 Seaport Boulevard), Strip (64 Arlington Street), or Del Frisco's (888 Boylston Street). Bon appétit.

Are you yearning for comfort food and could care less whether or not you have a tablecloth and when or if your water glass is refilled (because you brought your own)? Fantastic. Recharge your depleted brawn with a mouthwatering burger, or choose from an array of feel-good fare at the following local mainstays:

Craigie on Main and Alden & Harlow (853 Main Street and 40 Brattle Street in Cambridge, respectively, but worth the trip across the Charles), Sonsie (327 Newbury Street), Moonshine 152 (152 Dorchester Avenue), Contessa (3 Newbury Street), Hojoku (1271 Boylston Street), Back Bay Social Club (867 Boylston Street), or the Capital Burger (159 Newbury Street). Dig in.

If you didn't procure tickets to a Red Sox game, then consider attending the "Mile 27 Boston Marathon Post-Race Celebration" at Fenway Park (typically 6:30 p.m. to 10 p.m.). As a Boston Marathon participant, you can purchase an inexpensive ticket (additional tickets for friends and family can be purchased separately, and admission is free for children under 12). You'll be treated to live entertainment, concessions, ample beverages (Samuel Adams Boston Brewery is the lead sponsor), and access to the warning track (weather permitting). So if you're chomping at the bit to tell anyone and everyone exactly how you crushed Boston (or Boston crushed you), the Mile 27 event is the perfect place to find empathetic ears.

WHAT TO DO BEFORE YOU LEAVE

It's not uncommon for Boston Marathon participants to finish the race, make a beeline to Logan Airport, and then take afternoon flights back home. Many go straight from the finish to the airport without showering. If you're one of those athletes, your apology game best be strong. You will be writhing like a Cirque du Soleil contortionist to get your cramping legs comfortable in your seat, and the smells emanating from your sweat-stained skin and funky race kit will make you the scourge of the entire plane. There are plenty of horrible seatmates you can have on a plane, and you are now one of them. Congratulations.

Leaving in such haste seems poorly planned, especially to Bostonians, who tend to forget that Patriots' Day isn't a holiday in other parts of the world. But Marathon Monday is, indeed, a Monday (i.e., a workday) and most humans need to take care of business Monday afternoon and get back to their jobs by Tuesday morning.

If you're among the quick to leave, do yourself a massive favor and go to Flour Bakery (131 Clarendon Street, a stone's throw from the Boston Marathon finish line) and grab a box of treats (carrot cake, cookies, muffins, homemade Pop-Tart–like creations, Boston cream pie, and much more). If you're on the fence whether the Boston Marathon race experience has inspired you to run it again, Flour's baked goods will tip the scales in Boston's favor. And if you want to make amends for your sweaty funkiness, share Flour treats with fellow travelers in close proximity on the plane. All will be forgiven. Guaranteed.

If you're not on a quick flight out of Boston minutes after crossing the finish line and you haven't seen the Red Sox play yet, then you really should try to catch the Tuesday night game at Fenway to get the full-on, swaying-with-the-crowd-singing-"Sweet Caroline" Boston vibes.

It's one thing to hear the roar of the crowd and smell the beer and hotdogs when you're running on Beacon Street and quite another to hold court in the inner sanctum of baseball's most storied ballpark, yelling like a drunken sailor, doing the wave, and belting out a song like you're at a an open-air karaoke rave.

The Red Sox often wear special "Boston Strong" yellow and blue uniforms, and the winners of the prior day's race often throw out the first pitch(es), giving the whole game a Boston Marathon love-fest feel. So if you're looking to do that one thing that will endear you to Boston even more than you thought possible, get thee to Fenway Tuesday night.

CHAPTER 9

Now What?

You went to places, literally (like floating on a duck boat on the Charles) and figuratively (like the depths of your soul at Mile 24.5) you had never experienced and perhaps didn't even know existed. So many emotions. So much grit. All in an extended weekend. Outrageous. But you're home now. And you're probably icing your sore quads and wondering "now what?"

Your answer can send you down several different life paths. Let's explore a few alternatives so, as you ponder your next move, you orient yourself properly to ensure you at least set off in the direction you intend to go.

My favorite memory of my three Boston Marathons is the people; everyone is so supportive, screaming my name on my T-shirt and cheering for me running down Boylston Street towards the finish . . . it's the ultimate runner's high!

Tim McLean
8 Marathons
3 Boston Marathons

POST-RACE BLUES

Nobody wishes to slip into a dark depression after accomplishing something so meaningful, but sometimes you can't fully control what you're feeling (physically, mentally, or emotionally). If you undergo a post-race X-ray that proves you fractured your tibia, you would rest, heal, and rehabilitate before considering running again, right? When you suffer a physical injury, the path ahead is pretty straightforward (even if you may not follow it as prescribed). But what happens if the trauma is mental or emotional? That's trickier. What does that path look like?

Post-race depression is a real possibility. There's no stigma when you sustain a physical injury. So why is it taboo to discuss your well-being when you're mentally or emotionally hurt? After devoting four intense months (give or take) and reshaping your life to achieve a goal, you will leave Boston both euphorically supercharged but oddly depleted. It's okay. In fact, it's normal. After the highs of celebrating the accomplishment of such an important life goal, you're bound to crash a bit as you reenter your regular life, especially when one of your coping mechanisms, running, has been (temporarily) stripped from your daily means of relieving stress and improving your mental health.

If you feel overwhelmed and incapable of navigating your way through this dark time, you should seek help from medical and psychological professionals. You don't have to struggle alone. Another avenue available is to speak with fellow Boston Marathoners. Chances are they are experiencing many of the same feelings (positive and negative) as you, and it will be cathartic for you to externalize rather than suppress them.

Reversing your downward spiral begins with unpacking the "baggage" you're carrying home from the race. It's hard to move on to your next goal, regardless of what it is, when you have yet to unburden yourself from the heaviness resulting from your last one.

So how do you shake off your malaise? In the short term, one undebatable truth is you've freed up a significant amount of time and energy that you can now pour into something other than running tempos on tired legs, exhausting yourself on weekend long runs, and laundering copious loads of noxious running clothes. Pick up that book you've wanted to read. Get started on that hobby you've considered. Let your friends know you don't have to miss wine club anymore. Learning something new or reconnecting with friends are both great ways to lift your spirits and get you in a better frame of mind to kick-start your next move.

Do you know reason #6,324 why the Boston Marathon is amazing? It's spring, baby! That's right. Unlike fall marathons where you have to navigate the post-race blues while days shrink, cold air and winter settle in, and everything begins to turn gray, the Boston Marathon finishes just as days lengthen, trees and flowers bloom, and life in Technicolor reappears. Opt outside and soak up some sunshine, an incredible source of vitamin D (a proven antidepressant).

BUCKET LIST

It's quite possible that running a marathon (or, specifically, the Boston Marathon) was on your "bucket list" (the list of experiences you hope to achieve during your lifetime). If so, rejoice in checking the box. You will forever be a Boston Marathoner. Nobody can take that away.

To commemorate your milestone, you might want to consider a display case to showcase your finisher's medal and least-awkward race photo. You'll get plenty of mileage from sharing war stories from your Boston Marathon experience, but pointing to your medal on the wall adds a degree of validation to your words. It's not that your friends and colleagues don't trust you, but exhibiting proof separates you from the legions of fraudsters who say they've run marathons and haven't or say they've run marathons faster than they have.

MAYBE AGAIN

Many "bucket listers" are on the fence about whether they want to be "one and done" or whether they want to give the marathon (or the Boston Marathon) another try. As Olympic gold medalist (1972), silver medalist (1976), and marathon legend Frank Shorter said best, "You have to forget your last marathon before you try another. Your mind can't know what's coming." That is painfully true. It's difficult to sign up for your next marathon when your legs are "jacked up" from the damage they endured in your first go-round.

But a common fallacy of bucket-list marathoners is that once you run a marathon, you've "experienced" the marathon and there would be nothing new to experience if you were to run another. That is wildly untrue. As Boston Marathon streakers would be happy to share, no two Boston Marathons are ever the same. Sure, the course remains the same. But everything else changes. From the "Run for the Hoses" in 1976 to the "Duel in the Sun" in 1982 to the "Perfect Chaos" of 2018, the only thing that remains constant at the Boston Marathon is change.

My 46-year Boston consecutive finish streak (1974–2019) was inspired by the chance sighting of a fellow Artist Diploma student at the New England Conservatory finishing Boston in 1972, whereafter Boston became my annual rite of spring; and while a price was paid for this lifelong obsession, at age 80, with every mile of the course emblazoned in my memory, I feel great pride in the legacy of founding and directing for the past 22 years the exclusive Quarter Century Club.

Ronald Kmiec
92 Marathons and 10 Ultramarathons
46 Consecutive Boston Marathons
Founder, Boston Marathon Quarter Century Club

If you ran in the gray and ominous nor'easter of 2007, your experience would be quite different from the blazing sun and relentless heat of 2012. But it's not just the external factors like the weather that make each Boston different. "How" you arrive in Hopkinton affects your year-by-year race experience and performance more than the weather. Are you newly married? Divorced? Are you sleep-deprived because you just had children? Are you stressed in your last semester of graduate school? Are you unemployed? Did you just get married? Are you in the middle of a move? We humans can put up with plenty of inclement weather, but it's hard to run your best if your mind and heart aren't in the right place when you're standing in your corral on Marathon Monday.

If you BQ'd at Boston, it will be difficult to say "no" the forthcoming year. It's just so darn tempting to register and do it again. And then once you do it twice, you have a nascent little streak going, so it's hard to jump off the bus once you've said "yes" twice and the wheels are in motion for a third. But we're getting ahead of ourselves.

If you're thinking "maybe again" after your first Boston Marathon, you'll have five months until registration opens for the following year. Take the time to think through what's really important in your life and whether running again is a commitment you're willing to make. You have a taste of what it's like (pre-dawn runs, doubles, sacrificing time with family and friends, injuries), now picture doing that all over again. Is it worth it? That's your call. Boston will always be there for you when the answer is "yes." That's after you BQ or commit to raising significant money for a charity, of course.

STREAKING

The B.A.A. considers any athlete who has 10 consecutive official Boston Marathon finishes to be a "streaker." That may be the B.A.A.'s definition, but we all know streaking doesn't start at race number 10; streaking starts with the decision to run your second straight Boston. Once you have two in the bank, then you need to recommit each year to keep the streak alive. To be clear, year after year, that's never an easy "yes."

For starters, you'll need to BQ each year or run with a charity. Neither is easy. If you're hoping to BQ year after year, you may well be thrown a curve (e.g., extreme heat, injury) in April that will necessitate that you BQ at an early-fall marathon before the September Boston Marathon registration window opens. That may not work out as planned, especially if you're thrown another curve. And without a BQ, you'll have to run with a charity to keep your streak alive.

If you've never raised $10,000 or more in relatively short order, it's about as easy as running a PR. Not only are you tapping into the pockets of family, friends, and your immediate social network, but there are thousands of charity runners (roughly 6,000 in a field of 30,000, to be precise) who are all out on the streets of Boston and beyond raising money on behalf of their charities, too. So you're more or less competing with them to raise funds, making your task a skosh more challenging (akin to running that aforementioned PR on a not-so-ideal weather day).

Streaking across the quad can't hold a candle to streaking at Boston. Heather Schulz

When you're a streaker who runs for charity, you're reaching into the pockets of your family, friends, and network every year. From the point of view of the generous people donating their money to your cause, your yearly money grab polarizes them into two general camps: Either a.) you're a benevolent saint of a human who they're more than happy to support each year, or b.) you've become a bit of a nuisance asking for money each year, leaving your supporters wondering if the relationship you share has become a bit one-sided.

The problem is the charity runner doesn't know which camp the money is coming from, making the yearly fundraising a touch more stressful and the annual "ask" increasingly awkward, especially if the relied-upon yearly supporter finally says "no." Should Uncle Jim donate $500 like he did last year, or should he allocate his money toward the dental work he's been putting off? And what about those dozen or so corporate clients that have been reliably donating? What happens when you stop doing business, or, even worse, they all turn to you at once to raise money for them?

So streaking at the Boston Marathon is far more difficult than streaking at the Flying Pig Marathon in Cincinnati or your local 5k. Just because you want to streak doesn't mean your legs are fast enough or your network has pockets deep enough to ensure you can continue the streak that you start. That said, there is incredible camaraderie among Boston Marathon streakers, especially those who live in the Greater Boston community.

Streakers get to know one another and have implicit respect for each other. If you streak, you gain entry into a unique fraternity. And when you stop, your kinship doesn't go away. Your "membership" never expires. The question you'll face is whether or not the repeated sacrifices you'll be making are worth it. Depending on your response, you'll know whether or not lacing up makes sense. No one else can answer that question. That's on you.

WORLD MAJORS

If you finished Boston and you find yourself itching to run another marathon, a natural place to turn is to consider another one of the "Abbott World Marathon Majors" (abbreviated AbbottWMM, six of the largest and most renowned marathons in the world). Boston, Chicago, New York, London, Berlin, and Tokyo comprise the current list of big-city, destination marathons that deliver unforgettable experiences in their own unique ways.

Not only do you get to explore and enjoy some of the most impressive cities and noteworthy courses in the world, but you can work toward earning the highly coveted Six Star Medal, honoring the runners who complete all six majors. In addition to earning this impressive piece of hardware, you will be added to the Six Star Finishers' Hall of Fame, a database of all of the runners in history across the globe who have officially completed all six World Marathon Majors. That's pretty cool.

50 STATES

If you've been bitten by the marathon bug but world travel and streaking aren't your things, then you may want to meander your way around the United States with an eye toward finishing a marathon in all 50 states. It wasn't too long ago that marathons didn't even exist in every state, but times have changed, and now an ever-growing number of runners are tackling (or have already tackled) the 50-state challenge.

Marathoners who are racing marathons are hard-pressed to run more than two marathons a year. The body needs time to recover from hard efforts, especially when you redline and attempt to PR. Some would argue racing just one marathon per year is optimal.

So attempting to run 50 marathons in relatively short order (unless you're okay with the process taking 25 to 50 years) requires a shift in mindset from "racing" for PRs to "running" for enjoyment. If you're not okay with the clock above your head at the finish line reading a number that is far slower than your best, then the 50-states pursuit might not be for you. But if quantity is more important than quality, then start plotting your road trips or accruing frequent flyer miles straightaway.

SEVEN CONTINENTS

So you thought traveling the globe to run all six Abbott World Marathon Majors or hoofing around the United States to run marathons in all 50 states is challenging? Well, yes, they are. But if you're looking for something even tougher, you might want to entertain the idea of running a marathon on every continent. Or, even better, what if you ran seven marathons on seven continents in seven days? Mind blown, right? Well, it's a thing. And if you'd like, with a little bit of time and a significant amount of discretionary income, you can do it, too.

Who knew Boston was a gateway race to such insanity? You cross the finish line, think you can scratch "Boston Marathon" off your bucket list, and move on with your life, right? But, no. Here you are thinking crazy thoughts like running a marathon on every continent. You do know Antarctica is a continent, don't you? And the average air temperature in Antarctica ranges from -14 degrees F in January to -71 degrees F in September. Yes, those are negatives. And Antarctica is the windiest continent on earth, so windchill temperatures are dramatically lower. By comparison, the savage conditions in Antarctica make the "Perfect Chaos" of the 2018 Boston Marathon look like an idyllic spring day.

The World Marathon Challenge is the only annual event that delivers the opportunity to run seven marathons on seven continents in seven days. Not only do you have to run all seven marathons within 168 hours, but you have to travel from Novo (Antarctica) to Cape Town (Africa) to Perth (Australia) to Dubai (Asia) to Madrid (Europe) to Fortaleza (South America) to Miami (North America), making the logistical challenge as daunting as the physical challenge.

But, hey, if your heart is yearning for exotic endeavors in faraway places, you have proven your mettle on the roads of Greater Boston. You're ready to leave the nest. Go forth and conquer.

CHAPTER 10

Beyond Boston

There comes a time in your running career when you must leave the streets of Boston to the footsteps of others. Whether you're a one-timer, streaker, or anything between, you'll come to the conclusion that the next chapter of your life won't include the Boston Marathon.

You may continue running. You may not. You may even run more marathons, just not the Boston Marathon. The allure of different surfaces and distances may be calling you. Or maybe swimming, tennis, or mountain biking is in your future. No matter your reasoning, the Boston Marathon is fondly in your rearview, so what's next? What does life after Boston look like? Well, the sky's the limit. Take your deep reservoirs of determination and newfound grit in new, exciting directions. Here are a few suggestions to get you started.

OTHER MARATHONS

The Boston Marathon may well be the "Mount Everest" of road racing, but that doesn't mean there aren't plenty of other mountains to climb. Thanks to the running boom and resulting proliferation of races around the world, marathons are everywhere.

Do you want to run a marathon along the Great Wall of China? It sounds outrageous, but you can do it. Can you imagine how cool it would be to run the original marathon course that ends in Athens, Greece? Well, thanks to the Athens Classic Marathon (also known as "The Authentic"), you can do that, too. Have you heard of the Loch Ness Monster? You can take your smartphone and run the Loch Ness Marathon along the famous loch and try to capture a photo of Nessie if you'd like.

If you were in the habit of running the Boston Marathon year after year, your Boston buildup prohibited you from considering a lot of fun spring marathons. Late April's Big Sur International Marathon along the picturesque Pacific coast in California is a perfect example of what you've been missing. No one is going to say the Boston Marathon course is ugly. It isn't. It has its own unique charm. But charm and striking beauty are quite different, and Big Sur has the latter in bunches.

A world of adventure awaits you after you've chased your last unicorn.

If you'd like to turn back the hands of time, you can start and finish the Rome Marathon in front of the Colosseum. Yes, that Colosseum, the one that was completed in 80 CE and hosted animal hunts and gladiator fights. Whoa.

Or what about racing Tanzania's Kilimanjaro Marathon in March in the shadow of the world's highest freestanding mountain? Or running alongside camels in

January in the International Marathon of Marrakesh in Morocco? Or racing the Kieser Marathon on legendary Great Ocean Road along the southern shores of Australia, home of those cuddly koalas and gnarly surfers? Yep, you guessed it. Now that Boston is in your rearview mirror, you can spread your wings and do all of those, too.

MUT RUNNING

What do you do when the PRs you're chasing on the roads are no longer beatable? If your last Boston Marathon was a 3:44-high in near-perfect conditions and your 3:18-low PR at Berlin seven years ago is looking increasingly untouchable, you may have to "redefine" your relationship with running. One interpretation worth considering is to reformulate the surfaces and distances you run so you have new challenges in front of you (even though your road PRs are behind you). Say "hello" to your new friend, MUT (mountain, ultra, trail) running, a relationship filled with promise and opportunity.

The life cycle of a distance runner most often begins with school-sponsored track and cross-country races. Efforts are focused on improving PRs at distances on the track (both indoor and outdoor). Even fall cross-country is more or less a strength-building training cycle for athletes seeking to run faster on ovals over the winter, spring, and summer. Upon graduation, only the fleetest of foot are able to continue to chase PRs on the track via various pro contracts and sponsorships. But even the professionals eventually plateau, necessitating a transition from the track to the roads. And when PRs on the roads hit the wall, a natural progression for many is to change distances and surfaces again, seeking solace in MUT running.

The USATF recognizes MUT as a category that includes a diverse array of events (e.g., shorter races that go straight up mountains, trail races, 24-hour challenges, and 100-mile ultras). If you're one of those runners who always enjoyed hills, MUT is for you. If you always preferred cross-country over track, MUT is for you. If you enjoy hiking and traversing technical terrain, MUT is for you. And if you ever finished a marathon and thought to yourself, "I wish I could keep going," MUT is your cup of tea.

No matter how or why you arrive at MUT, it will provide you with a smorgasbord of opportunity to challenge yourself, satisfy your competitive spirit, and chase new goals. And if you thought camaraderie among road racers was strong, the MUT community is tight and wildly supportive of one another. Bonding among athletes in the parking lot of a local 5k creates lasting friendships. Can you imagine the level of bonding that occurs among competitors at the Barkley

Marathons, the legendary 100-mile ultra with more than 54,000 feet of "vert" that is so challenging that it often ends without finishers?

AGE-GROUP DOMINATION

What do you do when your road racing PRs are in the rearview but running up and down mountains on technical terrain sounds like a fate worse than retirement from running altogether? No problem. Welcome to the world of Masters running, where you will attempt age-group domination. Sure, PRs were nice, but chasing a time on a clock isn't nearly as fulfilling as chasing other humans your age so you can tower above them on the finishers' podium, right?

It's nice to get a finisher's medal, but every participant gets that bling. And even though winning the race outright (i.e., the Open division) might be a bit of a stretch now that you're 60, you can still win hardware by taking aim at the age-group podium. All you have to do is seek and destroy everyone (give or take one or two) who's roughly your age and, voilà, you're a medalist. You may not breast the tape at the finish line (only the winners of the Open division get that luxury), but there is an addictive rush to crossing the line and knowing that no one else your age crossed before you.

The tricky thing about age-group domination is it's often difficult to discern who is actually in your age group. You may recognize the faces of your usual competitors at the local 5k, but it's a bit of a guessing game at less familiar and larger races.

You've probably felt disheartened when you're passed in the homestretch by someone you believe is in your age group. It's a helpless, sinking feeling. But that dismay can be wonderfully transformed into elation when you see the race results and realize he or she is in an age group younger than yours. Not only can you breathe a sigh of relief, but you can rejoice in knowing the runner who looks your age is actually aging more quickly than you. That's a beautiful bonus to an already positive outcome.

The joys of age-group domination are endless. And, as a rule, the older you get, the fewer competitors you'll have in your age group. The key is to stay healthy as you age up, which is far easier said than done. Speed and talent won't do you much good if you're not durable enough to withstand the test of time.

AGE-GRADED RACING

If you think age-group domination is fun, just wait until you get hooked on age-graded racing. Age grading is a way to compare all of your past and present performances as well as the performances of all runners, regardless of age or gender. Each gender has an "ideal" time for every age, and your time is "age-graded" (i.e., your time is calculated as a percentage of the ideal time).

Your age-graded time allows you to compare your performance against other runners' performances even though they may be different ages and genders. The higher the percentage, the superior the performance. Even better, performances in races of different lengths can be compared to one another, too. For example, you may have thought your 2:47:05 Chicago Marathon (age-graded = 2:43:03, or 76.61 percent of the age standard of 2:08:00) when you were 40 years old was your best race ever, but it turns out your 18:31 in last weekend's local 5k at age 55 is far more impressive (age-graded = 15:33, or 81.16 percent of the age standard of 15:02).

As if ranking your own performances throughout your lifetime isn't fun enough, you can use age-graded times to compare your performances to other runners' performances, regardless of what race they ran or where they ran it. That's pretty cool. So, let's say you ran a 10k in 38:25 in Lincoln, Nebraska, and your bragging college roommate who ran the Paris Marathon in 3:10:27 has bet you a new pair of carbon-plate racers that his performance is better. Who's right? Well, if you're both 48 years old, your age-graded 34:09 (78.64 percent) crushes his age-graded 2:53:39 (71.93 percent).

According to the World Association of Veteran Athletes or WAVA (the world governing body for Masters track and field, long-distance running, and race walking), here's a general idea of how your age-graded time (expressed as a percentage of the age standard) stacks up against the rest of the running world:

>100%   Congratulations, you've just set a new world standard for your age.
100%   You've matched the world standard for your age.
>90%   World class
>80%   National class
>70%   Regional class
>60%   Local class

So, even though your actual finish times may get slower as you get older, you still can remain competitive and deliver your best performance of your lifetime long after your PR days are behind you. And if you find yourself in one of the categories above, you can parlay your intangible age-graded prowess into some tangible age-group hardware.

TRIATHLONS

If you've been running for decades, you likely have weathered dozens of injuries and niggles that have made you question whether there's a healthier way to achieve fitness than simply running. Overuse injuries accrue when you do too much of one activity repeatedly, a habit befalling the lion's share of runners. We've always heard too much of a good thing can be a bad thing, but we runners are a stubborn lot. So, what do you do when your durable, marathon-running body proves to be more fragile than you'd prefer? You transition to triathlons, of course.

Perhaps you swam competitively in your youth or were always jealous of those cyclists who serpentine their way up and down the Pyrenees in the Tour de France. Perhaps you just want a new challenge, one that tests you like you've never been tested before. Perhaps your legs are riddled with running-related maladies and you know the addition of two other disciplines (swimming and cycling) will force you to heal your weakened areas, strengthen neglected areas, and emerge (at least in theory) healthier. The greener pasture of triathlon looks so darn inviting no matter how you arrive at it.

It seems counterintuitive to believe that adding more training (hence more stress on your body) to your daily regimen will help you heal, but participating in two non-weight-bearing disciplines (swimming and cycling) provides your muscles, tendons, and connective tissues with a break from running's incessant pounding. You may even find that less running (coupled with cross-training) provides an unforeseen benefit: You become a faster runner.

You're probably no stranger to the expression "variety is the spice of life." Well, triathlon triples the fun, allowing you to pick and choose workouts across disciplines rather than throw on your shoes for yet another run. You may have been bored on occasion when running, but your new triathlon routine will provide you with the opportunity to mix it up and satiate your desire for adventure.

And if you thought the toys you got during the holidays were fun when you were a kid, just wait until you're an adult triathlete: multisport smartwatches, power meters, swim goggles, helmets, and more. Did you know the bike you rode in grade school probably weighed as much as you (ballpark 50 pounds or so) and modern triathlon bikes can weigh less than a third of that, even though you're a fully grown adult? Of course your titanium triathlon "toy" may be speedy and fun to play with, but it may set you back more than $15,000. That's a bike you won't be leaving haphazardly on your neighbor's front lawn.

PACING OR GUIDING

Since your PR days are behind you, why not help other runners realize dreams of their own? Sure, it's amazing to cross the finish line with a shiny new PR or BQ and ring the bell (literally, some races have bells you ring upon finishing with a PR or BQ), but it's oh-so-much-more satisfying to shepherd a herd of runners or guide a visually impaired runner to the promised land.

The Boston Marathon is special to me because it is the race that most represents a love of running, for everyone; I guide for my visually impaired teammate, Lisa Thompson, and we have been astounded by how joyful and welcoming Boston has been to us.

Alexi Pappas
Boston Marathon Guide Runner
Olympian, 10,000m, Greece (2016)
Author/Filmmaker

Have you ever tutored your 10-year-old daughter the night before an important test and then shed tears when you see the I-am-invincible look in her eye as she shows you the 100 percent inscribed at the top of her exam a few days later? That's what pacing feels like. It feels like you've done something selfless and awesome, a feeling you don't get chasing PRs of your own.

There are entire organizations that handle pacing for multiple races around the world, but many of the smaller races fend for themselves, enlisting the help of locals to pace races of various distances. If you're interested in helping others live out their dreams, pacing and guiding are noble pursuits that deliver "all the feels" of your PR-chasing days and more.

The best way to reinvigorate your love of running is to share it with someone else.

VOLUNTEERING

Another way to get your groove back when your legs aren't capable of their bygone magic is to volunteer at races and encourage fellow athletes as they take on challenges you're well-versed at overcoming. Being a volunteer can be a sweet gig, akin to being a doting grandparent; you get to spoil athletes with copious gifts (swag bags, electrolytes, water, gels, blankets) without being burdened by many of the pesky responsibilities like pre-dawn wake-ups or weekend long runs.

Volunteering is a rewarding way to interact with athletes, live vicariously through their agonies and thrills, rekindle your race mojo, and recharge your faith in the human spirit. And as an athlete who has benefited from the kindness of volunteers at countless races, you will find that making a deposit into the "karma bank" feels pretty darn good.

SPECTATING

Have you ever prepared and cooked an elaborate meal, sat down at the table alone, and eaten in silence? That's you racing to a PR, a lot of work for an expectedly satisfying, but selfish payoff. But have you ever poured your heart and soul into making a simple piece of buttered toast to nurse your daughter back to health, and then waited with bated breath as she took her first bite? That's you spectating after handing a plastic bag of Swedish fish to a struggling athlete. That's not a lot of work for a surprisingly fulfilling and selfless payoff.

What makes spectating so great? Spectating allows you to tap into the emotions of other humans without the need for any prerequisite interaction or relationship. Athletes stream by one after another, and you can instantly empathize with them. It might be a look of despair of a PR slipping away. It might be a fist pump in the air that communicates "I got this." It might be a grimace of pain as a calf muscle seizes up again. It might be a look to the heavens in memory of a loved one. And there you are, connecting and reconnecting, again and again, with people you don't even know. It's pretty wild. And hard to describe. But awesome. Undeniably awesome.

CHAPTER 11

Hall of Fame

Our Pantheon of Boston Marathon legends is chock-full of larger-than-life personalities, the kind that transcend wall-mounted plaques, glass display cases, or flattering words on a page. These icons built the Boston Marathon. Their legacy is responsible for our annual pilgrimage. Their passions and triumphs breathe life into ours. We follow their footsteps, layering ours on top of theirs to achieve our goals. And we honor them because our memories wouldn't exist without them.

Herein are Boston Marathon alumni deserving of the velvet rope to be lifted to the event's highest distinction, inclusion in its hallowed Hall of Fame.

Ellison "Tarzan" Brown—Two-time winner of the Men's Open division of the Boston Marathon, two-time Olympian (it might have been three-time, but the 1940 Olympics were canceled due to World War II), and two-time American men's record holder for the marathon. One of only two Native Americans (the other is Thomas Longboat) to win Boston and one of the most colorful characters in its history, he cemented his legacy by running barefoot to the finish in 1935, breaking Johnny "The Elder" Kelley's heart on Heartbreak Hill in 1936, and surrendering the lead by jumping whimsically into Lake Cochituate in 1938.

George V. Brown—Native of Hopkinton. Served as the starter of the Boston Marathon for 33 years, race manager for 11 years, and B.A.A. director of athletics for more than 20 years. Since 1905, for every year except one, a member of the Brown family has been the starter of the Boston Marathon. A bronze monument, *The Starter*, stands in Hopkinton Town Common in his honor.

Candace Cable-Brookes—Six-time winner of the Women's Wheelchair division of the Boston Marathon, nine-time Paralympian, and pioneer of Para Athletics. In addition to her prowess on the streets of Boston, she earned 12 Paralympic medals (including eight gold medals) and was the first woman to medal in both the Summer and Winter Paralympic Games.

Robert Kipkoech Cheruiyot—Four-time winner of the Men's Open division of the Boston Marathon and one of Kenya's all-time great marathoners. His 2006 victory in 2:07:14 broke the course record set by Cosmas Ndeti that had lasted 12 years. His win in 2008 made him the first four-time winner in the Men's Open division since Bill Rodgers.

Ted Corbitt—A pioneer in American distance running who completed 223 marathons and ultramarathons in his career, including 22 Boston Marathons between 1951 and 1974. The first African American to represent the United States in the Olympic Marathon. A lifelong champion of running and a student of the sport, he often ran more than 200 miles per week, and many of his inventions, including a carefully calibrated bicycle wheel to measure courses, are used to this day.

Gérard Côté—Four-time winner of the Men's Open division of the Boston Marathon, setting a new course record of 2:28:28 in 1940. Known as the most successful Canadian marathoner in Boston history, he endeared himself to the Boston community as much for his panache as his leg speed. His post-race cigars, fancy suits, and all-night partying were the stuff of legends.

Clarence DeMar—Seven-time winner of the Men's Open division of the Boston Marathon, more than any other runner in that division. Nicknamed "Mr. DeMarathon," he claimed his first Boston victory in 1911 and his last in 1930, won a bronze medal in the marathon at the 1924 Paris Olympics, and finished 33 Boston Marathons, completing his last in 1965.

Jean Driscoll—Eight-time winner (including a remarkable seven straight from 1990 to 1996) of the Women's Wheelchair division of the Boston Marathon, more titles than any other female athlete in any division. Additionally, she won 12 medals (including five gold medals) in events ranging from 200 meters to the marathon in four separate Summer Paralympic Games.

William Evans—Born and raised in South Boston (aka "Southie"), veteran of 54 marathons and 21 Boston Marathons, including a 2:53:45 Boston PR. In 1980, Evans joined the Boston Police Department (BPD), rising within the ranks to become interim commissioner before serving as its permanent commissioner from 2014 until his retirement in 2018. Evans finished the 2013 Boston Marathon in 3:34:06 before playing a vital role in the manhunt and capture of the bombers.

Jack Fultz—The 1976 Boston Marathon ("Run for the Hoses") champion in 2:20:19. Before you scoff at his winning time, consider it was 100 degrees F in Hopkinton on race day, carbon-plated shoes weren't even a twinkle in Phil Knight's eye, and cotton was still the running fabric of choice. Ouch. Fultz went on to PR in Boston with a 2:11:17 before teaching Sports Psychology at Tufts University and dedicating his life to the Boston Marathon: becoming a B.A.A. member, elite athlete liaison, and training advisor to the Boston Marathon's largest charity team, the Dana-Farber (Cancer Institute) Marathon Team.

Roberta "Bobbi" Gibb—A pioneer of women's marathoning and the first woman in history to run the Boston Marathon (1966), finishing in 3:21:40, ahead of two-thirds of the male runners. Recognized by the B.A.A. as a three-time pre-sanctioned era women's winner of the Boston Marathon. A bronze sculpture, *The Girl Who Ran*, honors her on the corner of Main Street and Hayden Rowe near the starting line in Hopkinton.

Before Bobbi Gibb became the first female finisher in Boston Marathon history, the longest AAU-sanctioned race for women was 1.5 miles.
Bobbi Gibb

John Graham—Founding father of the Boston Marathon, B.A.A. member, and inaugural US Olympic team manager. After experiencing the first Olympic Marathon in Athens, Greece, in 1896, Graham returned home inspired to create a Boston-based race that mimicked the undulations of terrain between Marathon and Athens. His opus and our holy grail, the Boston Marathon, wouldn't exist without him. The rest, as they say, is history.

Tom Grilk—The finish-line announcer with a 2:49:03 PR and the "your voice sounds familiar" baritone at the Boston Marathon from 1979 until 2013. A tireless member of the B.A.A. in multiple capacities since 1987, including as president and CEO before transitioning most recently to senior advisor. Ran a personal best of 2:54 at Boston in 1978. Coined the spot-on expression "In Boston, everyone owns the marathon" in his 2014 TEDx talk. He will be remembered for his countless improvements to the race during his tenure, but his phrase beautifully captures the heart of what the Boston Marathon means to the participants, nay stewards, who take ownership of it each year.

Robert Hall—The first sanctioned participant and champion of the Men's Wheelchair division of the Boston Marathon, winning in 1975 with a time of 2:58. Returned to dominate again in 1977, setting a new course record of 2:40:10. Known as the "father of wheelchair racing," he served as coordinator of the Wheelchair division of the B.A.A. and founded a company, Hall's Wheels, that pioneered lightweight racing wheelchairs, introducing designs and materials that are still used today.

Ryan Hall—Recorded the fastest time run by an American in the history of the Men's Open division of the Boston Marathon with his 2:04:58 fourth-place finish in 2011. Endeared himself to Wellesley College students when he playfully encouraged them to shout louder by cupping his hand to his ear in "I can't hear you" fashion as he ripped by at the front of the lead pack at 4:46/mile pace. Finished third at Boston in 2:09:40 in 2009, fourth in 2:08:41 in 2010, and 20th in 2:17:50 in 2014.

Ron Hill—Crushed the existing course record by more than three minutes with a 2:10:30 to win the 1970 Men's Open division of the Boston Marathon, the first time a runner from England emerged victorious. Raced 115 marathons, the last of which was a 3:12:46 in Boston in 1996. Represented England in three Olympic Games, finishing as high as sixth in the 1972 Olympic Marathon in Munich. With a PhD in textile chemistry, he experimented and led innovation in carbo-loading, technical fabrics, and shoe design optimization. Oh, and he was a prolific streaker, running at least one mile every day for 52 years and 39 days from 1964 to 2017.

Dick and Rick Hoyt—Father and son (diagnosed with cerebral palsy at birth) affectionately known as "Team Hoyt" who competed in tandem, with Dick pushing Rick in a specialized wheelchair as he ran. Finished more than 1,100 endurance events, including 72 marathons (32 Boston Marathons) and six Ironman Triathlons together. Ran a marathon PR of 2:40:47 at the 1992 Marine Corps Marathon and a Boston best of 2:48:51 in 1986. Immortalized in bronze with a statue near the starting line in Hopkinton.

Marcel Hug—Six-time winner of the Men's Wheelchair division of the Boston Marathon, world record holder (1:17:47 at the 2021 Oita Marathon), and Boston Marathon course record holder (1:18:03 in 2017). Nicknamed "The Silver Bullet" as a result of his trademark metallic helmet, he is one of the most highly decorated para athletes of all time, winning 15 World Marathon Major titles, and dozens of World Championship and Paralympic Games medals.

Ibrahim Hussein—Three-time winner of the Men's Open division and the first runner from Kenya and Africa to win the Boston Marathon. His first victory at Boston in 1988 (2:08:43) began an era of African dominance (30 African champions in 33 years).

Yuki Kawauchi—Winner of the Men's Open division of the 2018 Boston Marathon in arguably the worst weather in the race's storied history. Known as "The Citizen Runner" because he worked full-time for the government while running a prolific amount of races, averaging a marathon each month. Recognized by *Guinness World Records* as the first person to ever run more than 100 sub-2:20 marathons.

Mebrahtom "Meb" Keflezighi—Four-time Olympian (including a silver medal in the Men's Marathon at the 2004 Games in Athens), winner of the 2009 New York City Marathon, and winner of the Men's Open division of the 2014 Boston Marathon, becoming the first American male runner to win New York since 1982 and Boston since 1983. Affectionately known simply as "Meb," he is the only marathoner in history to claim titles at Boston and New York in addition to winning an Olympic medal. Achieved legend status when he sprinted to victory on Boylston Street in 2014, reclaiming the sanctity of the finish line a year after the 2013 bombing.

Johnny A. "The Elder" Kelley—Two-time Men's Open division winner, seven-time runner-up, and 58-time finisher of the Boston Marathon. Voted "Runner of the Century" by *Runner's World* magazine in 2000. His heart was supposedly "broken" on Heartbreak Hill by Tarzan Brown in 1936, but we all know those were just the clever words of a journalist, because "The Elder" personified the heart and soul of the Boston Marathon, his indomitable spirit woven into its fabric in perpetuity. Pay homage to him at Mile 19, where he is immortalized in bronze with the statue *Young at Heart*, depicting a 27-year-old Kelley in 1935 holding hands with an 84-year-old Kelley in 1992 as they cross the finish line in victory together.

Johnny J. "The Younger" Kelley—It's tough to be a legend in your own right yet have the misfortune of sharing the same name as the greatest Boston Marathon legend of all. Unrelated to "The Elder," he was nicknamed "The Younger" to avoid confusion. The winner of the Men's Open division of the 1957 Boston Marathon, gold medalist of the 1959 Pan American Games, eight-time national champion in the marathon, and the only male runner in history to have won the Boston Marathon and the Mount Washington Road Race (a historic, all-uphill, average 12 percent grade, 7.6-mile test of courage).

Jim Knaub—Five-time winner of the Men's Wheelchair division of the Boston Marathon, setting course records in three of his victories (including smashing the course record he held by more than four minutes with a 1:22:17 to earn his final title in 1993). An accomplished pole vaulter who finished fifth at the 1976 US Olympic Trials before being paralyzed in a 1978 traffic accident. In the 1990s, he held world records in every race distance from 5000 meters to the marathon.

Stylianos "Stelios" Kyriakides—Winner of the Men's Open division of the 50th edition of the Boston Marathon in 1946, upsetting his friend, runner-up and defending champion Johnny "The Elder" Kelley, by exactly two minutes (2:29:27 to 2:31:27). Known as the first charity runner in marathon history, he ran Boston to call attention to and raise money for his native war-torn Greece. The story of his heroism and philanthropy circled the globe, resulting in millions of dollars of contributions to Greece, the race becoming an even larger worldwide phenomenon, and increased participation of runners from more distant countries in Africa, Asia, and South America. Honored at Mile 1 in Hopkinton with the *Spirit of the Marathon*, a 12-foot-tall statue depicting him running alongside fellow Greek Spyridon Louis, winner of the first modern Olympic Marathon in 1896.

Jacques "Jack" LeDuc—The Boston Marathon starting line began in 1897 as a line in the sand, literally a line scratched along a dusty dirt road. By 1980, the starting line had become a simple, painted white stripe. Everything changed in 1981 when Jack LeDuc volunteered to paint the starting line. LeDuc, a 15-time Boston Marathon finisher, created his own designs for years until the B.A.A. selected a design that matched the finish line. LeDuc's enthusiasm for the Boston Marathon wasn't just displayed in the care and precision of his hand-painted starting lines; he became the "voice of the starting line" when he started announcing the start of the race. After 37 years, LeDuc retired from painting the starting line in 2018 (a road crew now handles the task), but his voice still echoes in Hopkinton on Marathon Monday and his legacy is forever etched in Boston Marathon lore.

Desiree "Des" Linden—Winner of the Women's Open division of the "Perfect Chaos" 2018 Boston Marathon (2:39:54), becoming the first American to win in 33 years. Born and raised in San Diego, Des has been adopted by Boston as if she were found swaddled in blankets in a basket on the front stoop of a "tripledeckah" in the Dot (aka "Dorchester" to the toonies). Two-time Olympian and women's 50k world record holder (2:59:54) with a marathon PR of 2:22:38 from her runner-up finish at Boston in 2011, finishing a mere two seconds behind the winner, Kenya's Caroline Kilel, after a sprint to the finish on Boylston Street. When not making Olympic teams, setting world records, and winning World Marathon Majors, Des enjoys cult status on the streets of Boston and glasses of the finest bourbons from her ever-growing whiskey collection (yes, bourbon's whiskey, Larry).

Tatyana McFadden—Five-time winner of the Women's Wheelchair division of the Boston Marathon and New York City Marathon, 20-time medalist at five Summer Paralympic Games, and nine-time winner of the Women's Wheelchair division of the Chicago Marathon. Born with spina bifida, a congenital disorder that paralyzed her from the waist down, she walked on her hands for the first six years of her life. Played wheelchair basketball at the University of Illinois and also won a silver medal in cross-country skiing at the 2014 Winter Paralympic Games in Sochi.

David McGillivray—Began with the Boston Marathon as technical director in 1988 before transitioning to race director in 2001, managing all technical and operational components throughout the most dynamic growth and innovation in the race's history. His list of athletic, philanthropic, and professional accomplishments could fill a Hall of Fame of its own. Has an active streak of 51 straight Boston Marathons, 16 with the field as a regular participant prior to 1988 and the

The jacket and bib worn by Boston fan favorite Des Linden, champion of the 2018 Boston Marathon (aka "Perfect Chaos"). Courtesy of Gloria Ratti collection

remainder at night upon completion of his numerous race duties. He, his race management company, DMSE Sports, and his DMSE Children's Foundation have raised more than $50 million for a wide variety of charities.

Paul E. "Jerry" Nason—Nicknamed "The Expert" because of his uncanny knowledge of the Boston Marathon, Nason served as *Boston Globe* sports editor for 33 years before retiring in 1974, a year after becoming the first nonrunner elected to the Road Runners Hall of Fame. It was Nason's description of Tarzan Brown "breaking Kelley's heart" on the final Newton hill that inspired the term "Heart-break Hill." Nason covered the Boston Marathon for roughly 60 years and authored the first widely distributed history of the race in 1970.

Catherine Ndereba—Four-time winner of the Women's Open division of the Boston Marathon, two-time silver medalist at the Summer Olympic Games, two-time Kenyan Sportswoman of the Year, two-time gold medalist at the World Championships, and former world record holder in the marathon (2:18:47 at the Chicago Marathon in 2001). Honored with the nickname "Catherine the Great" because of her dominance in the marathon at the turn of the 21st century.

Franz Nietlispach—Five-time winner of the Men's Wheelchair division of the Boston Marathon, 22-time medalist at the Paralympic Games from 1976 to 2008, and a pioneer in lightweight handcycle innovation. In addition to his success on the roads of Boston and beyond, he was dedicated to his native Switzerland, leveraging his athletic fame and business success to serve in political office in Aargau.

Uta Pippig—Winner of three consecutive Boston Marathons (1994–1996), three-time winner of the Berlin Marathon (1990, 1992, 1995), winner of the New York City Marathon (1993), two-time Olympian, Germany, 10,000m (1992) and Marathon (1996). As if Uta's dominance in the early 1990s wasn't impressive enough, her effervescent personality and infectious smile endeared her to the running world in general and Boston fans in particular.

Gloria Ratti—Described by the B.A.A. as "a trailblazer, leader, and loving matriarch of the New England running community," Ratti most notably pioneered timing and checkpoint practices along the course and single-handedly began assembling an archive of Boston Marathon mementoes that celebrated and preserved the race's heritage. Named by *Runner's World* magazine as "The Women's Running Trailblazer You've Never Heard Of" in 2021, Ratti was "the First Lady of our sport, no matter where she went" according to former Boston Marathon race director Guy Morse. With the charisma of a Broadway star, the heart of an adoring grandmother, and the moxie of a CIA operative who traveled the world, Ratti was one of a kind.

Fatuma Roba—Three-time winner of the Women's Open division of the Boston Marathon, Olympic gold medalist, and the first African (and Ethiopian) to win Olympic gold. Her three successive victories in Boston began an era of unprecedented African dominance (21 victories in 24 years).

Eugene Roberts—The first athlete to ever finish the Boston Marathon in a wheelchair, completing the course in a standard, hospital-issued wheelchair in 7:07:00 in 1970. And he did it in 38 degrees F with driving rain and sleet. Whoa.

Bill Rodgers—Four-time winner of the Men's Open division of the Boston Marathon, four-time winner of the New York City Marathon, former world record holder for 25k (1:14:11), and former American record holder in

Bill Rodgers was to the Boston Marathon streets what Steve Prefontaine was to the Hayward Field oval. Courtesy of Gloria Ratti collection

the marathon (2:09:27). Ranked #1 in the world in the marathon by *Track & Field News* in 1975, 1977, and 1979. A fan favorite in the Boston community, he and his brother Charlie owned and operated Bill Rodgers Running Center in Faneuil Hall Marketplace from 1977 to 2013. Always a fixture in the local running scene, he continues to inspire future generations of marathoners.

Joan Benoit Samuelson—Two-time winner of the Women's Open division of the Boston Marathon, Olympic gold medalist in 1984 (2:24:52), and winner of the Chicago Marathon in 1985 (2:21:21). Endeared herself to the Boston faithful when she emerged victorious in 1979 with a Boston Red Sox hat atop her head. Set the American record in the marathon at Chicago when she eclipsed the previous record, which had been held for 21 years. In addition to her success in the marathon, she won six Falmouth Road Race titles and a gold medal in the 3000 meters at the Pan American Games in 1983.

Winning the Boston Marathon twice placed Joan in the history books. Winning with a Red Sox hat atop her head birthed a legend. Courtesy of Gloria Ratti collection

Louise Sauvage—Four-time winner of the Women's Wheelchair division of the Boston Marathon, 13-time medalist (including nine gold medals) at the Summer Paralympic Games, and winner of the Berlin Marathon in 1997. Australian Female Athlete of the Year in 1999 and International Female Wheelchair Athlete of the Year in 1999 and 2000.

John "Jock" Semple—Controversial Scottish-American runner, physical therapist, trainer, and race official best known for attempting to tear off Kathrine Switzer's bib to prevent her from finishing the 1967 Boston Marathon. As co-director of the Boston Marathon, he developed a reputation for accosting runners he felt were disrespecting the race. He eventually reconciled with Switzer and became a fervent supporter of women athletes, particularly marathoners. The B.A.A. bestows the Jock Semple Award to local athletes who have made an impact in running.

Spencer—There are many colorful personalities who have enlivened the Boston Marathon's illustrious history, but there's only one mononymous figure worthy of inclusion in the race's Hall of Fame: Spencer, "The Official Dog of the Boston Marathon" (as designated by the B.A.A.). Beginning in 2015 (until he lost his battle with cancer in 2023), Spencer warmed the hearts of marathoners on Marathon Monday as he sat roadside in Ashland at Mile 3 displaying "Boston Strong" flags held securely in his canines. Video footage of Spencer in foul-weather gear in the driving rain and gale-force winds of 2018 went viral, catapulting his fame from motivational cult figure to full-fledged, furry Boston Marathon celebrity.

Bill Squires—Coached the Greater Boston Track Club during the era when it produced some of the best marathoners in the world (Bill Rodgers, Alberto Salazar, Dick Beardsley, Greg Meyer). A Greater Boston native, he had intimate knowledge of the nuances of the Boston Marathon course. He developed a "Heartbreak Hill simulator" for training, coauthored the book *Speed with Endurance* with Bruce Lehane, and received the Bill Bowerman Award from the National Distance Running Hall of Fame in 2002.

Kathrine (K.V.) Switzer—The first woman in history to run the Boston Marathon with a bib (#261) as an officially registered competitor. Because of her official entry and finish in 1967, the Amateur Athletic Union (AAU) barred women from all competition with men. Switzer lobbied with other female runners to allow women, but it wasn't until 1972 that the B.A.A. relented and established an official Women's division of the race. Winner of the 1974 New York City Marathon and named "Female Runner of the Decade" (1967–1977) by *Runner's World* magazine. To honor Switzer and her lifelong efforts to empower women, the B.A.A. agreed it would not assign bib #261 to any future runners.

Only two bib numbers have been retired by the Boston Marathon: Johnny Kelley's #61 (his number of starts) and Kathrine Switzer's #261 (the number she wore in 1967). Courtesy of Gloria Ratti collection

Wakako Tsuchida—Five-time winner of the Women's Wheelchair division of the Boston Marathon, first Japanese professional wheelchair athlete, and first Japanese athlete to win gold medals in both the Summer and Winter Paralympics.

Ernst van Dyk—Ten-time winner of the Men's Wheelchair division of the Boston Marathon (the most titles of any athlete in Boston Marathon history), two-time winner of the London Marathon, and eight-time medalist at the Paralympic Games. Named "Para Sportsperson of the Year" at the Laureus World Sports Awards in 2006. In addition to his wheelchair racing success, he has represented South Africa in Para Swimming and Para Cycling.

BOSTON CHARITY LEGENDS

Joseph Findaro—Doctors and nurses gathered around him at birth, not because he required medical attention but because his magnetic smile compelled them to draw closer. Offline, he is swarmed by alumni, colleagues, runners, and anyone fortunate enough to be in his midst. Online, social networks scramble to reconfigure their algorithms to facilitate his friends, contacts, and followers.

Joe Findaro is to the Boston Marathon what Kevin Bacon is to Hollywood. If you happen to whisper "I'm with Joe Findaro" when you walk into the Hynes Convention Center, half of the heads on the Expo floor turn to greet you. If you don't know Joe, either a.) introduce yourself to the persons standing to your immediate left and right at the Expo (they probably do) or, b.) wait. It won't be long before Joe, directly or indirectly, finds you.

Brett Gordon—Like bright paint on a freshly detailed car, the Boston Marathon's over-the-top personalities (Gerard Cote, Jock Semple, et al.) get a lot of attention, but understated heroes like Brett Gordon are the engine beneath its hood. Arguably *the* "Legend" among many Boston charity legends, Brett is a Six Star Finisher entering his third decade of running the Boston Marathon and raising more than a million dollars for local charities whose missions include alleviating poverty and homelessness (Project HOPE Boston) and preventing and curing liver disease (American Liver Foundation). Even when Brett became fast enough to BQ, he continued to not only run for charities but, in true Legend fashion, inspire his teams by raising the most funds.

Rich "Shifter" Horgan—If you participated in the legendary Thursday night runs on the marathon course from Woodland T station to Eliot Lounge (or Crossroads), you navigated icy roads, endured negative windchills, and shared beer and complimentary pizza with Shifter, arguably the most recognizable charity runner in Boston Marathon history. Shifter anchored the Dana-Farber Marathon Challenge (DFMC) team for 25 years, helping raise funds for Dana-Farber in pursuit of its ultimate goal, "a world without cancer." Shifter's distinctive bright-white hair served as a beacon on group runs, and his genuine smile, quick wit, and decades of anecdotes never failed to enliven his post-run celebrations.

Jake Kennedy—Ran 37 straight Boston Marathons, established a charity that hosts an annual Christmas Party for thousands of homeless Boston families, owned and operated a physical therapy business that healed legions of marathoners for more than four decades, endeared himself to all stakeholders in the Boston running ecosystem, hosted legendary Boston Marathon after-parties for local finishers, and streaked naked in Downtown Crossing to celebrate friends' PRs.

Jake eschewed warming up in Hopkinton because he was too busy taping runners' gnarled toes and threadbare hamstrings in Athletes' Village, massaging their strained calves on Hayden Rowe, fashioning last-minute makeshift metatarsal pads out of foam in corrals like MacGyver, and calmly reassuring first-time bandits and charity runners who were doubting their fitness that they would, indeed, make it over Heartbreak Hill to Copley Square.

Jake was old-school, a throwback to the days of cotton, tube socks, and beef stew at the finish line. And when he succumbed to ALS in 2021 (as had his father and youngest brother), generations of solemn (but grateful) marathoners from far and wide gathered to pay respects to the man whose generous heart made the fulfillment of their dreams possible.

Howard Weinstein, MD—If you're a Boston Marathon "purist" who feels charity runners don't belong in the race, you've never met Dr. Howard Weinstein, the founder of MassGeneral Hospital's "Fighting Kids Cancer . . . One Step at a Time"

Marathon Team. If there's one person who embodies all that is honorable about allowing charity runners to participate, it's Dr. Weinstein, a charity running legend and finisher of 30 Boston Marathons (and counting).

In 1998, Weinstein, an oncologist and the director of the childhood cancer program at MGH, captained an inaugural team of 10 charity runners who collectively raised roughly $50,000 to support pediatric cancer research and critical support services, a modest beginning for what has become an annual team of more than 100 athletes who have raised more than $18 million.

Many members of the team run on behalf of patient partners, children with cancer who are receiving treatment at MGH and benefit directly from the funds raised by the team. The cure rate for pediatric cancer patients has improved from 25 percent to greater than 85 percent since the team's inception. There's not a dry eye in the house at the team's Sunday night pasta dinner where patient partners and their families are introduced and honored.

And the man behind it all, Dr. Weinstein, isn't done yet. The MGH Mile-20 cheer section at the base of Heartbreak Hill (a block from Weinstein's house) gets louder by the year, and Dr. Weinstein insists he'll keep running until "the day every child's cancer is cured."

Errol Yudelman—Finisher of 111 marathons (including 20 Boston Marathons) and 17 ultramarathons (counting multiple Comrades Marathons); owner of a 2:32 PR; Capetown, South African born but longtime Newton resident; and legendary member of the Heartbreak Hill Striders running club. Errol was quick with a smile, a prolific racer, and a fixture on the Greater Boston running scene.

His spirit is woven into the fabric of the Newton hills, his backyard running playground. When Errol passed away in 2021, his friends, family, and fans installed a park bench a half-mile away from Johnny Kelley's statue at Mile 18.5 (the intersection of Commonwealth Avenue, Evelyn Road, and Fuller Street). The inscription on the bench reads "and here's Errol Yudelman nearing mile 18.5 with his joyful smile and South African shorts 111 Marathons—20 Bostons Forever Go Errol!"

If you're not smiling at Mile 18.5, check yourself. Errol smiled a lot, never more than when he greeted fellow runners, family, and friends in Newton. It's a privilege and a joy to run. Until life is over and you can't. Savor the moment. Channel Errol Yudelman. Smile through whatever you feel is suppressing your smile (leg cramps, nausea, or, as they would say in Boston, "whatevah"). Errol ran 10 miles on the morning of his death. Ten glorious miles. And then he was gone. That's right. Smile for Errol. Smile while you can. Smile because you can.

CELEBRITY FINISHERS

CELEBRITIES WHO FINISHED THE BOSTON MARATHON

Last Name	First Name	Profession	Year	Time
Aduba	Uzo	Actor	2015	5:03:24
Armstrong	Lance	Discredited cyclist	2008	2:50:58
Astin	Sean	Actor	2015	4:49:53
Bertinelli	Valerie	Actor	2010	5:14:37
Bremer	L. Paul	American diplomat	1991	3:00:34
Bruschi	Tedy	Football player	2019	4:35:35
Carpenter	Bobby	Ice hockey player	2016	3:46:53
Chara	Zdeno	Ice hockey player (Bruins)	2023	3:38:23
d'Arcy James	Brian	Actor	2021	3:30:22
Dempster	Ryan	Baseball player (Red Sox)	2023	4:42:11
Develin	James	Football player	2021	4:27:17
Dukakis	Michael	Governor of Massachusetts	1951	3:31:00
Elliott	David James	Actor	2000	4:57:23
Ferrell	Will	Actor	2003	3:56:12
Flutie	Doug	Football player	2017	4:50:41
Haaland	Deb	US secretary of the interior	2021	4:58:54
Holt	Brock	Baseball player (Red Sox)	2023	5:46:57
Johnson	Jimmie	NASCAR driver	2019	3:09:07
Ketterle	Wolfgang	Nobel Prize winner	2014	2:44:06
Landry	Ali	Model	2002	5:41:41
Lieberman	Daniel	Paleoanthropologist	2016	3:34:21
Lilly	Kristine	Soccer player	2012	4:27:45
Ling	Lisa	Journalist	2002	4:34:18
Lopez	Mario	Actor	2002	5:41:42
McIntyre	Joey	Singer	2013	3:48:11
Mullen	Dan	Football player	2016	4:28:35
Myers	Michael	Baseball player (Red Sox)	2023	5:59:31
Nikic	Chris	First person with Down syndrome to finish an Ironman Triathlon	2021	6:01:22
O'Brien	Vanessa	Mountaineering	2017	5:16:00
Patrick	Danica	Race car driver	2021	4:01:21

Last Name	First Name	Profession	Year	Time
Rakitt (Puig)	Monica	Tennis player (Olympic gold medalist)	2023	3:49:47
Reid	Harry	US senator	1972	3:16:00
Sanders	Summer	Swimmer (Olympic gold medalist)	2014	3:25:35
Segal	Erich	Writer	1964	2:56:30
Strug	Kerri	Gymnast (Olympic gold medalist)	2005	4:13:03
Sutter	Ryan	Reality TV contestant	2012	3:36:02
Turlington (Burns)	Christy	Model	2016	4:09:27

CHAPTER 12

The Boston Lexicon

Most sports have their own standard vocabularies, and road racing is no different. But, as we've learned, the Boston Marathon isn't ordinary, nor is its quirky vernacular. From "Beantown" to "Chuck" to "Smoot" to "WHOOP," our carefully curated dictionary defines specific terms you need to be your Boston best.

10 percent rule—One of the 10 commandments of distance running: "Thou shalt not increase your mileage more than 10 percent week over week." It is believed the ancient stone tablet inscribed with this edict was pried from Pheidippides's lifeless arms when he dropped dead in Athens in 490 BCE.

Age group—To run the Boston Marathon, you must be at least 18 years old on race day and run the qualifying time for your specific age group (18–34, 35–39, 40–44, 45–49, 50–54, 55–59, 60–64, 65–69, 70–74, 75–79, or 80+). Because time standards for older age groups get progressively more lenient, Boston Marathoners don't have to fake smiles on their milestone birthdays. Raise those sippy and Solo cups, kids. Grandma's going to Boston!

Bag check—On race morning, runners check their clear plastic Finish Area gear bags at designated areas on Boylston Street and Berkeley Street (roughly two blocks from the finish line). These bags (along with a preprinted adhesive label with your bib number) are provided by the B.A.A. when you receive your bib at the Expo. During relatively normal weather years, runners finish the race, get their gear bags, and move along to look for friends and family. In crazy weather years (hey, 2018, we're talking about you again), the bag check area looks more like an emergency room or open-air locker room with hundreds of athletes, male, female, and otherwise, stripping buck naked with absolutely no inhibitions in order to put on dry, warm clothes and stave off hypothermia. So if you've ever wanted to take off all of your clothes in public without repercussions, the Boston Marathon bag check area (if heinous weather necessitates) is your utopia within your nirvana.

Bandit—In Boston terms, a bandit is a runner who hasn't BQ'd, isn't running for charity, doesn't pay for entry, and yet runs the race bib-less anyway. It's not just like getting into the Super Bowl for free; it's like walking on the field in full pads and playing all four quarters while receiving complimentary food, drinks, and medical attention. Depending on who you're talking to, a Boston bandit is either the coolest person at your dinner party or the vilest person to ever walk the planet. And it definitely would be the latter if Boston hadn't been so surprisingly bandit-friendly throughout the 20th century.

Beantown—Contrary to what you may have heard, this is not where you'll be going to run the Boston Marathon. To be clear, no one who lives anywhere near Boston ever calls Boston "Beantown." Stop trying to make "Beantown" happen. Just stop. Locals know in a second you're from Paris or Tupelo or Munich or Seattle or Dublin or anywhere but Boston the moment this word spills out of your mouth.

Bombing—There have been unfortunate bombings all over the globe due to military actions, terrorism, and random acts of violence, but "bombing" in Boston terms refers to one singular event: the domestic terrorist attack that took place on Boylston Street at 2:49 p.m. ET on Marathon Monday, April 15, 2013. Bostonians initially reacted with grief and anger, but soon rallied to become resilient and strong, Boston Strong. Whether runners, volunteers, or civilians, most Bostonians can pinpoint where they were when they experienced or first heard of the bombing. Each April 15th, One Boston Day encourages acts of kindness and service to honor the tragedy's victims, survivors, and first responders.

BQ—How the cool kids say "Boston qualifying time," the marathon time that (for your age and gender) allows you to apply for entry into the Boston Marathon. Can be used as a verb ("have you BQ'd for 2023 yet?"), an adjective ("what's your BQ time?"), or a noun ("her BQ was a 3:38:40 at REVEL Big Bear, so she won't break fou-ah at Bahstin. No suh").

Bubbler—To you it might be a water fountain, but Bostonians refer to it as a "wadah bubblah." If you run along the Charles in January, you might hear the following, "I stopped at Dunks along the rivah at mile 12 'cuz the bubblah's off in the wintah."

Carrot—Have you ever been trying to find your rhythm in a race when, lo and behold, an extremely easy-on-the-eyes runner, the "carrot," finds his, her, or their way into your field of vision? You were debating the proper pace anyway, but now you know exactly what pace to run, the carrot's pace. Like Fight Club, there are rules regarding carrots: 1. Do not speak of the carrot. A carrot is a carrot. Everyone knows a carrot when they see one. 2. Appreciating for a moment is okay, stalking is not. 3. Do not turn around after you pass the carrot. Just don't. Oh, and if fellow runners are lingering behind you and/or breaking the rule and turning around to look at you . . . spoiler alert: You're the carrot.

Chuck—Seldom-used slang for the Charles River. Best to leave this one to the locals because you'll sound like you're from out of town if you attempt to use it. Even Bostonians favor "the rivah," but a well-placed "Chuck" by a local rolls off the tongue as easily as "wikkid" (e.g., "Go long on the carriage road in the wintah. Chuck's bettah in the summah.").

Corral—If you've ever wondered what it felt like to be branded livestock herded in a pen, your dream will come true in Hopkinton. When you stand in your corral, look around you. There will be runners of all shapes, sizes, ethnicities, and genders. But every runner in close proximity has BQ'd with a time similar to yours. You can tell whose BQ was faster or slower by looking at their brands (bib numbers). This all sounds dehumanizing, but thank heaven for corrals. Before their arrival in 2006, back-of-the-pack charity runners would shuffle forward for 45 minutes just to reach the starting line.

Crop dusting—A cloud of noisome gas "aerial applicated" by a flatulating runner. Because of the sheer volume of runners and typical stealth manner of application, the culprit is often unidentifiable and the victims are multiple meters (depending on hangtime, even more) in arrears. As a rule, don't do it. But if you absolutely have to, peel off to the side to spare fellow runners. Or do as actor and comedian Will Ferrell did before running Boston in 3:56:12 in 2003, when he said: "I'd like to apologize in advance to everyone running behind me," which was his way of proactively owning it before it even happened.

Crossroads—A now defunct bar that stood near the corner of Beacon Street and Massachusetts Avenue in Boston's Back Bay. Similar to the Eliot Lounge (until its closing in 1996), Crossroads was the meeting point for runners across the city on Thursday evenings. After changing clothes in its phone booth–sized bathroom, runners would take the MBTA Green Line D train to Woodland Station (in all manner of nasty New England weather) and run back to Crossroads (nine miles) for celebratory pizza and beer. Crossroads brought together runners from all walks of life and created lasting friendships and camaraderie among local marathoners. Even in the moment on those icy streets with negative windchills, you had the sense you were part of some strange slice of Boston Marathon history. You were. RIP Crossroads.

Doubles—Running twice a day. A training method most often employed by elites and PR chasers to increase mileage, promote faster recovery, and allow for faster paces. If you're running more than 100 miles per week, you'd average 14 miles per run if you didn't sprinkle doubles in your repertoire. Unlike the "doubles" followed by Bloody Marys and a long lunch at the local club, the running variety typically precedes foam rolling and deep sleep.

Downstep—The scourge of runners' racing photos, the "downstep" is when a foot hits the ground and the full force of a runner's body is being absorbed by the earth, resulting in the least aesthetically pleasing photos. The opposite of the downsteps are the floaters, images (typically the best ones) that capture both feet off the ground simultaneously.

Dreadmill—Yeah, yeah. We get it. You don't like the treadmill. Boo hoo. HTFU. Next.

Dunks—New England's native, fave coffee joint, Dunkin' (formally "Dunkin' Donuts" and always "Dunks" for short). If Dunks hasn't found its way to your neighborhood yet, you'll have a hard time avoiding it around Boston. You'll find one on every other block; Dunks is tightly woven into the culture of the city. There's a private club-like jargon to learn, too. For example, if you order a "coffee regular" (i.e. "kawfee regulah") expecting a black caffeinated coffee, try again. Coffee regular is caffeinated, yes, but it has wild amounts of sugar and cream in it (four creams and four sugars for a "lahge"). Best to learn the lingo before you go. Or, as Boston's own Oscar-winning Casey Affleck said best, "go back to Stahbucks."

Even splits—The holy grail of pacing. In Boston terms, running through the half marathon mark at the heart of Wellesley Square in the exact split it will take you to get to the finish. Even splits are difficult enough on a flat course, but, with the undulations of Boston and the unforgiving Newton hills, you have a Rubik's Cube of challenges that require divine intervention to even split, unless, in the eyes of Boston fans, you're divine already: In 2017, Des Linden hit Wellesley in 1:12:33 and made it to Copley Square in 1:12:33, finishing fourth in 2:25:06.

The Boston Marathon is special because it's a day when athletes from all over the world come together to celebrate milestones, challenge themselves, and create friendships and memories they'll hold for a lifetime.

Cris Gutierrez III
7 Marathons
4 Boston Marathons
Winner, "First to the Trackhouse," Boston Marathon (2023)

First to the Trackhouse—A race within a race for non-elites on Marathon Monday. The first runners (male and female) to make it to the Eliot Lounge bar within Tracksmith's world headquarters (the Trackhouse at 285 Newbury Street) after crossing the finish line are awarded a celebratory cold beer, a fancy post-run robe, a commemorative race portrait, and prestigious Eliot Hare trophy (created by Boston legend Bobbi Gibb).

To the victor(s) belong the spoils for finishing Boston, especially after dodging spectators and hurdling barricades to arrive at the Trackhouse first. Cris Gutierrez III/Lou Serafini/Tracksmith

Flat (insert name here)—We've all probably seen the self-indulgent social media posts of runners who take photos of their race-day kits (along with gear, bibs, and nutrition) lying flat on the ground. Some even wear the gear and recline on the floor. You know the ones with the captions "Flat Britney" and "Flat Scott" that, if captioned more honestly, would probably read, "Look at me, everyone. I have a marathon tomorrow. Would you please like my clever photo and wish me luck?" As mockable as they might be, flat runners do have benefits: making race morning easier, ensuring you don't forget any items, alerting spectators

You've had a rough training cycle when your "flat" photo includes KT tape, ibuprofen, and bourbon.

what you'll be wearing so they can spot you and cheer for you, and allowing you to discover gear you might like when you view other flat runners. Just be certain you obscure your bib number and name to make it difficult for nefarious people to copy your bib. You don't want to have two or three runners wearing the bib you earned (and paid for) on race day.

Green Monster—If you're a baseball fan and you're in need of yet another incentive to get to the finish in Copley Square, look no further than the 37.2-foot-tall Green Monster, the most famous outfield wall in baseball. As you crest the I-90 (Mass Pike) overpass (Mile 25), don't get mesmerized by the Citgo sign to your left like everyone else. Instead, look to your right, where you'll find Fenway Park, including a view of the back side of the one and only "Green Mahnstah." If you weren't able to get tickets to a Red Sox game while you're in town, this might be the closest you'll get (unless you have the energy to go to the "Mile 27" post-race party). Go, Sawx!

Heartbreak Hill—The most feared and revered hill in road racing, Heartbreak Hill is situated between Miles 20 and 21 (immediately before Boston College). On any other day, it's an unassuming rise on a picturesque street in a quaint New England town, but on Marathon Monday it's a challenge of biblical proportions, handed down from the heavens by the gods of running.

High—How the cool kids say a race time that ends toward the upper end of a range. For example, if you ran 3:03:58 at the Hartford Marathon, you wouldn't say you ran 3:04 (because you didn't) and you wouldn't say 3:03:58 (because that's just too precise and creepy), you'd say the far cooler "3:03-high." This expression simultaneously articulates you're hip to running lingo and that you've run so many darn marathons that remembering the exact seconds of each of them is an impossibility. You're a veteran marathoner, not Rain Man.

Hopper—As a heads-up to the non-Bostonians among you, the expression "in the hopper" doesn't mean "in progress" as it does pretty much everywhere else in the world. So if you're working on your race-day strategy but you're still ironing out some specifics, don't tell someone your strategy is in the hopper. In this neck of the woods, a "hoppah" is a toilet. So use the hopper if you have GI distress in Newton, but don't say your strategy is in the hopper, because your race is bound to end up there, too.

HTFU—Some acronyms you'd prefer to avoid (DNF), some you'd like to get to know better (HR), and others you'd sell your soul (possibly) to achieve (BQ). But if there's one acronym you need to embrace more than all the others, it's HTFU, shorthand for "harden the &%#@ up." Do you think Des Linden was monitoring her HR to determine her proper exertion level in Coolidge Corner in 2018? Not a chance. She leaned into the pain. That's where the breakthroughs are. That's where you'll find your PR, tucked behind the acronym that counts the most, HTFU.

Intervals—Most PR-chasing marathoners hit an inflection point in their training where adding more mileage (which used to generate faster and faster PRs) is no longer sufficient to PR. How do you get past this plateau? Well, one answer is to incorporate intervals in your training. Intervals are periods of high-intensity running alternated with low-intensity running, walking, or even rest. Unlike "repeats," which allow for full (or nearly full) recovery between efforts, intervals are performed with limited recovery time between efforts. Intervals increase your turnover, improve your aerobic threshold, and, arguably most importantly, teach your mind and body to become "comfortable with the uncomfortable" (i.e., red-line effort while remaining relaxed).

Junk miles—An expression for superfluous miles that don't produce a specific physiological benefit. Legends like Bill Rodgers, winner of four Boston and four New York City marathons, dominated the world on junk food and junk miles. By contrast, modern runners are often taught that junk miles are wasteful and "every run should have a purpose." Perhaps we should save the energy we spend worrying about what to call our miles and channel it toward actually running them.

Kit—What you wear when you race. Veikko Karvonen, the winner of the 1954 Boston Marathon, ran in shoes he found in a restroom. Considering today's plethora of gear choices and Boston's tricky weather, you'll be more inclined to throw extra items away in bathrooms. Make certain you test your kit with some long run dress rehearsals. You don't want any unpleasant surprises on Marathon Monday.

Leapfrog—Have you ever passed someone in a race only to be passed by them, and then you pass them, and then they pass you, and then . . . well . . . you know the rest. You're leapfrogging each other.

Low—Hip way to say a race time that ends toward the lower end of a range. For example, if you ran 2:47:12 at the Flying Pig Marathon (Cincinnati, Ohio), you'd say the far cooler "2:47-low." This expression simultaneously articulates your dog's name is Steve Prefontaine's middle name (Roland) and your son's name is Miles.

Marathon Monday—The third Monday of April, Marathon Monday is, among many Bostonians (especially students), as hallowed a holiday as Christmas or St. Patrick's Day. Sure, the race is responsible for and serves as the focal point of the day, but it's really a convenient justification for a statewide party that starts at sunrise (tequila sunrise to be precise).

Massholes—Nickname for natives (or residents) of Massachusetts. You'd think locals would take offense to the vulgar term, but it's actually embraced like a badge of honor. It's possible the name was first used by drivers in neighboring states who were appalled by the impatient, irrational driving of cars with Massachusetts license plates. Typically, Marathon Weekend brings out the best of Bostonians, but if you observe less-than-welcoming behavior, you know you've crossed paths with a Masshole.

Negative split—In its simplest terms, to negative split is to run the second half of your race faster than the first half. That's it. Easy peasy, right? Well, it's not, especially at Boston. Running faster on tired legs over the Newton hills while you're bonking is akin to winning a game of Whac-A-Mole on horse tranquilizers. Possible. Not probable.

Night run—In Boston, "night run" has special meaning. The very person who pays meticulous attention to every detail to ensure your Boston Marathon experience is everything you want it to be (and more) is the same person who finishes his race director duties in Copley Square late on Marathon Monday, drives back to the start in Hopkinton, and, for 51 straight years (16 by day and 35 by night), races the course back to downtown Boston. Boston Marathon race director Dave McGillivray's version of a "night run" is no ordinary night run. But in case you haven't picked up on it yet, McGillivray is no ordinary race director.

Nor'easter—If you're from the Boston area, you know these "wikkid stahms" all too well, but for the unfamiliar among you, a "nah'eastah" is New England's winter version of a hurricane, with all the usual devastation (coastal erosion, severe flooding, violent winds) plus the added bonuses of blizzard conditions, power outages, and multiple feet of snow. If a nor'easter is in the forecast, buckle up: You should know that, as the name implies, (strong) winds are from the northeast. That's not what you want to hear. Pray for prevailing westerlies on race day.

Numbah—At most races you'll wear a bib. At Boston, you'll pick up "yah numbah" at the Expo, pin it to yah chest in Hopkinton, and run "wikkid hahd" to Copley.

Overuse injury—The more you run, the more knowledge you'll gain about your body, including all of the delightful ways it can fall apart. Overuse injuries don't have a sudden onset. Overuse injuries are chronic, develop slowly, and typically last a long time. Oh, and because the human body is so beautifully interconnected, one weakness tends to enlist the help of another stronger area of the body to compensate, until it is overstressed as a result and weakens, too. Yikes. Welcome to running.

Patriots' Day—Technically, an annual holiday (observed by a handful of states) commemorating the battles of Lexington, Concord, and Menotomy, some of the first battles of the American Revolutionary War but, in practice, a perfect reason for Bostonians to start drinking at breakfast and cheer runners the remainder of the day.

Perfect Chaos—The 2018 Boston Marathon deserves a catchy nickname. Why should 1976 ("Run for the Hoses") have all the fun? *Outside* magazine's Martin Fritz Huber coined it perfectly: "The 2018 Boston Marathon was Perfect Chaos." "It was as though the marathon gods summoned a mid-April tempest," he added. So true. And it's time to honor 2018 properly and christen it "Perfect Chaos" so it can take its rightful place alongside the races atop the Mount Rushmore of Boston Marathons.

Pissah—Usually preceded by "wicked," pissah is quite versatile in Boston and has multiple meanings. Pissah can mean "really good." For example, "you pee-ah'd with 3:15-high? That's pissah, khed." Alternatively, pissah can enhance something awful. "Sully DNF'd in Ashland. Blew out his Achilles'. Friggin' pissah, right?" And if you're not confused enough already, pissah can describe a person who (or thing that) is wicked funny or off-center. "Ya heah that pissah Declan proposed to Angie at the finish. Couldn't get the ring ovah huh swollen fingah."

Positive split—Running the second half of your race slower than your first half. It sounds counterintuitive for a "positive" to be a negative, but much research has found that even splits or negative splits are optimal for running your best marathon. So logic would tell you marathoners avoid positive splits, right? Wrong. Studies have shown that more than 85 percent of marathoners positive split. If you couldn't negative split at Chicago, good luck trying to pull it off at Boston.

PR—Shorthand for "personal record," the American way of expressing the fastest time you've ever recorded in a race over a specific distance. Everyone else in the world has a habit of saying it wrong by pronouncing it "PB." In Boston, you'll be at the Expo on Marathon Weekend and hear something like the following: "So, I pee-ah'd and BQ'd at Hahtfid with a 3:32-low. Sully and I ah in Wave tree Corral six at Bahstin."

Pre-Sanctioned—Prior to 1972, women were prohibited from competing in the Boston Marathon. In 1996, the B.A.A. retroactively recognized the women who finished Boston prior to 1972 as finishers in the pre-sanctioned era. Bobbi Gibb was recognized as the champion of the "Pioneer Women's Division" in 1966, 1967, and 1968, and Sara Mae Berman was recognized as the champion in 1969, 1970, and 1971.

Quarter Century Club—Founded by prolific Boston streaker Ronald Kmiec, the exclusive Quarter Century Club is for streakers who have finished 25 or more consecutive Boston Marathons. Bennett Beach from Bethesda, Maryland, and Mark Bauman from Flushing, Michigan (54 consecutive), and Patty Hung from Orinda, California (37 consecutive), are the current record holders.

RBF—Acronym for "running bitch face," the seemingly angry face runners make when candidly caught on camera in race photos. RBF isn't a chosen expression. It just appears, like an unwelcome in-law with a bottle of rotgut tequila on Thanksgiving.

Run for the Hoses—The 1976 Boston Marathon, known for its legendary 100 degrees F temperatures before the noon start in Hopkinton. Winners Jack Fultz (2:20:19) and Kim Merritt (2:47:10) and the field benefited from the refreshing spray of spectators' hoses, and a generous sea breeze off the 43 degrees F waters of Boston Harbor cooled the course to a more manageable 68 degrees F near the finish.

Sawx—Boston is the home of multiple highly successful professional sports franchises (Celtics, Bruins, Patriots) that have won dozens of championships, but the one you'll hear the most about during the weekend of the Boston Marathon is Boston's most prized team of all, its beloved Red Sox, or "Sawx" as they're affectionately known by the team's most zealous fans.

Scream tunnel—You know how Reese's says chocolate and peanut butter are better together than either ingredient is separately? Well, the athletic equivalent is the Boston Marathon's legendary Wellesley College "Scream Tunnel," an unlikely, yet irresistible, combination of two disparate ingredients: a prestigious road race and a distinguished all-girls school. Beginning in 1897, the Boston Marathon's inaugural year, Wellesley College students have lined the Boston Marathon course en masse and cheered for the runners who pass their stately campus. You may have played other sports in your life and experienced some memorable athletic moments, but you'll still be taken aback by the awesomeness that is the Scream Tunnel. Huge kudos to Wellesley College for upholding the tradition and making the Scream Tunnel so special every year. The feeling as an athlete is so euphoric that you don't realize how good you have it until you exit Wellesley College and it's gone. But, hey, turn that frown upside down and remember the party at Boston College awaits. You still have more than half the race to go.

Smoot—Despite what your smartwatch's janky GPS tells you when you cross the finish, you're probably aware that the length of a marathon has been standardized to 26.2188 miles, or 42.195 kilometers. And, yes, you would be correct to assume the Boston Marathon measures the standard distance. But did you know the Boston Marathon also measures 24,794.3354 smoots? That's right. Leave it to Boston to be unique. Oliver Reed Smoot pledged Lambda Chi Alpha at MIT in 1958, and his fraternity brothers carried the 5-foot, 7-inch (1.70m) pledge, repeatedly marking the length of his body with chalk to measure the distance across the Harvard Bridge (over the Charles River on Massachusetts Avenue between Boston and Cambridge). The bridge was measured to be "364.4 smoots +/- 1 ear." The smoot markings on the bridge walkway are painted and refreshed each semester. And the "smoot" unit of measure was added to the American Heritage Dictionary in 2011. So keep topping off your carbs and don't bonk at 20,000 smoots in Brookline!

Supper—You're bound to spend some energy figuring out what to eat for dinner on Sunday night. There are plenty of carb-loading choices, including the North End (Boston's de facto Italian neighborhood), Eastie (East Boston, Boston's old-school, original Italian neighborhood), or the B.A.A.'s own pre-marathon pasta dinner at City Hall. But you're not doing it right if you're having dinner at all. True Bostonians don't have dinner; they have supper (pronounced "suppah"). If you're at the Expo and you overhear a runner say something like "aftah I get my numbah, I'll grab suppah up the conah at Rino's in Eastie," follow that runner. Cling to him like you're the last two Cheerios in a bowl of milk. He will lead you past City Hall and the North End to the best pasta suppah evah.

T—The oldest subway in the United States was built in Boston in 1901. Yes, it's the one Rosie Ruiz took when she cheated in 1980. Don't do that. You won't fool anyone, as she did for eight days before being stripped of her "title." Even though Boston is a very walkable and runnable city, you might want to go underground to get from point A to point B a bit quicker. When you do, please know that the subway in Boston is never referred to by that name. You'll be riding the "T." Not the MBTA. Again, not the subway. Not the train. Not the L. Not the Metro. Not the Tube. The T. Or, as a true Bostonian would say, "it's the friggin' T, chief." That is all.

Toonies—A "townie" is someone who grew up in Charlestown, the oldest neighborhood in Boston. In many locales, being a townie is a bad thing, meaning you're a lifer and never left the comfort zone of your hometown. Not so in Charlestown, where townies are royalty. If you live in Charlestown and your great-grandparents grew up in Charlestown, you walk the streets tall, without fear. Anyone who didn't grow up in Charlestown is a "toonie," someone from the outside. If you arrived in Boston to run the marathon and you don't have deep roots in Charlestown (yah know, by the shipyahd on the hahbah), you're a sheisty toonie.

You leave Boston with a cool unicorn tucked into the darkness of your suitcase, but the bling on display 24/7/365 beneath the bridge never experiences such indignity.

Trophy Room—Boston is filled with secrets (including a four-story "Skinny House" with an internal width of eight feet), but runners in town for the Boston Marathon might be more interested in the mysterious Longfellow Bridge Trophy Room. If you think your trophy case is impressive, wait until you see what's beneath the bridge, a cornucopia of bling the likes of which you've never seen. An anonymous local attorney started adorning the bridge's underbelly with trophies and medals to "spread the joy of winning." Others joined in the fun, turning the entire span of the bridge into a war chest of trophies and medals big and small. As you run west toward the bridge on the Cambridge side of the Charles River, take a quick detour (100 feet) to your right (across Memorial Drive). The lion's share of treasure is beneath the rafters on your right, not your left. Feel free to add to the collection, but refrain from taking anything so others can marvel at it just like you.

Unicorn—If you ask the B.A.A. how the unicorn was chosen as its symbol (and the symbol of the Boston Marathon), the answer, like the unicorn itself, is shrouded in mystery. The mythical creature, affectionately coined "Spike" by the B.A.A. staff, has become synonymous with the Boston Marathon, gracing its coveted finishers' medals, jackets, shirts, and, well, anything and everything to do with the race.

Despite the unicorn's worldwide prestige, the mascot's backstory is as mythical as the animal itself.

Weather stalker—Not only are you going a bit stir-crazy because you're in the midst of your taper, but you're also running a race in a transitional season in New England. Regardless of the time of year, weather in New England is wildly all over the place. It could be 78 degrees F, sunny, and calm on Sunday and 37 degrees F, sleeting, with 25-mph winds on Marathon Monday. That's New England. So if you're not already a "weather stalker," someone who incessantly checks multiple weather forecasts via apps, local news, or otherwise, you will become one over your weekend in Boston. Assume the absolute worst. Then lower your expectations to something egregiously heinous. Then, think something worse.

Wicked—If you believe *wicked* is too played out for you to actually hear it spoken while you're in Boston, you're wrong. It's used as liberally today as it was when it became cliché in the first place. *Wicked* is a distinctly New England intensifier used primarily because *very* ceases to exist in the Greater Boston area vocabulary. Best to leave *wicked* to the pros, the locals. Hearing *wicked* in the wild out of the mouth of a Bostonian is as quintessentially New England as seeing a whale breach on Nantucket Sound.

WHOOP—The Boston-based company responsible for erecting the shameful, bright-white neon WHOOP sign that now obscures our beloved Citgo sign. Yes, WHOOP capitalizes its name. Apparently lowercase letters are beneath them. There are several words for WHOOP's level of disrespect, and those choice words have all-caps, too.

Zombie shuffle—A way of running that expends the absolute least amount of effort. If you've hit the wall in a marathon, you may know this shuffle all too well. Your feet barely clear the ground, and it's hard to tell from your race photos whether you're running or waving the white flag and walking. It's easier said than done, but the best way to fight off the zombie shuffle is to keep your turnover strong. Your feet may not leave the ground very long and your stride may shorten (hey, you're tired), but if your cadence doesn't drop off too egregiously, you'll avoid looking like a zombie. Strike that. You'll avoid shuffling like a zombie. At Mile 25 outside Fenway Park, you'll likely still look like one.

AFTERWORD

An educator once said the best way to learn an important thing isn't to sit in a lecture hall and hear someone talk about it. The important thing should be placed in the middle of the room where everyone can gather around it, experience it, and learn from it together.

Fellow participants and I have found that the Boston Marathon is an important thing. The intention of this book was to place the race "in the middle of the room" where we all can appreciate it.

I will be gone soon enough. So will Des, Bill, Joan, Meb, Kathrine, Bobbi, and all the legends and luminaries herein. But the Boston Marathon and this book will live on.

There's only one Boston. Keep gathering around it.

Give it your heart and soul. Boston will pay tribute and absorb them into its own.

INDEX

ABOUT THE AUTHOR

Berg Photography

Marc W. Pollina is a writer, runner, and entrepreneur. He has completed 26 marathons, including 18 Boston Marathons, as a bandit, a charity runner, and a sub-3 qualifier. Pollina earned a BA in English literature from Hampden-Sydney College and studied digital transformation at MIT.

Marc survived a near-death childhood accident, recovered his soul from the cold grip of the financial services industry, and founded an innovative cyber-media startup prior to penning his nonfiction debut. He and his family escape to the Cape when they're not running to and from (and all over) Boston and New York City.